Trading Places

Trading Places

When Our Son Became a Daughter

A Mother's Story of a Family's Transition

Jane Baker

Braefield Press

Published by Braefield Press

Inquiries should be addressed to TradingPlacesBook@gmail.com.

Publisher's Cataloging-in-Publication Data

Baker, Jane, 1953-
    Trading places , when our son became a daughter : a mother's story of a family's transition / Jane Baker.
        p.cm.
        Includes bibliographical references.
        ISBN 978-0-9906267-0-1 (pbk.)

1. Baker, Jane, 1953. 2. Transgender children--Family relations. 3. Parents of transsexuals. 4. Transsexuals--Family relations. 5. Gender identity. 6. Mother and child. 7. Transgender people--Family relationships. 8. Transgenderism. 9. Transexualism. I. Title.

HQ77.9.B35 2014
306.874092--dc23   2014946884

Cover design by Jane Baker
Interior design by Sarah Ann Baker
First Edition
Printed in the United States of America

This book is dedicated
in loving memory
to Mom and Dad,
whose spirits are always with me.
They helped me with everything in my life.
Somehow, even now, they're still helping.

—and to my gentle companions
Sonny and Rose
who sat with me day and night
through the months and the years
whenever I worked on this memoir.
They never even noticed the transition.

Contents

Chapter 1   **Trading Places**
            An Introduction to My Story   1

Chapter 2   **Devastation**
            The Paradigm Shift   15

Chapter 3   **When She Was a He**
            The First Twenty Years   25

Chapter 4   **Dreams**
            And Other Stuff of Grief   41

Chapter 5   **The Devil's Advocate**
            No Stone Left Unturned   53

Chapter 6   **From Winter to Spring**
            Many Life Changes   79

Chapter 7   **From Summer to Fall**
            Don't Miss the Train—From Steven to Sarah   97

Chapter 8   **Liberation**
            Telling the Family   113

Chapter 9   **Making Peace with Religion**   135

Chapter 10   Queer Clarification   145

Chapter 11   **Merry Christmas 2009**
Turning the Corner   157

Chapter 12   **The Yin-Yang Milestones**
I Miss You Steve   171

Chapter 13   **Conceptualizing Gender Dissonance**   179

Chapter 14   **Affirmation**   187

Chapter 15   **The Year Long Test**
Finding Equilibrium   193

Chapter 16   **In the Mind of the Beholder**   211

Chapter 17   **A New Reality**   225

Afterword by Sarah Ann Baker   235

Appendix A   **Theories About the Causes of Gender Dysphoria and Transsexualism**   239

Appendix B   **Transphobia in Science and Medicine**   245

Appendix C   **What Percentage of the Population is Transsexual?**   249

Appendix D   **Why Doesn't Mainstream Society Know More About Gender Variance?**   253

Endnotes   257

Selected Bibliography   287

Trading Places

Chapter 1

Trading Places
An Introduction to My Story

Shortly before his 20th birthday, my son Steve told me he was a woman. The sweet, gentle boy I had known for 20 years announced that he was making plans to become a daughter. Learning suddenly and unexpectedly that my child was transsexual was the most heart-shattering experience of my life. Trying to come to grips with this news, I lost track of the regular course of my life and plunged into the depths of despair. Day after day for months on end, I'd wake up in anguish, wishing this news had been a mistake, desperately wanting it to just go away.

This book is about the transition that our family made together, from my point of view—through the eyes of a mother. In about two years, I ran the gamut from devastation to wary acceptance and finally, to the epiphany of affirmation. Out of sheer love for my little family and the determination to be happy again, I worked hard to get back in life's orbit. Although things are different than they were before, we are all finally happy in our new reality. But as a mother, I will always miss my sweet, gentle son, and a corner of my heart will bear a unique type of grief forever.

It's possible I'll never really understand this grief myself. To spare me the pain of losing my son, to try to stop Steven from leaving, I would have needed to ask him to look torture, even suicide, in the eye every day and live a trapped and tormented life. Though it took a few years, I can now ask with clarity, *how would this have spared me from grief?* Wouldn't this attempt to juxtapose our realities have ultimately led us all to an even greater grief? Death may have been more familiar than transition, but it would not have been a better fate.[1]

· · · · · · · ·

In the beginning, I knew absolutely nothing about transsexualism. The first images that flashed through my mind in the early days were those of burly men in dresses and heavily made-up be-wigged transvestites on street corners in South Hollywood, and their fringe position in the social hierarchy. I never thought of gender variant people as deranged—they were human beings, just like me—but I worried about their safety in an intolerant and brutal world. They never bothered me even though I couldn't relate to their plight, or their perceived "lifestyle." After all, there are many types of people that I do not understand. I just never imagined that my child would end up to be one of them.

When Steve told us about his gender dysphoria, I didn't want to buy new dresses for him the next day. I didn't immediately aim to become a poster mom or a crusader for the cause. I didn't think I'd ever write a book about it either. Instead I withdrew, frightened and isolated, and stayed in denial for months. Questioning the validity of Steven's condition, I searched for ways to stop this transition from happening.

This might sound like a story of sadness and even self pity. In fact, it is my intention to start my story with grief because that is exactly where my journey began. When I was drowning in devastation, I remember hearing calls from the people on the shore of the world I was leaving behind. But they couldn't just wish me back to safety. The world I left behind and the one I was about to enter both seemed a million miles away. I couldn't reach lifelines thrown in from a world away, and I didn't have a way to rescue myself, either. I needed to find lifelines within my reach, and I needed time to develop the will and the power to connect to them. Only then could I get through this and come out the other side still alive. Incredulous as I was at the start of it all, I wanted to know if it was possible to ever be happy again. Some of the parents who are interviewed in TV documentaries about transsexualism seem to have made peace with their transition; they seem well-adjusted and happy and proud of the immense courage of their transsexual loved one. But as I looked at those stories at the start of my journey, I wondered, *how did those parents get from devastation to affirmation? What was the whole story?*

In the meantime, the weeks marched on and our own story began to unfold. With love and resources and all the determination we could muster, we walked hand in hand and moved through the process together, all the while on totally separate paths. Our challenge was to judiciously balance everybody's priorities the best way that we could. It wasn't always easy.

Although they are controversial in the transgender community, those stereotypical but well-intended TV documentaries threw the first lifelines that managed to reach me in my ocean of despair. But it was the eloquent memoirs written by transsexual authors that did the absolute most to convince me of the validity of this grossly misunderstood medical condition. These writers were articulate, intelligent, logical people. They seemed a lot more like geniuses than nuts. The memoirs reached my soul, because the authors shared their years of pain trying to live in a body that did not match their brain. Born with a tragic mismatch, trans people do not change their outer gender by choice or whimsy, but only after intense and thorough soul searching. For years, many try to suppress their conflicting inner gender identity. Eventually some come to their limit of suffering and transitioning becomes inevitable. For others, it becomes a matter of life or death. Mikayla, the subject of one documentary said, "If I had not transitioned, I would either be dead by suicide or a walking corpse."[2]

I didn't want my child to sacrifice the essence of his life because a transition would be too hard on *me*. I came to realize that would be

3

selfish. But to make my transition easier, I did want to understand dissonance. Imagine what it would be like to blink open each day with the torment still there, desperately wanting it to just go away. This is a little like what I felt as I watched my disappearing son morph into a daughter. As my child became whole, I became the fragmented one instead. On some poetic level, I've traded places with her. But for me, unlike for her, living with the anguish was a choice. With time, determination, and education as my tools, I've been working through it.

• • • • • • •

The first full year passed, and in that time I compartmentalized: tragedy in one room, funny stories in another—but in the main living room there stood my daughter Sarah looking fantastic in body and spirit. You could tell by the light in her eyes that we were turning the corner in the right direction. I found myself sitting on that proverbial shore, still wet with the bitter waters of grief, but with sunshine on my back again—and now we too have a story to share.

I guess we are lucky to be traveling our personal journey of transition during this relatively progressive and hopeful time. As successful and well adjusted transsexual people are introduced to the everyday public, the myths and proclamations made by a previously ignorant society can slowly be dispelled. The condition can no longer be cast off to the fringe of society. Trans people have been living in mainstream society all along, and their voices have been getting more attention and publicity in the last 15 years than ever before. We are in the midst of mainstream America's transgender revolution.

In 2009, President Barack Obama's administration appointed two openly transgender people to Federal posts. The same year, Obama signed the Matthew Shepard and James Byrd, Jr. Hate Crimes Prevention Act, the first federal law in U.S. history to enumerate protection for transgender people.[3] Superstar Cher's beloved Chastity has become the son he always was, Chaz Bono. By 2011, Chaz seemed to be late night TV's most sought after guest, endearing himself to millions of viewers with his lovable personality and straightforward talk. Around this time in New York City, fashion model Lea T, a transgender woman, rose to fame. In 2012, Jenna Talackova of Canada made headlines as the first transgender Miss Universe contestant. In 2013, a transgender teen was voted Homecoming Queen at her high school. TV shows have increasingly featured transgender characters in dignified roles, and as I prepared to publish this book in 2014, trans actress Laverne Cox made the cover of Time Magazine. Documentaries and books on gender identity issues continue to gain public attention. Oprah and Larry King and other talk shows have featured numerous trans guests, and public exposure and acceptance continue to grow.

The best available estimate of the prevalence of transsexualism has made a dramatic leap from the farcical tally of 1 in 80,000 people all the way up to the more realistic 1 in 500.[4] Society is slowly but surely becoming more accepting and willing to recognize that transsexualism is a real medical issue. There is a growing body of compassionate supporters determined to educate the public and to encourage more trans people to come forward to be counted. One day, probably not too far from now, the statisticians may be able to tally their numbers much more realistically.

So the times might be better for people emerging with this condition, but it is still not so lucky at all for a person to be transgender. Progressive attitudes are fashionable and flourishing, especially in the younger generations, but there are still plenty of people out there filled with hatred for what they do not understand. If a heinous crime is committed upon a transgender person, most states still blame the victim, claiming they have tricked or deceived the criminal, who will then be excused from accountability for a hate crime. In fact, over half the states still allow private companies to fire a person if they discover the person is transsexual.[5] Research on transsexualism is under-funded, and health insurance coverage for transsexual care is rare. The public's initial interest in Amanda Simpson's prestigious and groundbreaking appointment in the Obama administration seemed riveted, not on her accomplishments, but on her before and after transition pictures.[6] The journey is still extraordinarily hard for transsexual people, and for the loved ones who travel this journey alongside them.

• • • • • • •

Over two years and a thousand baby steps into the journey, I attended my first support group meeting. It was supposed to be for parents and other loved ones of transsexual people, but the room was mostly filled with transsexual people themselves. I found myself surprised at how inhibited I was by this situation. We took turns sharing stories, and though I never lied, I couldn't be completely honest either. I looked into the eyes of these gentle souls and I couldn't hurt them. I couldn't tell them that I had once doubted the validity of their condition and vehemently questioned my child's claim to be transsexual. I did not describe the intensity of my resistance, nor my desperation, nor the chronic despair that set in as the transition marched on undeterred. I couldn't admit that I was the one who asked my child to go for a second opinion on this self diagnosis. I've come so far in my understanding of transsexualism that I was embarrassed to share my pain (and prior ignorance) with those who have suffered so much more than I have.

The flip side of this coin is that many of the people in my circle of friends were much more willing to think about and accept Sarah's transition once they knew I had fervently tried to stop it. Few would have taken me seriously if I had said, "We are cool with our son becoming a daughter." While some parents might have an easy time with the concept of transsexualism, I'm guessing there are others who would think we were nuts if we said it was easy. A distraught parent at the start of this journey may not simply look at the happy ending and be convinced that they will get there someday. I think they should know that it is normal to feel devastation during this process. Understanding that my feelings were part of a grief process really helped me get through it.

Today I stand in the middle of a bridge connecting two worlds, both filled with beautiful, sensitive, kind-hearted people; both fairly reachable to me. One is the world of transgender people, including young adults who come out and take unsuspecting parents by surprise. The other is the world of mainstream America, including some of those parents. But talking to each about the other has so far been challenging to me, as I strive to connect with each without losing ground or credibility. So I write instead, taking time to choose words more carefully, with less inhibition and much more honesty than if my words were spoken. The story of my transition is my shot at bridging some gaps. From the early days of having bad dreams of my son laying in a casket, to the happier days, over a year later, of shopping with my daughter for sparkly earrings like a couple of giggling teenage girls, the journey has been long, bumpy, and surreal. But I am getting through it with baby steps.

· · · · · · ·

The story spans the three year period of our lives from December 2008 through December 2011, though it's mostly about the first two years. I recall the journey sequentially, starting from Chapter 2, "Devastation," to Chapter 17, "A New Reality," and in most of the chapters in between. I also diverge from the storyline now and then to share history and personal commentary and some of the things I've learned in the last few years.

We were one of those families that never had a clue that our son was transsexual. Steve was almost 20 years old that cold winter night in January of 2009 when he shocked me with the news. In Chapter 3, "When She was a He: The First Twenty Years," the back story about Steve growing up, I describe my perception of a gentle and intellectual little guy. While he displayed no feminine characteristics whatsoever (even at age 20), he also wasn't a very typical boy either. He never seemed to fit in anywhere. This was not something I saw only in hindsight. My heartache for a perceived loneliness began all the way back in preschool.

In the beginning, I was sure this was all a mistake, that Steve was heading for disaster by becoming a woman. In Chapter 5, "The Devil's Advocate: No Stone Left Unturned," I reveal my resistance, and detail all my questions and arguments no matter how silly they look to me now. At first I knew absolutely nothing about transsexualism or gender dysphoria, and I believe that some other parents who find out by surprise also start out with no knowledge. For the first few months I went crazy trying to disqualify his diagnosis with my arguments. I thought, "If this transition ends up a mistake, it would be catastrophic! Someone needs to be sure no stone is left unturned!" My questions and arguments needed to be addressed, but ironically, instead of convincing Steve to change his mind, I was the one who became convinced. The real disaster would be if my child did not transition.

When we were strong enough to tell our extended family, we began a six month long series of disclosure meetings and letters that proved to be very healing and encouraging for us. Chapter 8, "Liberation: Telling the Family," describes a lot of interesting and sometimes quite startling reactions and responses. Almost without exception, to my astonishment and relief, our support kept growing—at least initially, when it mattered the most.

We've slowly become fluent in another language. Chapter 10, "Queer Clarification," is my version of a typical gender-book glossary based on my understanding and explanations from Sarah. For example, people who are not transsexual are *cissexual*—they feel harmony between their brain and body.[7] Most cissexual people don't even know there is a word for this harmony—they never stop to think about it. Chapter 10 also addresses some basic distinctions; for example, being gay is not the same as being trans, and both transsexual and cissexual people can be straight or gay or anywhere in between.

I wanted to share my ways of "Conceptualizing Gender Dissonance" in Chapter 13. For me to come to a better understanding of this condition, I use an exercise wherein I imagine switching places with my child. For Sarah to live, Steven had to die. As I grieved the loss of my son, I struggled to grasp the concept that my new daughter was the same person as my old son. Yet one reason for the transition was for *our perception of her* to become that of a different person. Steve didn't die, he just ceased to exist. My state of mind was in paradox for much of the first year 2009, and well into the second year too. As my child became less dissonant, I became more so—and I became able to empathize with dissonance. It is because of this exercise, which continues to this day on a maintenance level, that I decided to name this book "Trading Places." I highlight some of the memorable trades in Chapter 12, "The Yin-Yang Milestones." Every gain my trans daughter made seemed to result in a loss for the loved ones left behind.

I diverge from the story for a commentary in Chapter 16, "In the Mind of the Beholder." As we watch the gender documentaries together now, Sarah laughs at some of the shows, but I love them and take them very seriously. I continue to thirst for them, as they have been key to my healing, my coming to terms with this condition. It is most clear at these moments that Sarah and I view this family transition through totally opposite lenses. She's on the inside looking out, and I'm on the outside trying to look in. While I find every one of the documentaries incrementally affirming to me, she scoffs at the stereotypes they promote.

· · · · · · ·

Maybe I'm supposed to know by now that I never really had him, but I deeply miss the son I thought I had. I miss the person he used to be, the sweet gentle soul that I raised and loved for 20 years. The only person I knew him to be was my Steve. That this person was not complete and was tragically misaligned, with the most unlikely chance for any love in his future, was not a part of my reality, because I did not know it. I *did* know that he was mysteriously lonely and was a misfit in some profound way. So turning the page,

I am grateful to have made peace with the solution: the emergence of the daughter I now have, one I never knew I had all along. Our little family has found happiness again, but more and more pictures of the person I raised are coming down from my walls: pictures of Steve don't look like Sarah would have looked at those times. There is a very unique type of sadness for us as parents, even though the trade-off is, surprisingly, more happiness than we ever thought possible.

We have been given a gift, a chance to grow as individuals, and a chance to make a real difference in the world around us, even if it's just by example. We have been invited into a world of the most interesting, beautiful and courageous people in all of humanity. I count myself lucky to have a richer life now. Compartmentalizing myriad conflicting mental energies, optimizing happiness for us all, I live my new reality knowing that this is where we all must be. It all seems to be so much more natural this way. Surprised by my own happiness, I often smile and laugh about what life has given us, and what kind of growth was needed to adapt to it and move on. Dr. Marci Bowers put it succinctly: "I think society needs to stop taking itself so seriously. People are people and this is just part of the human expression."[8]

•　•　•　•　•　•　•

By now, as I am doing the final edits of this memoir (within the fifth year), I am so done with the journey that I almost don't want to finish writing the book. Each time I reread a chapter, it feels like I have moved on so far past that stage that I am tempted to rewrite the chapter from my newer, more enlightened point of view. Sometimes it seems like I have become a completely different person—I no longer feel the way I felt when I first journaled these thoughts. Although I have changed, if I was to delete my early thoughts, I would defeat the purpose of the book. I've come to a compromise: I point out and highlight those areas of my personal growth by writing commentaries about myself within the chapters

I am most tempted to revise (rather than completely rewriting them from my new point of view). I've been encouraged by trans people (and parents) on several occasions to leave the dark thoughts intact in the book. They know I've reached the other side, but the darkness was part of my journey to get there and I'm convinced that it is more helpful to share this openly rather than try to lighten it up. Additionally, in the spirit of teamwork and in some instances accuracy, Sarah has added her own commentary in some of the chapters and has also written the book's afterword.

Except for those cited as published source material, all names used in this book have been changed to protect privacy. I have also changed most people's personal details and the specific dates of some events, but the events themselves are accurate. This is my story. It is not meant to represent any other story. I've met other parents along the way, and though many have experienced similar emotional challenges, each and every story was unique.

I thank all the people who encouraged me to write this memoir in various simple ways, even just by asking about its progress, or expressing an interest to read it. Several people said, "We need more books out there on this subject." Those simple words were catalysts to me. It was easy to write at first, during the hardest part of the journey when I needed an emotional outlet the most. Journal writing was the single most therapeutic measure I took to mend my soul in private moments. But as I recovered it became tempting to move on and forget about the anguish of the past. It would have been pretty easy to abandon the work had it not been for the hundreds of hours already invested, and the few motivational words of encouragement that came my way from time to time. I thank my husband Ted for letting me take whatever time and energy I needed to write the story. He was happy that I found solace in this activity. As Sarah's other parent, he was the closest person on this earth who knew what I knew and vice versa. I thank my son Jeff for always having the right thing to say and for exuding profuse can-do spirit in almost any situation in life. Jeff was an easygoing comrade on this journey, and was quick to adapt to his new sister. After learning the news of the transition, he stepped out into life the next day with his sister, pushing aside and climbing on top of any figurative obstacle in his way. He is one generation past viewing this experience through eyes like mine, and he is one step closer to making a real and positive difference in how trans people are received.

I owe enormous gratitude to my dear friend Judy, my one true, reliable and constant companion on the journey. Right from the start she seemed to feel what I felt, as a mother herself and also as a very close second mom to Sarah. She was, and still is, always ready to talk, to listen, to lean, to be leaned upon. She has never tired of working through this life transition with me, and even today, we're still working. Through the first two toughest years and all 17 chapters, Judy kept me writing, always wanting another chapter to review, patient but persistent, optimistic and excited; she liked reading my story. "Don't give up," she'd say. "You have to do this. I think your story needs to be shared." So thank you, Judy. I'm finally doing just that.

But at the end of the day and at the heart of it all, I owe the whole story to my daughter Sarah. She wanted to keep us in her life, and so she worked with us, at a compromised pace, and with extraordinary patience and sensitivity. Before all this began, I had believed I was at capacity for pride in my child. I was not yet aware of the tremendous pride and happiness still ahead for us all. Thank goodness for the multi-dimensional growth that has come from this experience of transition.

It's equally important that I thank Sarah for her genuine interest in helping me get this book published. She was my proofreader and editor: dedicated, fair, honest, proficient. She read each chapter over and over through months of time, highlighting issues of grammar and tense, suggesting better word choice, pointing out areas to clarify. Most importantly, she worked to ensure my best chance of reaching the broadest range of readers without offending too many of them, especially trans people, and especially Sarah, herself. I think it's a pretty fitting end to my story to have its subject also be its best possible editor. Sarah is an exceptionally well read scholar currently enrolled in a PhD program at an Ivy League university. Thank you, Sarah, for most everything about this book.

Trading Places

Chapter 2

Devastation
The Paradigm Shift

The story begins in the early morning hours of January 7, 2009 at our home in Bloomfield, Michigan. It was a cold but peaceful winter's night. The Christmas tree was still up in the corner, twinkling with a thousand lights and all the same ornaments we'd put up every year for 20 straight years. A few of the ornaments could spin, and their tiny motors hummed softly. On the heater vent next to the tree sat our hairless cat, wearing a fleece coat. We were a non-conformist, bookish family, and we lived by a philosophy that optimized common sense, a free spirit, and the golden rule.

The Christmas tree never changed much in 20 years, which cast a Brigadoon-like enchantment over our holiday season. For a few weeks every year, we lived in a transcendent wonderland. Spirits of people from yesteryear would come alive and a tide of joy seemed to lift everything higher—senses, memories, dreams, beliefs. Santa Claus brought magic and toys to treat our two little boys, who wore pajamas with feet. In the great realm of nostalgia, one of these toys would achieve legendary status: the Big Loader. Seventeen years ago, this miniature heavy equipment vehicle shoveled and transported rocks from quarry to building site, where it would empty its bucket, then start all over again for our firstborn son, little Steve. He was spellbound by it for hours that Christmas of 1991. We knew there was something a little bit different about him right then: all the other toys still wrapped up and beckoning were oddly ignored.

Of course these days, the gifts under the Christmas tree are mostly electronic gadgets, or money or clothes. I know as I move through the holiday season, that the essence of each Christmas will also be moving from present to past to take its place as a memory of another bygone era. But the magnitude of the shift through Christmastime 2008 would be epic. We knew it would likely be our last Christmas with my mom, now in her fifth year battling cancer. What we didn't know was that it would also be our last Christmas with our sweet, gentle son, Steve.

●　●　●　●　●　●　●

It was not unusual for Steven and I to be awake and active at 2:00 in the morning because we were both night owls. My husband, Ted, and our younger son, Jeff, had already been in bed for hours. There was something magical about the absolute quiet and peacefulness of this time of night. For Steven and I, this would often be our special, uninterrupted time for those most private, intimate talks. We were then—and still are today—an exceptionally close and open family of four, except for one really big secret that Steve had been keeping suppressed for seven years.

Two weeks earlier, about two days after Christmas in late December of 2008, Steven had announced one evening, right out of the blue, that he was bisexual. All four of us were eating our home cooked dinner together, as we had done every night for the last 20 years. "I have something to tell you," he started. "There's really no easy way to say this." He had our attention; we all looked up from our plates. "I'm bisexual!"

We nodded, and continued chewing as though this didn't even blip the radar, trying for just a minute, to show no surprise. Steven was almost 20 years old, and had virtually no experience in romance or sex of any sort. We asked him, "How can you know this if you've never actually had sex with anyone?" We encouraged him to get on out there and try.

But he said, "No, not yet, not now. There's plenty of time

for romance in the future—" and with this, Ted and I were left perplexed. But this was not the big secret. It was true that he was bisexual, but there was more to tell. In fact, the bisexual announcement was a stepping stone and a litmus test for another big secret yet to come, the one about which this book is written.[1]

• • • • • • •

Although life was good, there had always been something mysterious about Steve. Throughout the years of his childhood, my heart filled equally with both pride and pain; pain for an unidentified yet palpable and profound loneliness that I detected within him even though he was unaware of it himself. With all the gifts and qualities of this highly intellectual person with a sweet and humble heart, he just never seemed to fit in.

For the last few years, Steve had been nurturing a peculiar interest in matters of women's rights and gay and lesbian issues. He had amassed substantial knowledge on these subjects. Earlier in the fall, he had a lunch date with a transgender young man, and was getting involved in LGBT issues almost obsessively. After announcing to us that he was bisexual, Ted and I realized his LGBT interest had not been merely academic. We were a little curious about the notion that maybe Steve was so longing for love and friendship, that he'd found it with a transsexual person.

So in the middle of this memorable night in January, Steve and I started to chat about various odds and ends, both of us lazy and draped on the blue-cushioned couches in the living room. Rose, our hairless cat watched from the heat register, comical and adorable in her new fleece coat with a ruffled collar; the house was otherwise dead quiet. With the Christmas tree twinkling, it could not have been more comfortable, except for the fact that my world was about to change. I decided to bring up Steve's recent bisexual announcement. The conversation rambled through various sexual and gender variant topics, as I was seeking greater understanding on many levels. We traveled to the subject of gender dysphoria, mostly because I was curious to know more about his transsexual friend, and the role of this person in Steven's life. I asked him to explain the difference between sexual preference and gender identity.

Steven explained to me that sexual preference is who you are attracted to, but gender identity is who you actually are. They are completely different concepts. Transsexual people are those with the misfortune of having the gender of their brain disharmonious with that of their physical body. They are people of one gender identity trapped in bodies associated with the opposite gender.

How did my child know so much about this stuff, I wondered; why was he so obsessively interested in all these sexual and gender issues? I gazed at him, as he laid supine looking up towards the ceiling on the longer blue couch, across from the couch I was on. I had become used to the idea that Steven was different, a little bit of a misfit himself, and wondered if he was now exploring this strange territory in hopes of finding a place to fit in.

At this point I was on the threshold of a seismic paradigm shift. I was about to take the first step of my own transition in a pivotal ten second window of a time that I now think of as the passage between "life before" and "life after." I remember, like it was yesterday, hearing my own heart beat, taking slow breaths as I waited for the answer to the question I next posed to Steve: "How about you?" I asked tentatively, suddenly and strangely suspicious. "Do you feel harmony between your brain and your body?" and of course I was expecting a fairly immediate answer.

But Steven didn't answer. Nothing was said in the seconds that followed, and I think I took another breath, but the room had become dead silent; even my beating heart stopped. I was in the portal now, in the midst of the shift. My last seconds of blissful ignorance disappeared; darkness and fear moved in to fill the space.

I almost regretted asking because when the next second had passed with still no answer, I knew this was going to be bad. Maybe if I had not asked, Steve would have taken additional time to change his mind about this disclosure. The light of the world I had left

18

behind was still glimmering. To run back to the way it was before was to do or to die. But I was frozen, paralyzed; I couldn't move. Yet it felt like I was being moved by a force that was not my own. My mind raced, *What's going on? Why was Steve taking so long to answer?* The lack of an answer was ominous, and I braced myself.

The answer finally came through the thickness of the interlude. "No," Steve said softly. "I can't lie to you," he was crying now, tears streaming down each cheek. Steven lay on the blue-cushioned couch, looking up at the ceiling, silently sobbing. We were two sorrowful beings in our darkest time shared together.

I sat frozen, stunned into shock. I tried to process what was happening, if it was even happening. My first inclination was to jump up and hug him and make him all better again. "Well we have to fix this!" I said or I thought—*but that was what we surely would do!* These were my first seconds lived in the new unknown world, as my old world unhitched itself from its orbit and hurtled away in the blink of an eye to the chamber of bygone days.

Steven continued slowly, carefully, "I wasn't ready to tell you yet but I can't lie. I do not have harmony between my body and my brain. I am a woman. I am a woman in a man's body. I've known about this for over seven years. I knew something was wrong at puberty. I have started to write a letter that I was going to give you and Dad in the next year. I really wanted to have the letter with me. It explains so much and would have made this conversation easier." Steven was distraught that the disclosure had not gone the way he had been so carefully planning. As unprepared as he was, occurring a whole year earlier than he had anticipated, he seized this opportunity nonetheless.

Within the first twelve hours of my new life, I had a few surreal moments where I felt the potential joy of this renaissance. It was as though, through the prisms of my tears, I was given a rare glimpse into the future through a crystal ball. Had my once seemingly misfit child finally found the reason behind his oddly isolated existence? For Steven had always had a mystery about him. If there was a "cure" for his enigmatic loneliness, and he would emerge a happy person, then was this really, quite possibly the answer after all these years?

Though it was short lived, I vividly remember the fleeting joy, the possibility that this condition was real and my son had it and by fixing it "she" would emerge as the correct person, the one she was meant to be all along. On this first day I had tears of strange joy mixed with tears of unbearable sadness, the first taste of what it would be like over the coming year, and the year after that, as the mom of a transsexual child.

• • • • • • •

Steve headed back to Ann Arbor the following morning to begin the second semester of his Sophomore year at the University of Michigan. As he said goodbye to me, we tenderly embraced and then I pulled back and looked deep into his eyes. My eyes welled with tears; it was eerily familiar, like that first bonding moment almost 20 years ago when the eyes of my newborn gazed intently into mine. "You will be the same person?" I whispered, I pleaded, like a mixture of a question and a mantra, though choking back the tears. I had an eerie premonition even on this first day of the journey, that no matter how hard I would fight this, and fight it I would, maybe this transition thing was meant to be.

"Yes the same person. I promise," he said. He meant it, though neither one of us knew it at the time but that was not a very realistic promise to make. Although he had to leave the place he was in, he had no experience, no holistic concept of the territory into which he was about to enter. In the end she would still feel the same inside, but to us she became a new person.

A flurry of emotions pelted my sanity in the week that followed, but like beads of water rolling around on Teflon, none of them penetrated; they just rolled about, skimming the surface. Shock was the protective barrier to my conscious mind, while my brain subconsciously went into overdrive to conceptualize what had just happened: unbearable sadness, panic, helplessness, hope, disbelief, belief.

When Steve announced his transgender condition, one of the first things I said to him was, "If you're going to do this, you have to do it right. You have to start taking estrogen hormones as quickly as possible so your shoulders don't brawn out, so you don't lose your hair." I guess this was my way of continuing to dote on my child even right at the very start of the journey. But those first fleeting moments of pseudo-excitement were short lived; time for rational thought would soon run out. I said these things so Steven would know that support from me would be possible, and that he would not lose my love. And then my head went under and I drowned for a year in a dark ocean of devastation.

• • • • • • •

Later that week, Steve sent us the "coming out to Mom and Dad" letter he had carefully and very lovingly prepared. It included the words, "I am still the same person I have always been: always your son, also your daughter." At the end of his emotional ten page disclosure letter, he included a long list of famous and successful transsexual people. To this day, I can't imagine how hard it must be to tell one's parents that you are transsexual. It would be 22 months before I'd ever be interested in a list of famous transsexual people, but at this moment it was way too much too soon. I was only on my first baby step.

For the next several weeks I began each day by waking up to a flood of anguish drowning my mind, consuming my existence. Was this my reality now? I'd lay there blinking. Am I crazy? Am I imagining this? I'd force myself out of bed, racked with malaise; I'd stand, then double over, then stand, take a step, and shuffle through the glue to change the calendar to the next day. I found myself stuck for a long time in a thick, dark, tangled mess of despair. With time, enough calendar pages turned, I hoped to slowly get used to it, though every morning I really wished it would just go away instead. Maybe one day life would be better—we'd be happy again—though at that time it was hard to imagine that would ever be possible.

• • • • • • •

By January of 2009, I was in the early stages of preparing for our younger son Jeff's high school graduation party to be held at the house that coming June. I had hundreds of pictures of the kids growing up spread all over the living room floor. To create Jeff's picture posters, I was using the photo displays I'd made for Steven's grad party as creative guidelines. My favorite display was a 30 foot banner of mounted pictures of Steven arranged in chronological order, starting from newborn baby to grown young man. With changes ever so subtle from one picture to the next, by scanning the banner from left to right, the baby grew up. This banner now spanned the whole length of the living room before me, filling my broken heart with indescribable loss. My photo festival of nostalgia had suddenly become a somber shrine of a family history in some sort of weird jeopardy—an existence now in question. This child growing up—who was he, who was she, and what did I really know about my own child?

For the last twenty years, through every minute of time, in every aspect of life and with every sense of perception, the child we raised was Steven. Everything was in his name: his birth record, his academic records, all of his awards, his achievements, naturally, obviously, everything ... everything that I knew about my child. How was I to reconcile our past with our future? When I took all those pictures of Steve over the last twenty years, was he really even there at all? In our reality, we had a boy, but she was a girl, who was transsexual, so we only thought we had a boy. Was our reality not reality? If our child was Sarah all along and I only knew of our son Steve, who did I know? Did I know a person who I did not know I knew?

Day after day, devoid of motivation, I'd sit in the living room and stare at the pictures in a trance-like state, not able to understand, barely able to breathe, my heart crushed with sadness. Steve was telling me he didn't want to exist anymore, that he was not happy as my Steve, as my son, and that he was never my son at all. Steve, as we knew him, was deliberately, and eagerly planning his own demise—the demise of his identity as a son.

Little by little, over the next couple of years, our sweet Steve would henceforth be disappearing, fading into oblivion, slowly fading away to only a memory. For the next several months I was besieged with torment and confusion, mired in a state of profound grief. The first and most significant part of my journey was to mourn the loss of my son.

It would be a long time before I thought about what it would be like to be a person living with gender dysphoria. It would be a long time before I would be capable of welcoming a new daughter who had come to take the place of my son. It would be a long time before I would acquire the ability to begin to merge the concepts of former son and new daughter—and in fact, I'm still working on that one today.

Trading Places

Chapter 3

When She Was a He
The First Twenty Years

The eyes are the window to the soul.

old English proverb

About 22 years ago and ten days earlier than expected, Ted and I rushed to the hospital after our firstborn broke my water at 4:00 in the morning. We had already decided to name the baby Steven, with a "v". We both loved this boy name, and without any deliberation it had been decided upon very early in the pregnancy. "No need to worry about a girl name," I assured Ted, as we headed to the hospital that very early winter's morning without any girl names picked out yet. I had always known, in some supernatural mother's way, that I was carrying a boy. What a strange twist of irony that would turn out to be.

Steve was born on March 10th, 1989 at 6:00 pm after 23 hours of labor. Ted ceremonially cut the cord and our little guy was placed upon my chest whereupon his gaze intently and deliberately met mine. I'm certain this was the magical soul-bonding moment so often spoken about, one that occurs in the first minute after birth between mother and child. From this moment on, a virtual umbilical cord would be replacing the physical one. Ted was given his turn to bond next, and I can still see that vivid memory of a very proud dad cradling his first child. He looked up at me with a blissful, ethereal radiance and whispered, *"My son... I have a son."*

• • • • • • •

Motherhood suited me well. I was a little surprised by this as I had not one maternal bone in my body before the kids were born. I was never the first one to want to hold someone else's new baby, but things were really different when the babies were my own. I took to it instantly and launched myself into the 20 year task with dedication and zeal. Once the kids were born they became the center of our universe. Ted and I didn't miss a thing; not one parent-teacher conference, not one band concert, not one soccer game. We were involved in every aspect of their lives. I loved those years of raising the boys.

"Whatever you're doing, keep doing it! Your kids are just wonderful people, so successful, so kind-hearted," a school teacher once told me. It wasn't the first time we'd been complimented this way; we were the quintessential middle class, happy family.

For 20 years we shared life with Steven, a sweet gentle soul with the rare mix of brilliant mind and humble heart. He was too kind for other kids to dislike, but he was too different for those kids to invite him over to play. Something was going on that made it impossible for him to bond naturally with peers. It was like he stood back and observed as the other kids grew up.

Through it all, I felt a profound loneliness and sadness laying dormant within him, even though he didn't seem aware of this himself. I wondered if a time would come when he might realize there was something amiss about himself. Maybe my son was simply unique and would never fit in or maybe he wanted his world to be this way. Sometimes other kids would reach out to include him, but the connections were fleeting and insubstantial. This is the essence of the Steven I remember. Had we raised Sarah instead, I would surely be remembering a different person with a different childhood story to tell. Steven was a misfit, and he was different, but I never once stopped and thought, "I wonder if my child is transsexual."

· · · · · · ·

Steve spent the entire first year of his life crying. He was in every sense of the word, inconsolable. He cried all day, and neither rocking nor massaging nor change of diet could make him more comfortable. During the day, he took no naps, so after exhausting himself he'd collapse and sleep for 13 straight hours at night. Since this was our first baby, we never quite realized how much easier a baby could be and figured this was an ordinary experience.

"It must be gas," some would say, but does gas really hurt that much, incessantly for months on end?

When I asked the pediatrician about Steve's colic, she laughed and said, "Your baby doesn't have colic! I would know because you'd be crazy by now." And so it was that only the passage of one year's time managed to fix Steve's colic.

I often look back to try to figure out the things I might have missed or misinterpreted during Steve's years of growing up. I wonder what possible signs of gender dysphoria or any biochemical or hormonal imbalance may have been manifesting itself in the baby years, or during childhood or youth. Could it be that even as an infant, he felt tormented in some fundamental physiological way? Was this incessant discomfort some first indication of the biological incongruity as yet unidentified? It's pretty farfetched, but I've tried to recall the things about Steve that were outside of the norm, whether or not they pertained to gender, and this first year was simply one of them.

· · · · · · ·

Almost overnight, Steve morphed from crying baby into a gentle and intellectual little man with almost no stage in between. By age two he was using three syllable words and people would stare at him spellbound when he talked with all those big words. With mature composure of a little man, he'd stand there spewing forth complex sentences to which many grownups had no response.

"It's in the DNA," Steve told the dermatologist as she investigated one of his freckles when he was about three or four years old. "Sometimes it gets scraped off, but it just grows right back the way it was. Freckles are in the DNA." The doctor just stared and said nothing.

"He's making stuff up!" said the first grade teacher, who called me one day, concerned when Steve tried to tell the class about the hexadecimal number system.

"It's a globally gifted specimen!" exclaimed the psychologist—academically referring to Steven's brain—after testing his intelligence quotient. "I've only seen a few of these in my forty year career!" Steve tested off the charts in every cognitive category. She shook her head and gestured her excitement. "Look out," she said, "you're in for a wild ride!" —an uncanny prediction for sure.

• • • • • • •

Sometimes a smart child will grow to acquire a level of arrogance to match. As Steve was witness to plenty of that throughout all the school years, he remained decidedly outside and above that fold. In fact, signs of extraordinary humility also rapidly emerged. As a kindergartner standing in line for something, any other kid could cut in front of him, and more often than not, Steve would end up last in line. He'd justify this peaceful behavior with, "it just seemed so important to the other kid."

When Steve was in first grade, we'd prepared all year long for a regional math games tournament held in the spring. In one round of a game at the tournament, Steve was assigned an opponent who did not know the game rules. So right there, during the competition, Steve taught him the rules of the game and showed him how to win it. In first grade! I stood there, exhausted after a year of training for this, incredulous that Steven had willingly forfeited a chance to parade on the stage to show off a first place ribbon. All the other mothers were beaming with pride— "My child is so smart!" they were probably thinking.

But for me, this was the dawning of a new awareness that Steven was smart in a different league, that he was not even worried about the competition. He actually had no real need to win this game at all. Instead, he gave his opponent the tools to win: "it just seemed so much more important to the other kid." So Steven stood back, like an outside observer, and watched as all the other kids grew up around him. Nothing seemed to threaten his intellectual confidence—not then, and not ever. I'd line his trophies up on a shelf over the years but they were really all just for me.

· · · · · · ·

Jeff was born in September 1991, $2\frac{1}{2}$ years after Steve. He had the classic second-born independence and devil-may-care adventurous spirit. He grew seamlessly from an easy going baby, to the person who ruled the house—which he did for the next 18 years. He managed situations with his charm and quick wit and ability to relentlessly argue us into exhausted submission. When he was a toddler I recall an incident where I had to scold him for something like running with scissors. He waddled over to me, smiling and confident, and hugged my legs, "Don't worry Mom, everything will be OK." I knew on that day that Jeff would be teaching me as much about life as I would teach him. I wondered what I had done to deserve this perfectly wonderful family.

The boys' temperaments complimented one another. They were both kind-spirited, generous, and friendly little kids and were very compatible and loving brothers. Jeff was an articulate, natural leader, very magnetic, quick witted and funny, and, he needed somebody to play with pretty much all of the time. A perfect balance to the pensive, precocious, more careful and serious Steven, Jeff's presence was electric and clamorous and large as life.

· · · · · · ·

The philosophy of our time was to expose the kids to as much as possible, packing every available minute of life with myriad enriching activities. I used to hang the family calendar on the refrigerator with a magnet the size of a brick. Ted and I were both engineers at Ford Motor Company, but I managed to work out a part time position with a flexible schedule which allowed me to balance my work with a hundred soccer-mom activities. The kids learned piano and karate and chess and tennis. We scheduled soccer games and science club and cub scouts and birthday parties. We did homework and made Christmas cookies, and every night, we ate home cooked meals together. Those were the busiest years of our lives.

As design engineers, Ted and I were proudly—and stereotypically—nerdy and unpretentious, which was a bit out of the ordinary in our relatively affluent community. We encouraged individuality, and embraced our unique and sometimes eccentric characteristics. Our functional and economical but very ugly cars stood out in the community parking lots filled with bus-sized shiny black SUVs, that always seemed to scream, "My husband makes more money than yours!" which, of course, was not necessarily true. I never walked lockstep with others of upscale society; I had no interest in fashion or status symbols—except for intellectual status. And in that area we fit in; we had our claim to fame.

Our family was exceptionally close and loving. We brought the boys up as people first and never, not consciously anyway, did we encourage gender roles. Miles of Hot Wheels car tracks wove their way past the science fair volcano and through the toy kitchen. The boys collected rocks and animal cards, Beanie Babies and bottle caps, and those collections were spread all over the house too. Although they were never denied anything blue or pink at the toy stores, the most desired toys were, in retrospect, gender neutral. They loved strategy games, and building sets, gear and magnet toys, Play-Doh and art sets and tons and tons of books. We had to bring crates to the library, and by second grade, I had to put Steven's lamp on a timer to get him to stop reading and go to sleep at night.

As I spin my wheels these days trying to figure out how we could have missed Steven's latent or emerging gender dysphoria, I sometimes wonder if our house was so flexible and gender-neutral, that perhaps the opportunity to feel misaligned never presented itself to Steven during those young years.

· · · · · · ·

As Jeff grew, so did his social schedule. We had the entire kindergarten class over for his 5th birthday party, because he was a social magnet. He traveled through the grades of school with loads of friends, girlfriends, and fan clubs, the telephone constantly ringing, and an insatiable need for play dates.

Jeff's lifestyle starkly contrasted with Steve's, who spent most of his childhood immersed in scholarly pursuit and didn't make a lot of close friends. When Steve was young, the other mothers and I would set up play dates, and of course we were all quite busy with those enriching after-school activities. Although Steve's lack of close friends was noticeable, I came to think of his social situation as a mere consequence of our busy way of life, combined with the temperament of a studious child who seemed content to spend spare time alone.

It didn't take long for Steve to start making a name for himself in our school district. Everybody was attracted to his intellect, and the fact that he was very generous about sharing it. He had absolutely no arrogance about him whatsoever. He was humble and kind-hearted, the teachers loved him, and all the kids liked him well enough. Everyone wanted him as a group project partner, but few ever called him up to play.

My heart was constantly heavy with an equal mix of pride and pain. As the years went by, it became clear that Steve lacked either ability or desire to pursue and build close friendships. My heart began to break at what must have been a profound loneliness so intrinsic, so fundamental, that Steven himself had not yet recognized its existence. Through the years I'd find the right times to ask him if he was happy, or if he was lonely, and he'd always say he was happy, never lonely—yet even in crowds, he always seemed so alone to me. Throughout all of Steve's growing up years, I desperately sought spots where he could belong. Most kids were busy being kids, whereas Steve seemed to grow up somehow separated from that course of life altogether.

Those years of superficial and fleeting relationships did not seem to affect his belief in himself at all, and he remained a content, self-respecting and seemingly happy child. It was almost as though he spent those years standing back and analyzing childhood behaviors like a young social scientist. He grew into a humble and fair-minded intellectual person, aware and respectful of the world around him, and genuinely interested in it. (It is interesting that today, she has chosen a career in social science.)

· · · · · · ·

I now wonder, of course, if the loneliness I privately perceived within Steven—even though he didn't seem aware of it himself—was due to his being transgender all along. Was it so much a part of his childhood existence that he never understood until later on, that this peculiar incongruence was not a normal way to feel? How can any of us really know if we are normal, after all? I asked him once, if he had grown up alone on a deserted island, would he have known he was transsexual? He admitted that although he might not have had a label for it, he would have known, absolutely, that something was wrong. Gender identity doesn't come from around us. It derives from within us.

Middle School

I spent so much time volunteering in the middle school, kids probably thought I was a teacher there. This was a time of fascinating adolescent social development. I witnessed the formation of groups and hierarchies that henceforth defined life paths or even destinies. The classification began, of course, with boy groups and girl groups. Within each group were pretty people and plain ones, hotties and hunks, nerds, jocks, and geeks. One by one they took social positions: followers and leaders, alphas and rebels, trend-setters, mischief makers, preps, politicians, bohemians . . . and Steve. Steve still stood alone, still belonging nowhere, to my chagrin, still not fitting in. Groups would reach out, the connections fleeting, futile, or superficial. And so even through middle school the phone did not ring for Steve. Nor did he ever ask for a play date. Not with boys, not with girls. In retrospect, he did not seem to really belong in either one of those groups.

At some point, for everyone passing through this window of time, the hormones of puberty would be unleashed—some earlier, some later, come they would, to ravage and overtake every young human life. The gender differences up to that point are not so great, not even noticed by many; but sooner or later, young men and women would emerge from their chrysalis of childhood.

At some point those hormones besieged Steven too, along with the horrible realization that the hormones coursing through his body were the wrong ones. By this time, gender dysphoria had begun to overcome Steve, but he would hide this from us for the next seven years. Even in a family as open and comfortable as ours was, Steve kept it to himself and tried to suppress it.

• • • • • • •

We bid farewell to many years of fun-filled family activities of Cub Scouts and then Steven, alone, entered the world of testosterone-driven, male-only Boy Scouts. When he dropped out only one week later, I'd chalked it up to a life schedule already over capacity. I was no longer surprised by this "not fitting in" business. But this particular scenario left me uneasy, and curiously aware that the reasons Steve didn't fit in with this scouting group were obscure and mysterious. Yet I never once thought to myself, "I wonder if he's transsexual," nor, for that matter, did I ever even wonder if he was gay, though neither characteristic precludes interest in Boy Scouts.

Track team, piano lessons, academic tournaments: these were all independent pursuits that worked well for a person who stood outside the bounds of the middle school cliques, interacting with people in all of them, but not a core member of any. With his Einstein hair style and T-shirt-based fashion statement, Steve continued to evolve as the school's gentle and beloved intellectual giant. He won the "Passion for Learning" award at middle school graduation, awarded to one student of each gender. Steve's name and the name of one other girl are engraved on a plaque permanently displayed in the middle school lobby.

I volunteered to make the 8th grade graduation video that year. I included a slide show comprised of each student's close-up picture. Sometimes it took a few retakes, but I managed to get flattering images of each student—every one except Steven that is. It was disquieting to me, that after a hundred or more attempts there was still something oddly peculiar about his images. His eyes didn't fit him. Those beautiful big blue eyes—they weren't right. They say eyes are the window to the soul. When I look back on that event knowing what I know now, I see her trapped soul was hidden in plain sight all along.

In spite of the mystery behind those blue eyes, Steve seemed fairly happy to me throughout the years of middle school. Could he go through all of his life not fitting in anywhere and not noticing? I wondered when the day would come that Steve would simply pop. But by this time, dysphoria had begun, and indeed he was acutely aware that something was wrong, terribly wrong; I just didn't know it and I wouldn't know it for seven more years. Like many transsexual people, Steven tried to suppress it. He remained alone with his tormenting secret for the next seven years, and privately, painfully began to withdraw.

High School

In high school, Steve joined the debate team, a fairly exclusive and interesting mix of geniuses and geeks. Surely, Steve would find his niche here in this elite intellectual hub of the school. But his character lacked the arrogant, cut throat dimension required to slaughter the opponent in the ultra-competitive world of high school policy debate. His claim to fame was behind the scenes research, which consistently helped win the team state championships but did not draw much individual recognition. Steve didn't crave the stress it took to earn him a regular spot in the top tier and the notoriety that came with it. And until his last year on the team, I think Steve was viewed as too passive. My heartache continued; even here in this intellectual clique, he didn't seem to fit in the way he should have ... *the way she would have.* But in those years, he finally made some true friendships; the kind that could last a lifetime.

These were also the years of steepest decline into the nightmare of a tormented life. Something went wrong with Steve during high school and bad things started to happen. We lost our close connection, our bond, our ability to talk intimately. The teenage years are not supposed to be easy, so in a way, I tried to view this unfamiliar, distant behavior as normal; even though almost nothing else was ever too normal about Steve. The distance between us grew mysteriously and rapidly. Through what remained of our connection, the sadness and confusion and torment of his secret was palpable.

By senior year Steve became masochistically immersed in his intellectual pursuits. He had a pathological intensity about his responsibilities on the debate team. Researching for debate then doing homework for five Advanced Placement classes left less than three hours to sleep each night. He began to sink into a serious and fragile state of depression. Like many transsexual people, it is possible that Steve was seeking to suppress his gender dysphoria by working himself to death.

From time to time, a girl would come into Steve's life and special relationships finally seemed possible. When Steve was building friendships and pursuing romance with these girls, he seemed happy, almost euphoric. But when the relationships ceased, in every case badly, his despair grew a hundred fold. Steven was close to suicide. Like many transsexual people, it is possible that Steve was seeking to cure his gender dysphoria with love.

• • • • • • •

Sometime in the fall of his senior year, his friend and teacher Ms. Lane asked him to stay after class; she detected a struggle brewing within him. When she asked him about it, he succumbed to his grief, grateful for a listening ear. Though he couldn't explain what it was, he told her that something was wrong. With compassion and delicacy Ms. Lane told me about Steve's inexplicable depression at the November parent-teacher conference, and it took me completely off guard. Naturally grateful, I was also bewildered. The mystery surrounding Steven was more widespread and ominous than I imagined. Thus began our heightened awareness of the worst year of Steven's life.

Steve's written compositions began to reflect darkness, despair, and suicidal thoughts, and the teachers were reporting these things to the counselors, who reported them to me. Then calls flooded in from the head of counseling, then soon, the school district's crisis counselor. Steve wrote depressing journals, and disturbing suicidal messages to his friend Holly in the middle of the night. Then one pivotal night in mid January 2007, his note to Holly alarmed her more than usual. I'm guessing she came to a point much like this: "Do I risk losing a friend or risk losing the life of that friend? Do I break confidence to help save his life, or do I bear the responsibility and guilt of not preventing a possible suicide for the rest of mine?" I had an email in my inbox from Holly the next day, just a few lines, and only that one time, and for this I'll be forever grateful. His close classmates, the teachers, the counselors and Vice Principal all watched over Steven, keeping me abreast via phone calls and email. Eventually, we heard from Steven himself.

An excerpt from Steven's letter to us, dated February 4, 2007:

I occasionally become depressed, nervous, panicked, or anxious—for no reason and at seemingly random times. I have fluctuating periods of vague, irrational, self-deprecating thoughts and feelings of entrapment. ... Holly recently told me she believes I have a form of clinical depression. Her assessment is not strictly true, given that the textbook definition of this condition is far more severe, but I may not be entirely well, either. ...

Several months ago, on a particularly bad day, Ms. Lane talked to me after school and asked if I was OK. I discussed some of these things with her. I didn't return for a while, but recently I've seen her three times in a similar context. Although she is reassured by the fact that I talk to people like Holly, she said on Wednesday that she wanted me to communicate with you. ... I agreed to do so.

Ted was particularly disturbed by "self-deprecating thoughts and feelings of entrapment" and we puzzled over this wording. Feelings of entrapment? Were we smothering him? Impossible! We kept no leash on either kid. We brought them up as free-thinkers. Common sense and kindness were their built-in guides. Despite the mystery of Steve's situation, this letter assured us he was ready for our help.

We dove head first into a smattering of conventional treatments. We found a therapist, we tried yoga, we got a light box to increase serotonin production to balance his circadian rhythm. His grueling lifestyle and sleep deprivation led to a diagnosis of Seasonal Affective Disorder or "SAD." This made sense I guess, since the feelings were less intense in the summer when daylight and sleep were much more abundant. But at no time, not one single time, did Steven ever mention his gender dissonance to us. Although the SAD diagnosis seemed a bit weak, we never deduced that "feelings of entrapment" could be due to gender dysphoria.

Steve played piano passionately. After eleven years of study, he was now at a concert level and he spent countless hours at practice. But when he would compose piano pieces of his own, they were more and more often dark and painful. His impromptu pieces were sometimes unbearably depressing. The sadness and torment resounded through the music, and through the proverbial cord that still somehow connected me to my child. I could hear the cry for help, and I could feel the agony, but I could not reach Steve anymore, nor the source of the pain within him.

· · · · · · ·

By the age of 18 his list of accomplishments was phenomenal and covered every discipline academically, musically, and artistically. Steve became a school legend. His class voted him (and one other girl) "Biggest Brain of the Class of 2007" and he was described by teachers as a "Renaissance Man." And through it all, the school had him on suicide watch. Tormented by unbearable despair, Steve wrote journals about wanting to die. The life went out of his eyes and darkness shrouded him and his soul. After all those years of not fitting in, something really was wrong, something dark and disturbing, and something within him had finally popped.

By the time Steve moved off to college later that year, he had already left us in spirit as well. The child we once knew was already disappearing. An enigmatic soul replaced that of our child and a mysterious shield had filled the space between us. I wondered why he chose to face his demons alone.

· · · · · · ·

In the summer of 2008, I attended a magnificent fairy tale wedding in Maine. The bride and groom had choreographed an exquisite dance event wherein the guests blew continuous bubbles at them as they embraced and danced and swirled in the spotlight to spellbinding music. Like fairy dust, the bubbles formed a blissful aura about the new couple joined in love. This was the most perfect manifestation of pure joy I had ever witnessed. As they danced,

I stood, transfixed, overwhelmed with emotion to see two young people express this level of happiness. I think any parent's dream would be to see all their children dance in magic bubbles like this. I knew to the core that this was in the stars for my Jeff. I also knew, by some kind of supernatural mother's intuition, that I would never see this kind of happiness bestowed upon my Steve. This juxtaposition of hopes and dreams, this bizarre premonition was a climactic moment and affected me deeply. Right then and there in those glorious bubbles, I was besieged by gut-wrenching sadness.

We clung to the dwindling thread of a hope that Steve would find a place to belong—maybe in college, maybe in career, maybe the next phase of life or the next. But our sadness anticipating a life of inexplicable loneliness paled to the fear of what depression could add to that. Is this the way we must live from now on? Forever on pins and needles, vigilant and alert to Steve's depression, always fearful of possible suicide?

Six months later we would learn that Steve wasn't chronically depressed at all. At great cost to heart and soul, we would learn that Steve had a curable condition. It was a strange mix of feelings. Would the lifelong dream of Steve finally belonging somewhere come at the cost of the dreams of which I'd once felt assured? Loneliness notwithstanding, I had assumed that no matter what Steve chose to do in life academically, he would succeed. But when I learned my child was transsexual, those dreams were shattered by justified fear. Through twenty years we had grown to assume that some doors would always be open to Steve, but now, wouldn't those doors close too?

· · · · · · ·

I spent countless hours looking back over the years to recall some kind of clue about gender dysphoria that I had missed. Steve did not have any feminine mannerisms whatsoever. He walked like a guy, he sat like a guy, his gestures and facial expressions were all guy. There was not a hint of a feminine spirit, no feminine tendencies or interests or aspirations. Not once in all those 18 years was there any indication of gender dysphoria or any gender variant issue at all. Nor did Steve exhibit any stereotypical effeminate mannerisms that might indicate he was possibly gay. He was a gentle and passive guy; maybe not a typical guy, but definitely not a girl either.

Had we known about the girl who lay dormant within, perhaps it would be easier to think back on our young child as a little girl. In her reality, she was a daughter, but in my reality, I raised a son, and my reality is just as valid to me as Sarah's is to her. Maybe someday when I have merged the two identities, I'll see the child Sarah in the memories of Steve, but I am not quite there yet.

One might think after reading this chapter which is drenched in loneliness, that I'd be happy to have found the reason behind it. And it's true there was an odd glimmer of hope and a fleeting moment of joy right at the onset. I hoped for twenty years that Steve would find happiness. I dreamed he would someday find a natural place to belong. Had he finally found this place in a self called Sarah? It's bizarre that the dreams I'd always wanted to be fulfilled for Steve finally might come true, but at the absolute cost of Steven himself. It would take years to appreciate that letting my child die was the only way to let my child be alive.

Chapter 4

Dreams
And Other Stuff of Grief

This might sound like a story of sadness and self pity, and in fact it is my intention to start my story with grief. When I was drowning in devastation, I remember hearing calls from the people on shore, but they couldn't just wish me back to safety. I needed to find lifelines, and the will and the power to connect myself to them, right there at that deep level of anguish.

I don't want to beat this discussion of my despair into the ground so much that I alienate the transsexual community and defeat one important purpose of the memoir. But I do hope to reach the soul of another parent, even just one, who might be struggling with accepting the concept of a transsexual child, and help to bring them through to the other side. In order to try to help, I feel I must first meet them on common ground, because that is what worked for me. So I write this chapter, which is dripping with grief, to give recognition to the darkest part of my journey. This is the common ground that many of us parents may experience.

I think many transsexual adults scoff at our struggle, bewildered that cissexual people find them so bewildering. The parents who are able to make this journey must have an element of trust in their child's self-assessment. But a relationship, and the trust therein, is a two way street. Our emotions are real too, and at the very least my story may offer insight as to why it took me so long—and why it might take many of us so long—to come to terms with our children's identities.

· · · · · · ·

I once heard of a letter written to Sarah that said, "Your parents must be very proud of you."

Well yes, our long-term goal was to return to days of happiness and pride. But the road to get there was long and difficult. When our son revealed his transgender condition, our first reaction was not pride. In fact, I doubt that "being so proud to introduce our new daughter" and "anxious to share the good news" are very typical or natural first reactions of many parents of grown-up transgender children. There are stages that some parents need to go through to come to terms with gender transition. These may include shock, denial, resistance, anger, and relentless, profound anguish—as was the case for me. It could take a while to gather courage and strength, understanding and acceptance. It took Ted and me a year before we could feel happy again. Now we can feel proud of our child's courage to transition, but it is important for me to disclose that pride was not the first feeling that we had. Loved ones are faced with a process: we have to transition too.

"You must be so proud of her," might be the right thing to say, certainly an easy thing to say if you are a student or teacher of gender studies, and look at it academically. But it is a little disconcerting to parents who are struggling. Should a supposition like this make them embarrassed or ashamed? Can parents be shamed into a better state of mind, into a quicker acceptance of their transsexual child? Should one be wondering, "Why is it taking me so long to come to terms with this?" or even, "Am I a bad parent for questioning this?"

There are no rule books on how a parent is supposed to make this journey. Models of the stages of grief are meant to be guidelines only, suggesting six or seven distinct and very normal emotional states that people typically experience after a great tragedy or trauma or life-altering event. Sometimes these stages overlap, sometimes they circle back. There is no definitive sequence or duration of these stages, and sometimes people get stuck in one.

I don't know about all the tragedies of life, although I am often reminded of them by well-meaning consolers helping to put our grief into perspective. I do know that ours belongs to a very unique corner of humanity. There just isn't much data collected yet to see whether we fall within the norms of the typical grief analysis model. Transsexualism is one of the most derided and misunderstood medical conditions known. As parents, in addition to the personal trauma and sadness, we also have the unusual burden of dealing with the rest of society as well. Most notably, this includes how society's influence affects our ability to come to terms with our children's transitions in the first place. I wonder if parents of transsexual children who cannot move past the denial or anger stages of the process are possibly stuck there because of the conscious—and unconscious—influence of society.

As a matter of fact, I'm not so sure this would be a tragedy at all, were it not for the rest of society.

• • • • • • •

One day in February of 2009, a solid month into the darkest leg of the journey, Steven decided to come back to us. He changed his mind! This had all been a mistake! He cut his hair short and styled it like my handsome 20 year old young man again, parted neatly on the right. It was just like the last beautiful boy hair cut he'd ever had, the one that I loved so much. He had on his boy clothes, the khaki tan dress pants and a collared short-sleeved button-down shirt. Sheer euphoria erupted within me flooding my body and soul. It was like Steven had come back from the dead. I sobbed, ecstatic with tears of great joy, my arms stretched out to embrace him. This joy was compounded by the fact that I had been, just moments before, living and breathing a profoundly grief stricken existence.

Steven was coming home to me, returning to the place he had established as our son, not just with his hair cut but with the total decision to be a son. He had his past and his future with him too! He walked toward me through the golden wheat field, a slight breeze made the grain sway, the sun was shining down upon us. He approached me through the field, slowly and deliberately, carefully, his hands brushed the tops of the tall grasses. It seemed so ethereal! Was this in slow motion? Where is this field?

Even within the dream I figured out it was a dream. I was seeing the vision of my lost son, because by that time the Steven I knew was beginning to fade away as he started preparing himself for transition—hair grown out long, eyebrows thinned out and shaped. I was seeing the vision of a person who no longer existed, a person who was lost to me, one for whom I so deeply longed. This tormenting dream showed me the person who I could never have again. As I came to wakefulness I crashed down into my bed of sorrow; the dream made me feel like once I awoke, Steven had died.

The dream cast a spotlight on the before and the after very clearly. There was no plot to the dream, just the overwhelming joy to see my Stevie once again, and the unbearable sadness I felt as I watched him disappear upon waking.

The following day, suffocating with grief, I decided to share the dream with Ted. But he erupted with anger chastising me for even thinking, much less saying, that I felt like Steven had died. "He is not dead!" Ted bellowed, and his face got red and angry. But scolding me did not make me get better. It did not make the impact from that dream go away. Instead, I was blindsided by the fork in the road that suddenly appeared before me. My husband and I would part ways at this fork, but only for a short while.

I needed to mourn the loss of my son. The feeling that my child had died was real and with or without my only friend at the time, I had to work through it. Wouldn't it be easy if someone could just command another person to get through hard times? There would be no grief whatsoever in the human experience. But alas, Ted wasn't going to get me through this stage by forcing shame on me. So without further ado, I moved him out of my way and into another place, then shut the door on him. This was a pivotal point in our relationship and for the next four months Ted and I walked the journey on separate paths, isolated from each other and completely alone in the world. Although it was more lonely, it was better this way. As strange as it may sound, grieving separately enabled our marriage to stay intact.

For many of us parents, the cessation of a son—even though he is replaced by a daughter—feels like the death of that son. I've heard it mentioned repeatedly by parents of older trans children in documentaries and books. It's like a death: we go through mourning; we mourn the loss of our former child. Grief counselors today have parents of transsexual children filling their waiting rooms. Steven is not really dead. But Steven has ceased to exist.

My emotions were a turbulent ebb and flow of the classic initial stages of grief for the first year of the journey and well into the second. Which feelings seemed to be dominant from one day to the next, from week to week, were sometimes vague at the time. But in hindsight, I recognize them all from the Kübler-Ross Model: Denial, Anger, Bargaining, Depression, Acceptance.[1]

Although Steven was not really alive anymore, he was not really dead either, in the more familiar albeit less fortunate sense of the word. We didn't have it quite so bad, so permanently sad as those who experience a real death, but we did have a few extra factors unique to our journey alone.

At the start of it all, I was fraught with anxiety as my hopes and

dreams for my child got swallowed up by a torrent of panic and fear.
I used to wonder, "Will he win a Nobel Prize someday? Will he be
a famous statesman?" I was now wondering, "Will she stay alive
from one day to the next or will somebody try to kill her?" Once a
beloved member of the community, will she now be viewed as an
oddity, a curiosity, on the fringe, mentally ill, an aberration? Who
will hire her now?[2] Companies in most states can still fire a person
for being transsexual![3] What will become of this once promising,
magnificent mind? Will she find work in the public eye, or will she
work in seclusion? Even if she cures cancer, will the world see a
hero or a transsexual first? Which friends will stay and which ones
will turn away? Will people be malicious and cruel to her? Will life
be even more lonely than it was before? Will our family abandon
us, disown us? Who will love her romantically? Will she be limited
to fringe groups to find companionship? How many times will she
be hurt, abandoned, rejected? Will she look like other women, or
will she be discovered and shunned? Will she be a victim of a hate
crime? Beat up? Killed?

This hurricane swirled around inside me for several months.
I spent countless hours on the internet trying to come up with
other possible reasons why Steven was feeling gender dysphoric. In
my eyes, Steve was a guy through and through. There had been
absolutely no signs of feminine behavior whatsoever, no clues during
childhood or at any time, that there was a woman in there. I was in
denial. No doubt, denial is a dominant stage for parents of grown-up
trans children—at least for those of us who never saw it coming.

As I investigated this condition, anger began to bleed into the
denial. Why was Steve doing this to himself? Why was he doing
this to us? Why did he keep this from us until the age of 20? A
part of my pain stemmed from the betrayal one can feel when one
learns that a close person has been keeping such a large secret. I
questioned how close we really were, and sometimes felt angry that
we had been living something akin to a lie. For 20 years I knew
my child as a son; I had been allowed to have visions of a grown

up son, hopes and dreams for his success, maybe as a husband or a father, or maybe a single man, but a successful man who would surely contribute great things to our world. In moments of panic, I threatened to sue any therapist who would confirm a transsexual diagnosis. I declared I would stage an intervention! I felt like sending him to South Hollywood to witness the life on the streets, the transvestite community, and the drag queen bars, to get a snapshot of what his future world might be like. (The words in this paragraph describe strong emotions I never shared with Steven at the time. As I review them, I want to delete them, because they reveal my initial ignorance about some of the kindest, most courageous and misunderstood people on earth. But these thoughts were a part of my private torment in the early stage of the journey and I want to tell my story truthfully.)

I had a growing awareness that Steve was merely placating us every step of the way, only telling us enough bits and pieces to gradually pull us in, and I felt duped. He pretended to move slowly, to wait and be patient while we worked to validate or invalidate this condition, to allow us to think we had input in the matter. But his plans were already completely designed, timeline set, destination certain. Steven was the one driving this train all along, slowing down only long enough for us to either get on board or get out of the way. He wanted our blessing, not our permission.

I felt desperate and trapped and angry. I found one outlet by generating reams of documents of evidence and arguments that would surely refute Steve's self diagnosis. But after a six month flurry of panic, it became clear that this activity would do nothing to bring Steven back. It was like trying to walk down an upward moving escalator. Every step down that I took to refute this condition seemed to bring me closer to the top. My investigation led to my education and the awareness that I was the disaster that needed to be stopped. Instead of convincing him that he was wrong, I convinced myself that he was right. The byproduct of this panic-like stage of the journey is my chapter called "The Devil's Advocate."

My devil's advocate efforts evolved into the bargaining stage of my process. I had hoped to stop the transition by rooting out some disqualifying factor, and identifying another diagnosis. At the very least, I had hoped to "bargain down" the degree of transition. I believed that only "intense" transsexuals would not find peace until genital surgery, and I was going to prove that even if Steven was gender dysphoric, he was definitely not a "severe" case. I tried to bargain this transition away right up through September 2009, around the time of our visit with another psychologist for a second opinion. But I grew weary of the battle, and ever more aware that Steve's plans to go forward did not depend on my research, not one little bit. He was looking for our blessing, but not our help validating the diagnosis, and certainly not our permission. He started hormone treatment even before our visit for the second opinion.

· · · · · · ·

I am beset with a paradox, a kind of infinite loop in my logic: *I am the mother of a son who once existed and a daughter who exists now instead of him. But if she was Sarah all along, and if Sarah was not Steven, then she was not the person I knew. But I knew this person. The person who I knew was Steven. If Sarah was not Steven, then she was not the person who I knew. But I knew this person. The person who I knew was Steven. . .*

Sometimes trying to make sense of it all would bring me to the brink of delirium. I got tired of the fight, tired of the futility, tired of the relentless sadness, tired of feeling an unjustified anger. It was exhausting to comprehend that my son was becoming a daughter but would end up the same person. Humans overcome adversity every day. My task was to come to terms with a paradox. My child needed to change identity in order to stay the same identity. And this would have to occur by merging two mutually exclusive realities.

Somewhere in the vortex of panic and exhaustion and futility, I wondered if this is why some parents give up and abandon their child—is it perhaps a matter of their own self preservation?

· · · · · · ·

I went to a funeral that year. The funeral home was packed with visitors, mostly young people around 19 or 20 years old. It was crowded, standing room only in all the rooms, all except one room which had no visitors. I entered the empty room, Steven's room, and he lay there, as a boy, dressed in his old clothes and old haircut, my child, my sweet gentle soul. But no one came to visit him. I could hear the crowds in the hallways behind me, but I was the only one in that room. Even in death Steven was alone; no one wanted to visit my dead son. My heart grew bigger, suffocating my lungs, choking off my breath, it began to pound its way out of my body. The loneliness was larger than life. Was it because my son was dead? Or because he was a lonely person in life? Or because even in death my lonely son was still alone? Heavy with grief, I turned to stone, permanently to stay with my son.

When I woke up, I lay there blinking, heavy as stone, my heart still pounding. I think, with this, I was finally at the bottom of the pit. There was no place left to go but up.

Sometimes you have to feel as bad as you possibly can before you can start to feel better again.[4] By wallowing in the dark for long enough, the dark energy would be depleted. Sooner or later I would start to get tired of filling every one of my cognitive chambers with despair and anguish. I did in fact, have some control over my own cognition. I first needed to be convinced that Steven was transsexual. In parallel with that, enough time needed to pass. I would build new memories with Sarah, and in 20 years I will have known her for as long as I had known Steven. But I knew the most important factor in my cognitive shift would be to allow happiness to gradually dominate—to just "go with it" and start feeling the joy this transition is actually meant to bring. If my child is really transsexual, then gender transition is the cure. Theoretically, I should be happy about this in the end.

· · · · · · ·

As a parent of a grown-up transsexual child, my losses are unique and paradoxical. There is the loss of a child I perceived as a son. There is the loss—at least a questioning—of a history that had been perceived as happy. There is a loss of everything ever imagined about our son's future as a husband, a father, a man. There is a loss of what could have been—a lost opportunity to raise our child as a daughter, a lost chance to let her grow up whole. I wonder how different her childhood would have been had she grown up as Sarah. As strange as this question seems to sound, would she have been more normal? Sarah came to be at 20 years old. She literally missed her girlhood.

· · · · · · ·

From my journal at the time I was writing this chapter on grief:

> Even now, 21 months later, I find myself in a place of retreat and isolation; not clinically depressed, but in a melancholy state of reflection. The fanfare is over now, most everyone knows our story, the dust is settling around us. The rest of the world has to move on, like in any personal tragedy, leaving us to suffer in solitude, however much we still suffer.
>
> So, sick and tired of the senseless misery, I've built a happy place to go, because I see my child is happy or because I finally get it or, most ideally, both. I've learned to live compartmentalized. In my retreat, I feel

productive to write this memoir. Most days are fulfilling and energetic. The world around me is returning to life and even seems pretty much like it did before, although I'm aware I'm looking at it through a different set of lenses now. I still miss my son; I think I'll miss him forever, my sweet awkward misfit, my angel, my baby. Where did he go? When I lay on my death bed, I wonder if I will still be looking for him. It's been a year now since I've seen Steven, although I just saw Sarah yesterday.

Trading Places

Chapter 5

The Devil's Advocate
No Stone Left Unturned

The value of learning is that it is one of the most powerful ways to move beyond your fears and misconceptions to a place of understanding and acceptance.

Mildred L. Brown & Chloe Ann Rounsley[1]

For most of my life I knew absolutely nothing about gender dissonance. Not once did I ever look at my baby, my little boy, or my teen, and wonder, "Is this person transsexual?" I never spent a single minute preparing for this day because I never saw it coming. Except for death, disease, or disappearance of a child, I wondered if it was possible for a mother's heart to be more broken. In the beginning I wondered, "Why is my child so desperate to take an already perfect life and deliberately, willfully ruin it? He was making a mistake and we have to stop it!" As a mother, it was my duty to intercept what I perceived as disaster. I did not yet realize that to prevent the transition would be the real disaster.

During the first several months after finding out about Steve's gender dissonance, I left no stone unturned in my mission to disprove it. While Ted accepted Steve's transgender announcement with blind faith, I aggressively played devil's advocate. It was imperative that I become convinced that this was not only a real condition, but one that my child legitimately had. I told Steven that I could no more easily have enabled my toddler to run into traffic than enable my grown son to change to a daughter. These concepts had seemed equally disastrous to me at the start of my journey. We have a unique bond, in that my child knew (and patiently, somewhat grudgingly accepted) that I would investigate and exhaust all other options. I spent hundreds of hours reading books and online articles. I immersed myself in the study of how gender dysphoria is typically diagnosed, and what qualifies—or disqualifies—a person for treatment. I was sure my copious arguments would reveal that Steve was not transsexual in the least, but simply a sweet, gentle guy. I vigilantly questioned the diagnosis and ensuing process every step of the way.

As mentioned before, I think many transsexual adults scoff at parents' struggles, bewildered that cissexual people find trans people so bewildering. But a relationship, and the trust therein, is a two way street. Parents' emotions are real too, and so is the transition we must make along with our children. Though many of the questions I asked then seem silly to me now, they seemed reasonable at the time and it was important to have them addressed so I could move forward. To censor and soften the text and write from a happy, healed, and more educated perspective would be a disservice to an interested reader who wants to know how it felt at the time, and would defeat my purpose in sharing this story at all.

This chapter diverges from the main story line of the memoir, but learning about the condition was a big part of my thought process and essential to my growth. In order to illustrate the progress I made, I wrote parts of this chapter from two perspectives—from where I was at the start, and from my more knowledgeable point of view today. My early thoughts, except for the questions themselves, are italicized. Sarah also wrote comments about a few of the questions.

· · · · · · ·

1   What does gender dysphoria feel like?

One young trans woman was asked her whole life about why she wanted to change her body. She described an "intensely strong conviction" that she was not a man, not male, and a sense that she was female instead.[2]

This idea was elaborated by trans author Joanne Herman:

> I felt like a car running on the wrong type of gas. I did not fully understand how wrong it was until I replaced testosterone with estrogen when I transitioned genders in 2002. I now have an amazing sense of well-being and harmony that I never knew before. Now my body just hums.[3]

I learned of a trans girl, born genetically male, who prayed as a child that God would turn her into a girl. I read about one trans boy, born genetically female, who was waiting for his penis to grow. He figured that by puberty, surely it would grow, but instead breasts grew, which was devastating. Steven was particularly uncomfortable with the facial hair that came in. He said when he looked in the mirror it always seemed startling. While puberty can be an exciting time for some people, during which a cissexual girl might get her first bra or a boy might start to shave, it is often the worst time imaginable for a trans person. They already may know they are in the wrong body as a child, even when the bodies of both genders are nearly the same. But the development of unexpected secondary sex characteristics at puberty—the wrong ones—exacerbates the dissonance, causing great emotional distress. Cissexual people do not experience this, as their bodies deliver what their brains expect.

From Julia Serano, *Whipping Girl*:

> For me, the hardest part about being trans has not been the discrimination or ridicule ... but rather the internal pain I experienced when my subconscious and conscious sexes were at odds with one another. I think this is best captured by the psychological term "cognitive dissonance," which describes the mental tension and stress that occur in a person's mind when they find

themselves holding two contradictory thoughts or views simultaneously—in this case, subconsciously seeing myself as female while consciously dealing with the fact that I was male. ... But most of all, it felt like sadness to me—a sort of gender sadness—a chronic and persistent grief over the fact that I felt so wrong in my body.[4]

Jan Morris painted an exquisite 194 page picture of what it was like to be transsexual in her classic and eloquent book, *Conundrum*. As a woman who spent her first 40 years in a man's body, Jan described feeling like an undetected "spy in a courteous enemy camp," in an observer's role only. While she felt herself to belong to no segment of humanity, she longed to belong somewhere.[5] The dictionary describes identity as "the condition or fact that a person or thing is itself and is not something else." Jan wrote about her identity, "I realize now that the chief cause of my disquiet was the fact that I had none. I was not to others what I was to myself. I did not conform to the dictionary's definition—'itself and not something else.'"[6]

A paragraph from Sarah:

We all know our gender identities intuitively, in a way that cannot be explained using step-by-step reasoning. Just as I know where my hand is and that it is my hand and not someone else's, I know that I am a woman. Cis readers may not have spent much time examining how they know their own gender identities, but most will find that they feel a similar conviction. It may not be possible to describe to a cis person precisely what gender dysphoria feels like; it may have to be sufficient to say that it hurts to experience dissonance between your actual identity and a false identity projected onto you by others.

2   How is a person with gender dysphoria medically treated?

The World Professional Association for Transgender Health (WPATH) Standards of Care (SOC) is the most common explicit protocol used by therapists, endocrinologists, and surgeons to treat patients with gender dysphoria.[7] Before September 2011 (when I was first learning about transgender health) WPATH was known as The Harry Benjamin International Gender Dysphoria Association.[8]

The Standards of Care start with at least three months of therapy, usually with a psychologist or specialized social worker. The therapist will work to determine that the patient is of sound mind and does not appear to have any other pathologies. The therapist will advise the patient of the many difficulties and risks of this perilous journey. The therapist must be sure the patient knows what they are asking for, and that the end result may not always bring the level of happiness expected. In therapy, they talk about family and how to transition at work, and about the risks of being targeted in a hostile world. The therapist may serve as a gatekeeper, making sure the patient is well-adjusted and well informed. But the therapist cannot decide whether the patient is a man or a woman; one's awareness of one's gender—and whether or not one is transgender—is fundamentally personal. This is a self-diagnosed condition.

Once the therapist gives the green light, the patient is referred to an endocrinologist, who prescribes hormone treatment. Hormone treatment is the absolute most necessary ingredient to alleviate dysphoria in almost all transsexual patients. This is usually considered the most important step in transition, and the first one that requires a gatekeeper's referral. Facial hair removal and facial feminization surgeries for male to female patients and breast removal for female to male patients may be significant as well. But these procedures don't require permission from anybody and can occur as the opportunity arises. Genital surgery may be pursued after living a full year in every aspect of life as the intended identified gender. Genital surgery requires a visit to and a letter of referral from a second doctor.[9] Presently, the waiting list for surgery in the United States is long and bookings are made well over a year in advance. Since the clitoris and penis are homologous organs, surgeons make use of them in typical procedures. In male to female patients, tissue that had made up the penis and testicles is used to build the vagina, labia and clitoris. Physical sexual arousal is thereby preserved. In female to male patients, metoidioplasty enhances the erectile capable clitoris which has already become enlarged due to testosterone. As an alternative, in phalloplasty, a penis is created from surrounding tissue, the blood supply of which has been kept intact. How one is perceived by society as a man or as a woman is not dependent on the appearance of genitals. Some trans people never have genital surgery.

It was easy for me to learn about the Harry Benjamin Standards of Care on the web, and I downloaded and printed out a full copy.[10] I eagerly pored through it, studied every word, every detail, desperately seeking the part of the process where Steven would be disqualified, the part where the therapist would discover that Steve was not transsexual at all but had intellectualized this idea to subconsciously escape another disorder.

Harry Benjamin was a pioneer, a leading endocrinologist and the first doctor to offer compassionate recognition and a dignified approach to treating transsexual patients. All psychological attempts to treat or "cure" gender dysphoria in the past had failed. So in c.1948, Dr. Benjamin decided to approach this condition as physical-medical rather than psychological. He offered hormones to his transsexual patients, from which they reported great emotional relief. This was a revolutionary turning point in the treatment of transsexualism. His guidelines for treatment became known as The Harry Benjamin Standards of Care.

I think it is fair to say that most people honor Dr. Benjamin's contribution in this field and appreciate the progress he made for this cause. Nonetheless, many trans people today consider the standards (first named in his honor) to be more like an obstacle. They believe they should not be forced to go through this regimen (or any regimen at all) to prove to another what they already know to be true about themselves. Sarah specifically endorses an informed-consent model of trans-related medical treatment, to bring it in line with most other forms of medical care. In her view, therapy before and during transition should be optional.

But for me in early 2009, having just discovered that my son had a gender issue, the Standards of Care did not seem stringent enough! They simply looked like a list of common sense measures and very high level, general criteria. I wondered, "Where were the definitive tests listed? Where were the detailed physical tests that would ultimately prove Steven was not transsexual? Where were the clear-cut evaluation criteria that would reveal Steve's mistake?"

3   What types of physical tests are performed to confirm a diagnosis of gender dysphoria?

Do they test for a chemical imbalance? Do they test hormone levels? Do they perform neurological tests? Will they x-ray to check for an intersex condition?

The answer to all of the above is: They don't do *any* physical testing whatsoever. There are no physical tests that "prove" that an individual is transsexual. The only thing needed for access to professionally prescribed hormone therapy is the green light from a gender therapist. Endocrinologists test patient hormone levels for dosing, not for diagnosing.

This was not the answer I wanted to hear at the start of my journey. I was looking for some tangible validation. I was shocked that no physical tests by a physician or psychiatrist are required to be allowed access to any stage of gender transition at all, including genital surgery.

4   What chromosomal tests are performed to identify the cause? Will karyotyping reveal a genetic abnormality?

In the beginning, I desperately wanted there to be a clear-cut DNA abnormality to substantiate a transgender diagnosis. I hypothesized that maybe transsexual people are chimeras with the DNA of both genders. After all, they found a case of chimerism in one intersex individual.[11] I wondered about mosaicism, in which some cells of the body deviate in chromosomal makeup or genotype from those in the rest of the body due to a mutation.

But it doesn't matter. No DNA testing is done to validate a diagnosis of transsexualism. As it turns out, this is a good thing because the last thing a trans person needs is another test to pass. Even though chromosomal substantiation would have helped me accept the condition easier, ideas like this can be controversial or offensive to trans people themselves.

I've since learned that gender identity is far more complicated than XX vs. XY karyotypes. There are plenty of cissexual men with XX karyotypes, and with XXY karyotypes (i.e., Klinefelter syndrome), and cissexual women with XY karyotypes. About one out of every 500 boys is born with Klinefelter syndrome. More often than not, these folks aren't gender dissonant at all.[12] The biological connection to gender identity is multidimensional; I address this complex issue in more detail in Appendix A, "Theories About the Causes of Gender Dysphoria and Transsexualism." I still believe that society will accept transsexualism more easily when more conclusive scientific evidence is published to help explain it. However, while physical evidence may help people understand the condition better, it would be a violation of human rights to use any such findings to build more roadblocks in a treatment path already far too difficult for transsexual patients. Physical evidence is not needed to prove to a trans person something he or she already knows.

5 Why not give male to female transsexual people more testosterone to see if it will help them become more comfortable living as male?

Surely it seemed like these guys who claimed to be women were just too low on testosterone! But Steve laughed when I first asked about this, and assured me that he had more than enough testosterone.

I've since learned that the idea of increasing testosterone intake to try to "cure" a male to female trans person is not only a misconception, it could be catastrophic. A low testosterone level is not what causes dysphoria, but a high testosterone level would probably exacerbate it. A male to female trans woman already has too much testosterone washing around in a brain that expects and needs estrogen.

Scientists are currently investigating a hormone receptor theory as a possible cause of transsexualism.[13] A simplified account of the idea might go something like this: Everybody has a certain number of estrogen and testosterone receptors in the brain, and the brain expects to receive a corresponding dose of each sex hormone to match these receptors. In a cissexual person, the brain gets what it expects. In a transsexual person, the theory is that the brain does not receive the hormone levels that it expects of either estrogen or testosterone. A neurologically female brain, while expecting estrogen, is instead swamped with testosterone if it is trapped in a male body. The result is a powerful sense of dissonance.[14]

6   How long does a person typically have to go to therapy before being allowed to take hormones?

I had hoped this would take years, and that the therapy would eventually cure Steve.

The Standards of Care recommend a minimum of three to six months of therapy by a gender specialist. Steven's therapist was ready to allow hormones after just four months. I asked her how she determined that Steve passed the evaluation and was a valid candidate for transition. She replied, "I listened to him. There is nothing wrong with his mind." It was his body that was wrong.

In the beginning, I thought this was extremely lax, and made fun of therapists who (figuratively speaking) put signs on their lawns: "Get your hormones here!"

Today I understand why four months seems extremely stringent from the viewpoint of a transsexual person. As a post-menopausal woman, I don't have to visit a therapist at all to be "allowed" estrogen supplements for my medical condition. Transsexualism is also a medical condition, so transsexual people should also theoretically receive treatment without a gatekeeper determining its validity. However, as a mom who was faced with a sudden transition in the opposite direction, the therapist's work was a vital step in my process of leaving no stone unturned.

7 Wouldn't a smart patient just fabricate the right answers in order to convince the therapist to allow hormones?

Indeed, a smart trans person will figure out what to say in order to be granted professional hormone treatment. Is this deceitful? Or is this the right of a person trying to obtain the treatment they need and deserve from a sometimes resistant, often uneducated medical system?

There are still therapists out there who believe they get to decide the gender of their patient. I read of a case of a trans woman who was denied hormones for weeks because she wore pants to her therapy sessions. One day, exasperated, she decided to attend her therapy session in full womanly regalia—dress, heels, and makeup—and with this facetious display, the therapist was finally convinced.[15] Yet as a cissexual woman, never once in 58 years have I ever gone to see a doctor in a dress and heels.

You couldn't pay a cissexual person a million dollars to change physical sex, yet trans people, who are willing to pay, are often denied. Trans people already know who they are but they still bear the burden of proving it and convincing a gatekeeper to allow them access to medical treatment.

8 Doesn't the therapist need to talk to the parents to see what kinds of toys and interests the patient had as a child?

I was absolutely certain that a diagnosis with such serious life altering consequences would require investigation into a patient's past and require input from parents and other loved ones.

Assuming the therapist would be as thorough as possible in her position as gatekeeper, I prepared a comprehensive list of Steven's childhood activities and male characteristics. These would surely stump the therapist and disqualify Steve as a candidate. He played with Hot Wheels, Thomas the Tank Engine, Dungeons and Dragons. He even wanted to drive a steamroller when he grew up! He ignored dolls and ignored the pink aisles in toy stores.

Indeed, the therapist did talk to Steven in depth about his childhood, and Steven didn't have to lie about any of it. He was a little boy, he was happy as a boy, and he felt no dysphoria at all until puberty. As it turns out, it doesn't much matter what kinds of toys young people play with at all. Some trans children don't think about their gender and may not yet know they are transgender, as was the case with Steven. Many children who do know are quite successful at hiding it, and sometimes continue to suppress it well into their thirties or forties. And toys like Hot Wheels and dolls are only associated with boys and girls because of stereotypes anyway.

There are no tangible check points that an adult trans patient must pass, like proof of cross-dressing as a child, or validation from parents. Modern therapists do not (or should not) ask for such evidence.

9 Do some patients try to transition because they think this will enable them to "fit in" better?

Had Steve reached a point where he became so desperate to belong, to connect to people, that he thought he'd fit in better if he tried life as a woman?

Actually, yes, because she was meant to live life as a woman. Her innate gender identity—her neurological sex—was female. In retrospect, this is most likely the reason Steve never fit in as a child growing up.

10   There is not one single feminine characteristic about my son. He has no feminine interests, aspirations, or mannerisms. How can a person like this claim to be a girl?

It's not about being feminine. It's about being female.[16]

Some trans women work hard to "bring the man out" of themselves by engaging in ultra macho activities like racing dirt bikes or playing football. Sensational documentaries often shine the spotlight on trans women in prior manly roles.[17,18] It's not uncommon for trans women to join the military, to work in construction, to believe that they need to work harder than most men in order to become the man to match their body and to obliterate the feminine spirit that lies within them. Some trans women who transition later in life attend body image classes in order to un-learn a lifetime of masculine mannerisms.

Although Steven never quite seemed like a typical boy, he never once seemed like a girl at all. But being a woman is not about being feminine; it's about being female.

A paragraph from Sarah:

> Questions like this one reveal a double standard—few would ask them of a cis woman who fails to exhibit consistently feminine mannerisms. If a cis woman fails to comply with feminine stereotypes, do you wonder if she is secretly a man? Or do you allow her some flexibility because stereotype compliance, however strongly our culture may encourage it, remains at least somewhat optional in most people's minds?

11   My child has always been very successful. Wouldn't it be true that a dissonant person would be immobilized by depression and unsuccessful in life?

Actually, it's common for transsexual people to throw themselves into activities to block out thoughts about their dissonance. Steven was an overachieving superman in high school, but the pace of his life nearly killed him.

From an article by Jamison Green:

> It is very difficult to isolate one's experience as a transsexual person from one's life experience in general. And unfortunately, many people have tried to analyze and generalize about transsexual experience to the extent that they try to create patterns that we are all supposed to follow. This makes it difficult for people whose trajectories don't follow the prescribed path. For example, early on (back in the 1970s) I understood transsexual people to be so unhappy that they were suicidal. I was not suicidal, therefore I must not be transsexual. I held off for another 10 years before seeking treatment, and I might have done numerous other things in that time had I transitioned earlier. ...[19]

12 Aren't people more legitimately trans if they were gender non-conforming as children? Doesn't it raise a flag of caution when people don't even feel gender dysphoric until they are teenagers?

Many cissexual people still view trans people who felt gender dysphoric as children to be more legitimately transsexual. But it is just as common for trans people to first encounter gender dissonance at puberty when the wrong sex hormones flood their bodies, and unwanted secondary sex characteristics develop instead of the ones they expect.

The process of coming to a realization about one's own gender is confusing and takes time to sort out. And many kids—cis and trans—don't have much of an understanding of their gender identity until puberty.

Many kids in our culture today are not forced to adhere to stereotypical gender rules. I guess now that I think about it, we gave our kids a free-thinking, fairly gender-neutral upbringing. Perhaps there was no reason for any gender dysphoria to surface in an environment like the one we provided.

Mainstream media sources love to spotlight little kids who display transgender tendencies, because society accepts them more easily. But it is a myth that a person who experiences dissonance as a child is more "trans" or has a more genuine case of gender dysphoria than one who figures it out later in life.

13 If a person starts to believe they are transsexual at puberty, the time of sexual awakening, could it simply be a misdiagnosis for some sexual disorder?

At first I was interested in testing for other types of sexual disorders, particularly because of the timing of the self-diagnosis. It was reassuring to me that Steven picked a gender therapist who had a degree and expertise in human sexuality. Surely she would explore that arena and root out some hidden sexual dysfunction as the real reason behind Steve's dissonance.

Sexual dysfunctions may be investigated along with all other psychiatric disorders. But being transsexual doesn't really have much to do with sex at all. Transsexualism is not about sexual disorders and not about who a person has sex with. It's about gender; it's about who a person is.

14 How can people know they are gender dysphoric if they have never had sex with anyone?

In my naiveté, I had initially figured that transgender people would use sexual experience to help verify their transgender self-diagnosis. I asked Steven, "As an 18 year old male, when you were with girls you liked, didn't you ever think about having sex with them?"

Steven responded, "With this male body, I can't imagine having sex with anyone."

Steven's experience was not universal. Many trans people force themselves into a "normal" life, get married and have plenty of sex.

Some hope the experience will cure them. Some may pretend to be the other repressed gender during sex. Transsexualism is about who people are on the inside, whether they are sexually active or not.

15 How can people claim to be transsexual if they are married or have fathered or given birth to children?

Although Steve doesn't have a spouse or children, I am curious about the trans people I've learned about who do.

Many trans women and trans men try to repress their gender dissonance for years in a loving relationship and hope that love will "cure" them. Mainstream media sources love to spotlight these stories because they are sensational and shocking. There are a lot of publicized cases of middle aged "men" who have seemingly perfect lives—great wealth, loving wives, beautiful healthy children, successful, fulfilling careers—but still feel the need to transition. None of these things actually cure or permanently repress the extraordinary pain of gender dissonance. I've heard many stories about retired people and grandparents transitioning, and I've personally encountered a person who was transitioning at age 80.

16 What if a transsexual person is really just a gay person seeking easier social acceptance?

At first I hoped that Steven was gay instead of transsexual.

Gender identity defines who a person is; sexual preference defines who that person wants to be with romantically. They are not the same thing.

The idea that a male to female trans person could actually be a gay man is counterintuitive. Homosexual men are still men, and are usually quite happy with their male bodies. By definition, gay men want to be with other gay men with male bodies like their own. Going through a gender transition would make this type of partnership unattainable.

Many people confuse the concept of gender identity with the concept of sexual preference. I talk about these concepts more in

Chapter 10, "Queer Clarification."

17 Doesn't the need to transition reinforce gender stereo-typing? Doesn't it contradict feminist ideology?

Doesn't transition make the statement that men cannot be "womanly" and must therefore become women to display feminine attributes more acceptably? Wouldn't it be taking more of a stand against gender stereotypes to proudly live as a feminine man?

This question almost seems too silly to include in my book—except for the fact that it was an important source of confusion for me in the beginning: I wondered if Steve was succumbing to social expectations by transitioning into a woman because he was not a macho man. But transsexualism is a painful medical condition, it is not a choice on any level, and it has nothing to do with stereotype conformity.

A paragraph from Sarah:

> I, too, struggled with a misplaced sense of tension be-tween my commitment to gender equality and my need to transition. For example, in September 2007, I wrote, "I can't even admit that I want to be a woman because it feels sexist to express a preference." Even at the time, I acknowledged that internal gender identity is different from social gender stereotypes, and that having a strong gender identity says nothing about one's endorsement of such stereotypes—but I had trouble applying that abstract understanding to my own situation. I accepted the identities of other trans people, but scrutinized and challenged my own identity in ways that were sometimes logically inconsistent. Regarding this double standard, I wrote, "I can't allow myself to accept myself." Of course, I eventually ran out of energy for pretending, and could no longer hold such inconsistent views about my own identity.

18 What are the odds my child will be happy with therapy alone?

I read in some articles (including the SOC version 5) that some transsexual people obtain adequate relief just by going to therapy.[20,21] *For much of the first year, I clung to the hope that Steve would be in that group and be satisfied with a lifetime of therapy. As the months went by, Steve continued to remind me that cases like this are rare; almost no one is happy with just therapy. He could see that I needed to process the transition slowly, and I needed to hope, just a while longer, that my son would stay with me. It would have been too hard to tell a mom that the son she thought she had was never really there in the first place.*

I now believe most transsexual people want to actually live life in their true gender; they don't want to just talk about wishing to do so. From what I know today, I would guess that the early standards mentioned the possibility of obtaining adequate relief from therapy alone as a result of pressure by family or religious groups.

19 Can my child find adequate relief just dressing up from time to time?

I've heard trans people describe their former lives, when dressing up was the only outlet they had: "When I looked in the mirror I finally saw myself." But dressing up in private for a couple of hours a day seems temporary, like putting on a band aid to cover a wound, or at best just like therapy. It seems more ideal to live life without the wound at all. There is more to living life with harmony between mind and body than just wearing the right clothes and privately looking in a mirror.

20 What are the odds my child will be happy with hormones alone?

I heard that many transsexual people are content with life on hormones alone, and do not have genital surgery. At first, I was hoping that Steve would be one of them.

Hormones are key to aligning the body with the brain. Hormone treatment on most trans people relieves their dissonance and improves psychological well-being immensely. How one is perceived by society as a man or as a woman, while sometimes dependent on hormones, is not dependent at all on the appearance of genitals. Some trans people view genitals as irrelevant to identity, and others may not have easy access to surgery even if they want it. But many trans people continue to experience severe dissonance with mismatched genitalia. In some states, gender markers on legal documents cannot be updated without proof of some qualifying gender alignment surgery (such as genital surgery). Heterosexual marriage is allowed with proof of genital surgery in most states (except Texas). An account that frames "being content with hormones" and "wanting to have surgery" as opposing experiences oversimplifies a much more complex set of circumstances. I don't think there are documented odds about either.

21   Can my child try to be content living androgynously?

I tried to negotiate a compromise with Steven, hoping he would remain "partially" a boy.

Androgynous people have ambiguous or blended gender traits and expressions; they are not clearly masculine or clearly feminine in appearance or in behavior. While androgynous people fall under the transgender umbrella, they are not the same as transsexual people. A transsexual woman is strictly a woman and does not want to be perceived as ambiguous. (Chapter 10, "Queer Clarification," addresses some terminology and basic distinctions between different kinds of transgender people.)

22   What if my child has a mental illness?

I explained to the therapist that we had some history of mental illness in the family including depression and bipolar disorder. Shouldn't these conditions be investigated by a doctor who is trained in psychiatric disorders?

Therapy does seek to verify the absence of pathologies, but only to validate a presumed soundness of mind. Transsexualism is a medical condition, not a mental illness.

Before undergoing genital surgery, the SOC protocol does require a second evaluation by a clinical psychologist or psychiatrist. Steven was given a diagnostic exam to screen for psychological disorders. We were told that this test would rule out most mental illnesses—and at the time this helped me to feel that no stone would be left unturned. But while such tests can establish a benchmark for a patient's mental health status, they are not intended to provide alternate reasons for why a patient might feel gender dissonant. A transsexual person will still be transsexual whether or not the person also has obsessive compulsive disorder or bipolar disorder or a broken arm for that matter.

Though transgender conditions are still listed in the DSM-5,[22] they have a classification and a chapter of their own and are separated from pathologies and paraphilias. Transsexualism is more widely recognized today as being due to a medical condition and the terminology "disorder" has been eliminated from the description.[23]

23 Why does just one single therapist get to decide the fate of my child (and the fate of all the rest of us for that matter)?

Isn't the therapist worried about catastrophic consequences if this is a mistake?

It is true that just one therapist is needed to serve as the gatekeeper to professional hormone therapy.

I asked Steve's therapist about the enormous responsibility she had as a gatekeeper. Dr. Smith replied, "That's why we have the 'real life test'" as a final validation of the self-diagnosis. The protocol requires that patients live a year in their desired gender before genital surgery is considered an option. While the therapist may clear obstacles from the path, it is the patient's decision to walk it.

It is noteworthy that Dr. Smith has not had a single suicide in her career treating transsexual patients. In other words, a good therapist should be able to discern that blocking access to hormones and transition is more likely to have catastrophic consequences than allowing access to treatment.

24 How many people want to turn back once they start the "real life test"?

In the mid to late twentieth century, it was said that few people who started transition could make it all the way through. I now hear that very few people who start will ever turn back. Once they get to the point of the real life test, they are already sure they are transsexual. Of the roughly 300 patients Sarah's therapist has treated, only two turned back after starting their real life experience (and those individuals were under extreme pressure from family and religious groups). Society itself is a roadblock, and this was much worse twenty years ago. I suspect fewer people bothered to try to transition back then. It isn't enough to be born with a painful medical condition—transsexual patients also must deal with a cruel world. Unlike most other medical conditions, this one is often met with hostility.

25 How does estrogen change the body of a male to female trans person?

At the start of the journey I was worried that my child would never look like the woman she was inside. Today, I find it hard to imagine her looking like a man.

Transsexual women usually take both estrogen and anti-androgens to stop further development of masculine secondary sex traits such as broadening of the shoulders or hair loss. If the testicles are removed in an orchiectomy, the anti-androgens aren't needed and the estrogen dosage can be reduced. Estrogen redistributes body fat and reduces muscle mass and upper body strength. Sarah's once square shoulders seemed to get soft and round. On estrogen, body hair thins while head hair thickens. Skin softens and fatty tissue is redistributed to the hips and face. Sarah's face shape actually changed from a sharply angled diamond to a soft and lovely round circle. Breasts grow, penis shrinks, and, after about six months to a year on hormones, a trans woman becomes permanently sterile. Most of these changes are noticed within weeks, and they continue evolving for several years.

26 How do estrogen and anti-androgen hormones affect the temperament of a male to female transsexual person?

Donna Rose:

> Although the physical changes are certainly significant and oh-so-welcome, the mental and emotional changes dwarf them in comparison. A sense of well-being and contentment somehow seems to take hold. A flood of new emotions and sensations is suddenly unleashed. For someone not used to it, looking at the world through an estrogen-filled lens is a very intense experience.[24]

Julia Serano:

> In retrospect, when testosterone was the predominant sex hormone in my body, it was as though a thick curtain were draped over my emotions. It deadened their intensity, made all of my feelings pale and vague as if they were ghosts that would haunt me. But on estrogen, I find that I have all of the same emotions that I did back then, only now they come in crystal clear.[25]

In many of the cases I've learned about, one dramatic change that comes about with hormone therapy is the sharp (and often welcome) changes in sex drive. Before anti-androgen hormone treatment, some male to female trans women reported masturbating many times a day, thinking about sex 24-7 like a testosterone-loaded cissexual male might do. Some trans women report a decrease in sex drive when their testosterone levels drop with anti androgen treatment, and trans men often report just the opposite—a sudden increase in libido coincident with increase in testosterone levels. It's notable that many trans women also report an increase in sex drive. Even if testosterone is linked to sex drive, feeling comfortable in one's own skin is also linked to sex drive. It is impossible to predict which of those influences will be stronger.

I've heard it said that a transitioning person goes through a "second puberty" in many ways. Emotional changes, sometimes volatile, are evident in social interactions. In our house, as the "thick curtain lifted," Sarah was finally able to express many of the emotions she likely possessed, but suppressed, for the last ten years. Steven never shared these with me as a teen or young adult; he interacted agreeably, even submissively. Sarah conversely, is sometimes terse, sassy, unyielding, and when we interact now, I am the submissive one. Unleashed assertiveness and a razor sharp brain will be useful tools as she steps into the next phase of life; I'll never worry about any battles of wit and reason she may face—in general or regarding transsexual issues.

Through the eyes of a mother, I see a completely new person in her that I did not see in Steven. Although I am happy and relieved, the absence of Steven is palpable.

A paragraph from Sarah:

> The most important effect of hormone treatment on transsexual people is the level of psychological comfort it provides, regardless of whether the individual in question is male or female. Having the wrong hormones is extraordinarily uncomfortable, causing dissonance and stress. Hormone therapy can therefore make trans men *and* trans women more comfortable with themselves, more in touch with their emotions, less sad or angry, or more assertive. In some cases, trans people and their friends and family try to ascribe these changes to the particular hormone being taken. If a trans man becomes more assertive as he transitions, people may assume it

is because testosterone causes assertiveness. If a trans woman becomes more emotional, people may assume it is because estrogen causes emotionality. Neither of these things are necessarily true—but it is clear that being comfortable in one's own body can both facilitate assertiveness and allow one to express one's emotions more freely.

27   What characteristics don't change with estrogen?

Facial hair has to be removed by laser (if one is lucky) or electrolysis (which can take hundreds of hours over a couple of years and cost tens of thousands of dollars). An Adam's Apple can be softened in a "trachea shave" surgical procedure. Vocal chords lengthen irreversibly at puberty so a trans woman has to learn to modify her voice. The overall skeleton does not change, which means that characteristics like height and handspan are more or less fixed. Some trans women have facial feminization surgery to flatten their brow, lower their hairline, and soften their jaw, chin and nose.

Skeletal growth and masculinization of the face of genetic males could continue well into the mid-late twenties with default testosterone left unchecked. But these developments will cease with estrogen and anti-androgen treatment in people who transition young.

28   How much of the process is reversible if my child starts to transition then changes his mind?

If estrogen is stopped and testosterone resumed, muscle mass and body strength build up again, breasts shrink, and genetic hair loss will resume. But facial hair removal, sterility, and surgery of any kind are mostly permanent.

29   What are some theories about the causes of gender dysphoria and transsexualism? Is there a genetic link?

For decades, scientists believed the sole determining factor causing differentiation in gender identity was the fetal testosterone hormone wash which occurs around week 14 in a fetus developing male gonads.[26-29] If the brain fails to masculinize during this hormone surge, some sexually dimorphic areas of the brain may continue to develop as female. For example, one sexually dimorphic area of the hypothalamus in transsexual women is similar in volume and neuron density to that of cissexual women.[28,30] In 2003, scientists found a possible genetic link to transgender identity in 57 different genes.[29] More recent studies have shown a link between genes related to androgen and estrogen hormone receptors and transsexualism.[31,32] Evidence from several studies suggests that trans women are likely to have a longer version of the androgen receptor gene than cis men.[31,32] This may cause reduced testosterone signaling during fetal development and may be responsible for the under-masculinization of the brain during the fetal gonadal hormone wash.

I've been told by my proofreaders that my lengthy description of biological and genetic causal theories reads like a textbook and that few will want to read about androgen receptors and neuroscience in the middle of my personal story. I put my expanded discussion of this topic in Appendix A for those few who might be interested: to me, it is the most important question of the chapter.

I've noticed that some trans people seem to discount the importance of identifying neurobiological and genetic links to transsexualism. "Why not just take us at our word?" they seem to say; and for the most part, that is what we must do. But biological links would help people understand why their loved ones must transition. Biological evidence would also challenge health care providers who still treat gender dissonance as a mental illness and have built their careers on *blocking* transition because of this mindset.

30   How can I know that my child will be happy?

If only I could have known for sure that this transition would make my child happy, it would have been so much easier to get through this. But nobody gets to know that answer. Transsexual people don't even know ahead of time if the world after transition will be a happier place. All they know for sure is that they cannot stay in the place where they are.

· · · · · · · ·

Is it more caring to make a leap of blind faith? Or, is it more caring to be sure transition is not a mistake? There are probably many parents who can get from shock to acceptance with a leap of faith instead of intensive questioning. Everybody is different and a lot of people are stronger than I am. Still, I suspect that most parents of trans children have wished—at least once—that their child did not need to transition.

My intense period of investigation and questioning ultimately led to the comprehensive level of understanding I sought and needed. I was told over and over again that my desperate and unrelenting questioning made all the difference in the world in convincing friends and family that I'd done thorough work to "legitimize" and validate my child's condition. I'd done all I could to thwart disaster. The irony is that I could have contributed to a disaster if I remained stuck living in a state of ignorance and resistance.

The knowledge I've gained through my process of questioning and bargaining is a powerful tool that I now use to support my child and others like her. I've built myself a bridge between the darkness and the light.

Trading Places

Chapter 6

From Winter to Spring
Many Life Changes

2009 would have been a significant year even without Steve's gender transition. It was the year my mother died, and with our dad already gone, my brother and I became orphans. It was the year of Jeff's high school graduation, so with Jeff off to college in the fall, Ted and I would become empty-nesters.

We were in the midst of the worst economic crisis in the United States since the 1930s, aptly named "The Great Recession." The job and housing markets in Michigan were in the worst condition out of all 50 states. For a hundred glorious years, the Detroit area had been the automotive capital of the world. But in the last few years, many once iconic automobile assembly plants had shut down, leaving acres of parking lots empty and cold. Houses were in foreclosure, shops were out of business and boarded up, and people were fleeing our state in droves to find a better life. Michigan was beginning to seem like a ghost town.

In February, my mother moved into our house after $4\frac{1}{2}$ years of battling stage-IV ovarian cancer, and we became her nursing home. Her bone marrow had stopped producing red blood cells due to all the years of chemotherapy, and she advanced into stages of Leukemia as well. Monthly blood transfusions replaced chemotherapy and time was running out. The oncologist estimated that we could have her until May or June at the most. With this in mind, Ted and I agreed to forever shield her from the pain of knowing about Steven's transgender condition. I guess I believed that if the cancer didn't kill her first, this news surely would have.

"Who is that pretty girl?" my mother playfully asked one time when Steven entered the living room where she and I were sitting.

Steve and I froze for a second and our eyes quickly met. We wondered, "How did she figure it out? Did she, perhaps so close to death, suddenly develop supernatural abilities? Could she see what was happening on some ethereal level?" It was a startling moment to be sure, but I quickly dismissed it as a jibe on her part about Steven's lengthening hair. By this time, it had been about a year since his last hair cut. He had been changing before our very eyes for some time now and a lot of things started to make sense. For many months before we knew about this, he had been shaping his eyebrows into thin, delicate arches. He had always been a hairy guy, and by middle school he had a thick unibrow. His new femme eyebrows were shocking and disturbing to me. The area above his eyes that had been cleared of hair was more pale than the rest of his face, casting a spotlight more dramatically onto the new look of his eyes. With his long curly hair and feminine eyebrows, and his slight build of 5'7" and 125 pounds, a person with blurry vision just might see a woman instead.

But we had agreed to mercifully spare Nana from the news. She was frail and dying, with only weeks left in her life. In retrospect, it was strangely perfect timing. Steven was seeking therapy as recommended by the standards of care, and was still presenting as a guy. And I desperately clung to the hope that after enough therapy, when my child's transsexual assertion would surely be disproved altogether, all of this trouble would go away and we'd never have to worry again about telling anybody.

Ted hated keeping Steve's transsexualism a secret, but his discomfort presented a quandary since we weren't ready to disclose it to anyone yet. Ted especially hated keeping this colossal secret from Jeff; he viewed it as deception unprecedented in our close family. But I disagreed; I viewed it as the way to optimize everyone's best interest. With Jeff's high school graduation only a few months away, I wanted to avoid any risk that this news would crush his spirit or create challenges for him in an insensitive high school environment. As an active school community member, I also feared for my own psychological well-being. Would someone probe me about Steve's transsexualism many months before I was ready to talk and before I had made my own peace with it? Would there be talk behind my back? A thousand senior year events and celebrations seemed to offer me a respite, a sanctuary—but only if no one knew our family secret.

• • • • • • •

Around this time, February 2009, I had the first death dream, the one in which Steve came back to me through the golden field, with his boy hair cut and tan Khakis. This was a watershed event, which upended and redefined the team dynamic I had with Ted. We would henceforth not be traveling through this early stage together as companions on the same path. We were always within arm's reach, except for a thick, invisible barrier between us. While this new barrier in our relationship shielded the marriage from damage—or even involvement—it added profoundly to our individual loneliness. We were already at the bottom of the pit of darkness as it was. Because we weren't ready to share this news with anyone else yet, this was a time of great isolation.

I lived in a cave with stone walls so thick that news from the world could not penetrate. Stacks of unopened bank statements had been shoved into drawers, lost and forgotten. I remember getting a call from a friend, "The stock market is crashing! Banks are collapsing!" and perhaps our life savings was gone. But I was totally oblivious to events in the outside world beyond my reach. Even after the words were spoken, they just kind of hovered there, somewhere between the voice of one person and the stone ears of another.

· · · · · · ·

During these months, as my mother's life waned, I lived and breathed a totally grief-stricken existence. I was devastated by Steven's plan to transition, and the sadness weighed me down like a lead shroud. Moving through the days became mechanical when absolutely necessary, but more like dragging anchors through glue otherwise.

I'd wander through Meijer and Costco, picking up the cancer drugs and protein drinks and Depends. Dragging anchors through the glue, I'd sometimes turn down the beauty and makeup aisle. "What would it be like," I wondered academically, "to shop this aisle for Steve?" Another me would then step out of my body and say, "Condition yourself! Walk the aisle and pretend it's fun! This stuff is sparkly and pretty, and you never had this chance before because you thought you were raising two sons." It was as though there was a part of me who knew all along that Steve's transsexual assertion wasn't going to go away, and I began to prepare for that.

People with multiple personalities work for years trying to become whole again, and here I was, in the beginning stages of creating a second me. I suppose I was starting to compartmentalize.

I'd drive home and give my mother her food and drugs and exercises. Then I'd dart to the computer to add several more pages to my journals of anguish. "The research and documentation would be ready," I said to myself as I pounded the keys, "when the time comes to meet the therapist. We would be able to prove that Steven was just a guy, a sweet and gentle soul, but still, just a guy." 18 months later I remained unsuccessful: I never got my sweet Stevie to come back. But from all of that effort I produced instead the chapter of this memoir called "The Devil's Advocate."

· · · · · · ·

My best friend Judy is as socially aware, altruistic, and effervescent as Oprah Winfrey. Judy has an extraordinary calling, marked by a sense of urgency, to reach out and help people and make the world a better place. The most important part of her substance is not her articulateness or her wealth of knowledge or her infinite energy but her genuine interest in and acceptance of people from all walks of life. Her opinions are strong and engaging, and her voice is an effective mix of boldness and warmth. She can easily persuade a person—or a whole room full of people—to stop in their tracks and listen, spellbound. Although I can still battle with her, it is not easy. She is a powerful force to have on your side.

I desperately wanted to cry on her shoulder the very first week of this journey. But it was morally prohibitive for me to share this information with any other person until my son Jeff was in the know. Yet one day Judy called me up and out of the blue told me about a friend whose 25 year old son wanted to change into a woman! What are the odds of that, I wondered to myself, for Judy to have two really close friends with transsexual kids?

"So how is Steve?" Judy asked, suddenly stopping her story about the other transsexual family. "Does he have a girlfriend? I noticed on Facebook that he is a part of Affirmations! How is he involved?" she probed, as the blood ran out of me. Affirmations is one of our local LGBTQI organizations.

"He speaks and writes as an advocate for this community," I said, managing a passable response, by now concluding that Judy had figured it out or was at least suspicious that Steve was gender variant. It was comforting to have a secret confidante, but at the conclusion of the phone call, she wrapped it up with, "Steve is such a sweet and gentle soul. I hope someday he will marry one of my girls." So I wasn't so sure that Judy really knew, and I wouldn't be sure until several months later, when Judy became, at long last, a great companion on this journey. Until then, I retreated behind my shield in isolation.

I thought a little about Judy's other friend with a transsexual child. I had learned that although this friend and her husband love and accept their child, they have not paid to help him transition. I wondered about this mixed message—but also wondered, with great anguish, if perhaps we were handling our situation the wrong way. By doling out money, we were enabling a transition that might have ended up disastrous—one that we could have tried to prevent by withholding the money instead!

· · · · · · ·

Taking care of my mother during her last months of life was extraordinarily difficult for me, even without the paralyzing trauma born of Steven's gender announcement. People were so proud of me and called me an angel and the perfect daughter. The truth is, I barely survived those months, and hearing those words truly gave me encouragement; I wanted to live up to the honorable reputation I was establishing for myself.

Mother-daughter relationships can be complicated. My mother and I got along a little like oil and water, but our loyalty was unconditional; we were bonded at a deeper level than just being able to see eye to eye. We had seemingly few priorities in common, and scant ability to connect like best friends might. It seemed like our conversations were always little mini-arguments. I believe we saw the world through constitutionally different eyes. When I would try to say this to her, I'd see blank eyes looking back at me. Nowadays, as I continue in life without her, I just look in the mirror and find her in there, her eyes still looking back at me.

Mom was a Pollyanna, an eternal optimist with a cheerful temperament, even through the grueling days of cancer. She lived her life putting everybody else's needs before her own, making excuses for everybody's mistakes, letting them off the hook—almost to a fault. In stark contrast, my disposition has always been much more pensive, sensitive, and intense. Our temperaments were so different, I often found her boundless optimism to be annoying, even grating, and this challenged my composure around her. I sometimes wanted to grab her by the shoulders and shout, "Doesn't this cancer *ever* make you mad?"

My teenage years must have been difficult for my mom, but no matter how snotty I was, I couldn't seem to break her. One time I got pretty close though. I remember a confrontational incident from about 30 years ago, where she said to me in frustration, "I hope someday you have a daughter!" I think I finally realize her pain. Though our relationship was close on so many levels, she longed for a storybook best friend relationship with me, her daughter, and my heart breaks now because I wish I had tried harder to give her this kind of happiness. She was a gentle, generous, tolerant person.

I reflect now and realize that she was the person who taught me to accept people as they are, a quality within myself of which I am most proud. She led me to recognize and appreciate that people are born with many characteristics already set in place by nature. If she had not died from the cancer, I now think she *would* have made peace with her grandchild's gender transition. But I didn't think this way in the beginning.

She loved little kids, including both of her own, and she seemed to have a good relationship with my brother. But I was the only one to give her grandchildren, and, in spite of having to deal with me, she spent her golden years with us and her two grandkids. She had openly hoped, at each pregnancy, that one of my babies would be a granddaughter. She bought little dresses to have on hand for when the baby girl arrived, but alas, a boy was born, and then another. I am not a religious person, but I wonder if she is looking down upon us now, with her impish grin. We finally have our girl.

Alone with primary custody of my mother and her care during the years of battling cancer, my days were consumed by these mental and physical responsibilities without much respite. I'd never be able to repay the lifetime of support she had given me and my kids, but this was my opportunity to try. Even though it was hard, it was the right way, the only way to be living my life at that time. Maybe now in retrospect, I can finally see that we were best friends after all.

• • • • • • •

Days filled with doctor appointments and errands and organizational tasks effectively precluded my ability—or desire—to deal with the idea of Steven's proposed gender change. The unbearable sadness was relentless, and sometimes in order to survive I suppressed it. But in no time at all, it would loom large again like turbulent waves first receding then crashing back with a mighty force. To expel the chaos out of my head and sort it all out on paper, I continued to write, and wrote copious notes and journals. I'd bring the Harry Benjamin Standards of Care to the oncologist and hospital and doctor waiting rooms, combing through it in all those hours looking for the clue, the evidence that would disqualify Steve.

· · · · · · ·

All through the spring of 2009, Steven was visiting his therapist, Dr. Sylvia Smith. After interviewing two, he had selected one with whom he had the most comfortable rapport, a social worker rather than a psychologist, much to my chagrin. I speculated—correctly— that he had thoroughly investigated gender therapists in the area and selected one who had the reputation of being very transition-friendly. I'd ask Steve with a mix of bitterness and helplessness, if she had a sign on her lawn, "Get your hormones here!" He would laugh and assure me that she did not dole out hormones like candy; this process was thorough and cautious. (Years later I discovered that this therapist is world famous and transsexual people come thousands of miles to be lucky enough to meet with her.)

Week after week I would view the online bank account that I shared jointly with Steve, and I could see when the therapy visits occurred. Insurance paid nothing for visits to social workers; we had to pay the full charge for each visit. I would ask Steve now and then, "How's it going with Dr. Smith?" and his answers were vague. I remained hopeful, even certain, that the therapist would easily figure out that Steve was not transsexual, that he was just a guy and all of this confusion would go away. I was certain that

I'd be ready and able to sue any therapist who thought otherwise. (At that time, I didn't know that the therapist does not make the diagnosis.)

Avoiding the Therapist

Steve could see how overwhelmed I was with the care of my mother, and he never pressured me to attend a therapy session during the spring of 2009. When I had a moment off from nursing duties, I didn't want to jump into something possibly even more emotionally taxing.

So it was like a lucky star that Jeff got cast as the lead character, the boy-wolf Mowgli, in the high school spring production of *The Jungle Book*.[1] What a dream come true, to have something important to do that was actually delightful. When I wasn't with my mother, I'd be at the school, immersed in production meetings and costume design and dress rehearsals. The school community was a second home to us, and for me in particular for just one more season, it was my sanctuary, my respite. I had a place to go where Steve essentially still existed.

People at the school would sometimes ask, "So how is Steve doing? Does he like the University of Michigan?" and I'd think, "Steven is virtually dying. My heart is a knot of agony." But out loud I'd hear myself say, "He's doing great!"

Immersed in my mom's care and Jeff's graduation events, I was too busy, too emotionally taxed, to deal with Steve's transition. The visit with the gender therapist would have to wait. Besides, the therapist would clearly see that Steve was just a guy. There was nothing feminine about him at all; he was simply a very sweet and gentle young man. She would see he wanted to transition only for convenience and that he was not a valid candidate for hormone treatment.

In retrospect, I was deeply immersed in the denial phase of my journey. Every single day from January to June, with the light of morning, my eyes would open and I'd linger in a sort of trancelike state between sleep and wakefulness, between shock and incredulous daze. *Is it really true, or did I just dream it? Does Steven want to become a woman? Is Steven really transsexual? I can't handle this, it's just too hard. I can't do it.* The reality of my life with a transsexual child would flood my brain. I laid there in momentary shock, wherein I tried to absorb this concept as the new reality of my life. The hope that it was just a bad dream fizzled away as my waking consciousness took over; with one more arrow stuck in my heart, I'd face another day.

Transition-related thoughts got a minute or two every morning, but then I had to block them away to tend to the routine activities of my daily life. On those days when emotional tidal waves broke through the dam, I'd research and write my journals. I had amassed about 40 pages of questions and arguments to share with the therapist, who I planned to visit someday, but not quite yet. When the therapist would ask for my help to verify that we never saw any signs of gender dysphoria in Steven as a little boy, I'd be prepared. I'd help to invalidate this transsexual theory once and for all. Steven had misdiagnosed himself, and this would all go away.

What a huge emotional expenditure for which there would be no refund when it was established that Steven didn't need to make this journey after all. I wasn't willing to spend it all at once, since sooner or later, one way or another, we would surely stop pursuing the crazy notion that Steve was a woman.

My alter ego—the other I who emerged that January day while shopping at Meijer—was also acutely aware that if the dysphoria wasn't going to go away, one of the things that needed to happen for me to come to terms with it all was the passage of time. I'd get used to the weight of those arrows, and learn to live life with a heavier heart.

The next week I was at Meijer again, pushing the shopping cart through the glue. I picked up my mom's cancer drugs and her protein drinks and Depends. I pushed through the aisles, fixated on the young mothers with little kids, especially the little boys. "Be wary," I thought, "you don't know what will become of them." I'd see the young men, and think with great envy, "You look so happy just being a guy. Why do so many people seem so happy just as they are? Why can't it be that way for my child?" It seemed like suddenly everyone represented something that we could not have anymore, ever again, for Steven—strangers at Meijer, TV show characters, people I knew. I was going through a "why me?" stage of grief.

Suddenly I also began to notice something else just about everywhere I went those days. With magic eyes combing intensely through the maze of faces, like in a Where's Waldo puzzle, I began to notice a lot of other transsexual people (or so I thought). At Meijer and Target, at the pet store, at the hospital among the nurses and staff, even among the children at school, I saw people I thought might be trans. When I thought I'd detected one, I wanted to give them a bear hug and say, "I am a member of your club too, because my child is transsexual just like you." I'd watch them at work, happy and laughing, helping customers, blending right in. I'd wonder about their story and if they'd finally found peace within themselves and a place to belong, after so much work and leaving so much behind to get there. Nobody else seemed to notice a thing, but I was more special than most at this point, with eagle eyes, like Waldo's own mother herself.

Maybe none of those people were transsexual at all, but the odds are, some might have been— along with many others that I presumed not to be. Transsexual people are out there everywhere and in every walk of life; they've been among us all along. An overwhelming sense of admiration and pride began to seep in. The seeds of realization of the magnitude of their journey were starting to take root.

I beefed up our cable TV subscription to have access to more of the health and educational channels, where I'd noticed documentaries on transgender issues suddenly appearing with greater frequency. The very first one I watched reached deeply into me, and captivated me as a lifeline; it left me thirsting for more. I wanted to learn more, to see more stories, and I began to crave these documentaries. They were key to my growing awareness and understanding of this condition; they were my first lifelines. It was imperative that I hear about the whole story, the sadness and the anguish and the struggle; it was only here that I could find a tangible (and believable) connection, where I could be reached on common ground and then gently led out of the darkness.

During the early months, I watched documentaries and surfed the internet looking for words from other parents. I wanted to hear what they had to say about the process of coming to terms with their trans children in all the gory detail. I didn't want to see just the end of the story, some well adjusted happy parent, perhaps on a national speaking tour or marching for PFLAG[2]. A happy-go-lucky attitude would not have reached me. Such an attitude would have been still alien to me, and perhaps even repelling. I knew that a child's transition had to take at least some getting used to. What was it like to come to terms with a child's transition? Did it seem, at first, like your child had died? How did you get to be happy again?

The public library in a professional community is such a beehive of activity, it's often hard to find a place to park the car. Ours is over a hundred thousand square feet, with several hundred thousand publications within it. Nervously looking at the catalog monitor and over my shoulder at the same time, I searched for books on transsexualism. I found only four or five of these books on the shelves. I sandwiched them in between a couple mystery novels, used self check-out, and put the whole stack of books into a library bag. And then I drove home, and put the bag down where it sat for two weeks while I circled it. One day I bravely opened the bag and there inside, right before my eyes, lay the next lifeline and the beginning of a whole new phase of this journey.

The first book I read was *Transparent: Love, Family, and Living the T with Transgender Teenagers*, by Cris Beam.[3] It was a real story, not a primer, a political commentary, or a textbook, but a real first-hand story with heart and soul. I would learn in the months and years ahead that personal memoirs like this would be key in changing my life. Documentaries opened the door, and for much of the first year they were about all I could manage, spoon fed to me in little chunks. But memoirs ultimately brought me inside the world of transsexual people.

• • • • • • •

One day in March of 2009, I noticed a withdrawal from Steven's bank account, over $400, payable to the University of Michigan Health Systems—a huge medical charge! My stomach knotted and I got dizzy, clammy with sweat: *Was Steve starting hormone treatments already?*

I knew he was attending therapy sessions quite regularly, but I was counting on those taking months and even years, as surely the therapist was working hard to determine that Steve was just a guy and would never be a real candidate for hormones.

Beset with panic, my heart raced as I dialed the phone to call Steve—*pick up pick up!* "What's going on?" I asked frantically, when thankfully he answered the call. And right then and there, I learned that Steve had begun laser treatments to remove his facial hair.

I had a sinking feeling, naturally, but it was abated by my relief to learn that at least he wasn't starting hormones yet. He pacified me, choosing words he thought I could handle at the time: "Don't worry, Mom, I'm not at that point yet. There is still a lot of time." Of course, I hoped he meant that he wasn't at that point because he was still thinking of turning back, or because the therapist was not willing to give him the hormones. But it was getting a little harder to pretend that the dysphoria would go away; the laser treatments were permanent physical changes.

In retrospect, swallowing the news of the laser treatments was one of the first major milestones for me. But it was made to feel relatively easy when compared to the much more daunting prospect of estrogen hormone treatments. Having laser hair removal is irreversible, but there are probably a lot of guys who would love to quit the shaving routine. So this would still be OK when Steve returned to being a guy—and I was still hoping, indeed I was quite sure this would happen after enough therapy.

"Why are you starting this now? Shouldn't you wait until after you've tried to live as a woman, after you know for sure you want to change?" I asked, calming down, but still alarmed at how quickly this process seemed to be unfolding.

"I can't go out in the world and live as a woman if I look like this! That would be humiliating. I would not look like a woman," he said with his usual logic and common sense. He had a point, except that I was still pretty sure that he'd not like living as a woman and would change his mind and have to live as a guy with no facial hair.

But my alter-ego knew that the young man I once knew and loved was starting to take permanent, physical steps toward fading away into oblivion.

That spring and summer, between college semesters, I'd still have one more season to see men's shaving stuff on his bathroom counter, but I felt a deep sadness. Who would think the sight of a razor in a bathroom could have such a profound effect, nearly bringing me to tears? How much time did I have left before the laser treatments finished off the last of Steven's masculine facial hair and one more aspect of the boy I thought I raised would disappear forever? And what of my memory of this rite of passage of my adolescent boy turning into a man, this quintessential milestone? What had Steve been thinking about it all that time? Unbeknownst to me, it was a torturous ritual endured behind closed doors for many years right here in our loving home.

● ● ● ● ● ● ●

Steven moved home from university for the months of May and

June 2009. He could see how overwhelmed I was with the care of my mother, and he had never pressured me to attend a therapy session. Strangely, the therapist hadn't called me yet either, to hear my input on the gender matter. I watched him come and go and noticed that the visits to the therapist had clearly stopped. I didn't ask. I clung to my last opportunity to truly believe, or truly pretend, that after a few months of therapy, Steven had a change of heart and had abandoned the notion of becoming a woman. I allowed myself to feel immense relief as if my wish had come true.

We didn't talk about the transition much during this time. My mother was dying, and we were heavily immersed in the sadness and the stress of her last weeks of life. Steve, being a kind-hearted, patient person, stayed out of the way. He could see I was at emotional capacity with regard to dealing with tragedy.

It was heartbreaking that I was not able to give my mother the full attention she deserved. The dark pall that hovered over my head in the spring of 2009 because of the figurative (and literal) loss of my son, was competing with, sometimes eclipsing the actual loss of my mother.

Mom died on Memorial Day, almost five years to the day after being diagnosed with ovarian cancer. It was miraculous that she lived as long as she did. When diagnosed in May of 2004, the doctor had thought she only had six months left. But she was a strong person in so many ways: mind, body, spirit, and determination to live. She was so positive and cheerful, she even smiled in her sleep. If I'm ever in her state of health I think I'll be a grumpy old goat for sure.

All day we dealt with funeral decisions and phone calls. The next day we went to Jeff's College Freshman Orientation in Grand Rapids. The next day, we were back in town for funeral planning. The next day included both funeral planning and Jeff's Honors Convocation. The next day, Friday, Steven went to his fourth laser treatment, while I continued with the funeral planning on some type of adrenalin. Saturday was Mom's funeral. Steven stood at the front of the room with face burnt tomato-red raw from the laser and gave a beautiful eulogy to his Nana.

On Sunday, Jeff officially began the next chapter of his life with Commencement, our culture's symbolic and emotionally moving rite of passage. The all night senior party on Monday was an extravagantly planned closing of the past chapter. Starting on Tuesday and for the next two weeks I began to pull together an enormous graduation party for 300 guests in our backyard. This same type of party had taken me several months to plan for Steve. The days were interspersed with estate work and funeral thank-you notes. I felt myself to be extraordinarily fragmented. We did the best we could to prepare, in just a few days, for a party that was supposed to be about the size of a wedding. But I never had a chance to send most of the invitations, missing dozens of friends, so consequently only half the people showed up. On the day of the party I stood there surprised at how many chairs remained empty. I was dazed and exhausted, but in a brief moment of lucidness, I realized how much I had compartmentalized. I never had the clarity of mind to absorb the loss of my mother, and I always had an excuse to avoid dealing with my transsexual child.

Timing: A Blessing in Disguise

Was it the best timing or the worst timing for all three of these things to happen at the same time in our little family? I went into a trance-like state and then handled these events automatically, like a robot. Those few weeks in May and June remain burned in my memory as the most unfortunate—or fortunate—juxtaposition of events I will ever likely encounter in my lifetime.

In retrospect, the timing was incredibly merciful. If I was a religious person, I'd call it divine intervention. Nana was spared any knowledge of Steven's transsexualism. We had thus far remained steadfast in our plan to spare her from this pain. We wished also to shield Jeff until the last of his graduation events had passed, for his benefit as well as ours. Besides, all along, I still hoped that Steven would change his mind given enough time. He probably wasn't going to go through with this gender transition anyway.

• • • • • • •

When the dust had finally settled after this cacophony of events, I stopped and looked around and there was no place left to hide.

One day in June, I worked up the courage to ask Steven if he had stopped visiting the gender therapist, hoping he'd say yes, that he was deemed an invalid candidate for transition, and that he'd changed his mind.

"It seems like you haven't visited Dr. Smith in quite a while," I began. I thought I was braced for the answer I didn't want, but this road had been full of land mines for me, and I was now stepping into another one.

He replied, "That's true, we haven't had a session in awhile. We are waiting."

Why would they be waiting? I thought, as I absorbed the words, knowing full well another heart-stopping pivotal moment had arrived.

"It's time for you and Dad to come to therapy with me. Dr. Smith and I are waiting for you." And with that, my heart sunk like a stone.

Trading Places

Chapter 7

From Summer to Fall
Don't Miss the Train—From Steven to Sarah

"It is time for you to come to therapy with me." This ominous message meant Steven had not changed his mind. Instead, it was time to tell us about the next step of the process. Was it actually possible that Dr. Smith was ready to give Steve the green light for hormones? If Dr. Smith had cured Steve of his gender dissonance, they probably would *not* need to meet with us. Still, I clung to the hope that they had come to some intermediate solution where Steve would be content to be androgynous around his family and close friends or lovers but continue to present as a man in the outside world.

· · · · · · ·

By the time summer came, Nana had passed away and Jeff had graduated, and I woke up one day to find myself in a different stage of the transition. With nowhere to hide and nothing blocking my view, I stood squarely face to face with a situation that I liken to an idling train—not stopped and not in reverse. It was waiting for me to either get on board or get out of the way, but in either case, it was going to take off very soon. "It's important to keep moving forward," the person driving the train said finally and firmly. Ted and I often remarked on how the transition seemed to be moving way too fast as it was. But Steve was eager to start moving even faster.

Still clinging to the last threads of hope, I continued to try to convince Steve to reconsider this transition, that he might be heading for disaster, and that this might not be the golden key to happiness. But he had a response to everything, as always, assuring me that all the options and all the pitfalls had been considered over and over again. Growing exhausted by the futility of it all, my desperate pleas began to dwindle in frequency over the summertime. These discussions started to seem more for my benefit than for his. I had a growing awareness that Steve was merely placating me, patiently waiting as I worked through my part of the process.

I give Steve credit for his immense patience. We deserve credit too, as we navigated the first half year such that everyone's interests were fairly optimized. I had believed that Steven was moving as fast as possible, and was therefore not impeded by our steep learning curve and slow pace. Ted and I felt pushed about as fast as we could reasonably handle, considering the magnitude and suddenness of this change. In retrospect, our process seemed brilliantly choreographed. A 20 year old adult doesn't legally need the blessing of his or her parents to transition, but transition is often a painful journey and no one should have to go through it alone. We had been the most important people in Steve's life, so it seemed to be in everyone's interest for us to be included and comfortable with each step of the process, increasing hope for a win-win outcome. But I would learn some years later that Steven felt he was generous to wait the four months of summer for us to come on board, that time had never moved *so slowly* for him. That would be like me saying I felt generous to give the resources needed to enable the transition to occur *so rapidly* in the first place. I think giving parents the time and education they need will assure cohesiveness on this mutual journey. It never felt like any of us were pacing our steps out of generosity so much as out of love and the determination to transition as a team.

We made the first appointment with Steve's gender therapist, Dr. Sylvia Smith, for June 18, 2009, just a few days after Jeff's graduation party. I was sure that the arguments I had so carefully prepared would invalidate Steve's self-diagnosis and disqualify him from the transition program. Before the visit, I emailed Dr. Smith a condensed, six page letter of introduction created using material from my 40 page "journals of anguish." This letter included a list of some of the toys Steven played with as a child—rocks, gears, little cars and trains, the Big Loader steam shovel. I planned to point out his clear lack of interest in anything traditionally feminine. In fact, I had a million points and arguments to challenge the diagnosis and to prove that Steven was just a gentle guy. But I was nervous, sapped of energy, giving up and giving in. My alter ego—the one who was coming to terms with having a daughter—was becoming a bigger and bigger part of me.

Ted and I sat mostly silent on the drive there, thinking about what it would be like to finally meet the person who had capacity to change the course of our entire life. I remained composed but inside I was bewildered and sickened that a total stranger could think she knew Steven more than we did. I didn't know much about what Ted was thinking; our communication on this had been frozen for months, since my first death dream. But I felt powerless and angry and numb.

I could see why Steve liked the therapist. She was a friendly looking, middle aged woman who practiced out of her home in Ann Arbor. Her den was warm, crammed with soft cushioned couches, piles of books, and interesting but not-too-distracting knickknacks. I liked her too, but she was not there for me. She was first and foremost Steven's advocate and fiercely guarded him like he was her own. And once in her presence, Steve turned into a total stranger. Like a lawyer and client, they were unwilling to relent to my anguish.

I had imagined and hoped that Dr. Smith would be more successful at getting Ted and me on board, and would be sympathetic to our struggle as parents on this journey. I had thought she would know the kinds of things we would need to hear, to convince us more completely that Steve was transsexual. But she expressed concern that my letter to her had a lot of emotion in it, and said that it didn't provide a neutral environment, and so she wouldn't share too much of it openly in session. This was a stonewall to me; it is pretty hard to deny that emotions are a big part of this process for parents. In retrospect, it may have been impossible for her—in this shared therapy session—to deal with me without compromising her genuine dedication to my child. She worked on behalf of transsexual patients seeking relief from a painful dissonance. (To be fair, we could have visited her separately to work through our trauma as transitioning parents heading into a dissonance of our own.) I liked that she didn't need to take charge and that she wasn't arrogant or intimidating. She was warm and kind hearted and she listened compassionately. She was extremely generous with her time and I never felt rushed. But she was also quite firm in her position behind Steve. Although she tried to address all of my questions, she sometimes seemed to miss the gist of them. She startled me by her tendency to jump right in and defend Steve even if it didn't seem warranted at all.

"Try not to think of it as losing a son. You are in fact gaining a beautiful daughter," she suggested at one point. It was a good concept to bank for the future, like a savings bond; in 20 years we might cash in on the gain. But those words seemed insensitive and brutal at the time. I looked at my son in his grey plaid shirt and blue jeans, a beautiful work of art, built with twenty years of everything Steven.

I said to Steve, "There is not one thing about you that seems like a girl. You are my sweet gentle guy." He gave me a look of disgust and tears began to flow. *Who is this person?* I wondered to myself as I sat there stunned. I looked around desperately for acknowledgment, for backup, but Ted sat there frozen and mute, spinning in some orbit of his own; a stranger. The therapist jumped in to rescue Steven from me, leaving a dagger in my heart, my life draining out.

Where did everyone go? Steve and his therapist, his new

alternate-parent, were suddenly strangers—cold, frightening, and unfamiliar. I felt ganged up on by three imposter people whose bodies had been taken over by aliens. No one seemed to recognize the language that I spoke. Dr. Smith was there to support Steve and, once in her presence, he disappeared from mine. I didn't feel any closer to understanding the condition; instead, I felt completely shut out and alone.

As we were walking out, I asked "Do you have any children Dr. Smith?" I continued the question silently in my head, ". . . and is one of them transsexual?" It was eerily chilly the way she chose to respond, sort of turning her back and walking towards the door to lead us out. Without eye contact, she summarized quickly, dismissively, that they were all grown up now and living far away. Even with her infinite knowledge and expertise on the matters of transsexual patients, she cannot really know what it is like to be the parent of one.

In time I would learn to appreciate that Steve found one of the most highly recommended and respected gender transition therapists in the country. I would learn that many patients travel thousands of miles to meet with her for assistance in treatment. But that time was still many months away.

· · · · · · ·

By mid-summer 2009, Steven's plan had become crystal clear. He was the one in control all along; he was driving this train on a journey already mapped well into the future. Ted and I never had a choice in the matter at all, and Steve knew it right from the start. All Steve wanted from us was our continued presence in his life and, at the very minimum, for us to accept what he was doing and love him just the same. He seemed sensitive to our trauma; he wanted us to be comfortable with each step of the process before moving on. But he also gently and consistently reminded us, "It is important that we keep moving forward."

"God grant me the serenity to accept the things I cannot change. . . "

We all know this prayer in various personal contexts. I am not a religious person, but seeking peace through this mantra was what I tried to do next. For me, moving forward at this point meant letting go of the resistance. So I took a few months off and just coasted through life. Ignoring the transition didn't seem so bad once I started to realize that there wasn't a lot I could do to stop it. It was a relief to finally quit the investigation. I had turned over every stone and was tired of the work, exhausted from the fight, and I succumbed both defeated and liberated.

Steve went back to Ann Arbor where he had been granted a prestigious summer internship at a research institute. This delighted me and alleviated my worries that his career opportunity would be limited to Wal-Mart greeter. I was sure that once the research team got to know him, they would still offer him permanent work, even after he became a woman. The future did not seem so bleak anymore.

There was plenty to keep me busy that summer, and I let "time heals all" start to work its magic. The Class of '09 graduation parties filled all of June and July. This was a time of bittersweet good-byes. I had come to know hundreds of kids during the years that Jeff was growing up, and now I was saying farewell and good luck to all of them—and their parents as well. This was the end of an era. I did not expect to see many of these parents regularly anymore, as our time shared together had been mostly because our kids grew up together. My heart was heavy with our family's secret; I didn't want to think about who might be uncomfortable with our situation, and whether anyone would abandon us. I couldn't see myself wanting to extend my arms around the old school friends who would be drifting away naturally from this point on anyway. It was better for me to focus on building new relationships in my life going forward.

In retrospect, keeping my old world alive would end up keeping "my son Steve" in my life a while longer. It helped provide an interim platform for me to start to gradually merge the son-person and the daughter-person into one person.

Jeff

After the last graduation party was over, it was time to finally tell Jeff about Steven's transition. In the event that Jeff would want to turn a new page and start a new life, like I imagined myself doing, we wanted the break to be as clean as possible for him. He would begin college in another month; he could tell his first college roommate and the new people of his future that he had a sister.

On July 1 of 2009, Steve took Jeff behind closed doors and presented him with a letter that had taken six months to compose. The meeting took barely an hour. Jeff reacted with maturity beyond his years, and said, "Our relationship isn't built on gender. It's built on friendship." Steve reported that if he didn't know any better, it seemed like Jeff had also spent six months composing such an eloquent response. Then they played a game of chess. Jeff appeared to take this news in stride, but declared in the days to follow that he would still call his trans sister whatever he wanted and at this point, she was still "Steve."

I don't think Jeff gave it much conscious thought at all in the first few days. It was almost two months later when he came to me one day and asked, "Say Mom, what's Steve going to do with his genitals?" I had thought this was one thing most people wondered about right away, but in Jeff's case it validated my suspicion that he was letting the news sink in much slower than he originally led us to believe.

When I talked to Jeff about his feelings from time to time after that, he reassured me that people of his generation are much more tolerant and many just seem to "get it," at least in educated and progressive communities.

It was easy to predict that once Jeff knew, the leak from that point on would flow unchecked and the rest of the high school community would soon know. As sure as the sun rises every day, in only a matter of minutes, Jeff's friends began to learn about Steve's gender dysphoria too. After carrying the secret for seven months, I was well aware that such news is not easy to keep contained. By now I was like a horse at the gate, so tired of being confined.

Telling Jeff was a significant milestone wherein we connected our nuclear family back together again. Additionally, with the inclusion of Jeff, the road was cleared for us to move forward and disclose to others. It was a great liberation.

Judy

Some people are born with ability to suffer through their own share of tragedy and still have the capacity to suffer the tragedies of others. And so it is with Judy, for when I finally could cry on her shoulder, I swear she took half the burden from me right then and there. There would be no other reaction quite so genuinely similar to mine, nor would there be a greater companion for me to travel with on the rest of this journey.

I popped out of my rabbit hole and arrived at her house on July 7, 2009. I told her that I had come to tell her something huge. "There's no turning back once you hear this news." I had her attention. We settled into chairs on her secluded backyard deck. "It's about Steve," I began. Her eyes searched my face for clues. The intensity of what she found there was palpable. A minute of silence went by, as she braced herself, then finally said, "Tell me. Just tell me."

I said, "You know your friend Alice? You know how her son wants to change to be a woman?" Our eyes were locked now, we didn't blink at all. I let this sink in, then I just let it out, "Steve wants to change too."

We stared at each other for a minute more, as I watched the news seep into her body, and like infused with new blood, she seemed to change color. In the minutes that followed it became clear to me that she didn't know about this last spring, as I had once suspected. With great sadness and love she embraced the challenges born from this news. Then she took my hand and jumped down the rabbit hole with me. This isn't something that too many people would do.

Some time later she said to me, "What are the odds that I would

have not just one but two very close friends with this condition?"
(I would eventually learn she had three friends with transgender
children.[1]) For Judy, a popular person with a lot of friends, the odds
are actually pretty darn good. According to one credible estimate,
the prevalence of transsexualism is possibly one in 500.[2]

I didn't need to talk about the transition too much more that
summer. I told Judy long before I was ready to tell anyone else.
I told her not for liberation but because I was seeking help, even
though I had absolutely no idea how anyone could help me. I think
that just not being alone anymore was a start. Her perseverance
in supporting me throughout the journey was a lifeline. Eventually
many things would help me emerge from the darkness, and Judy's
companionship was truly one of those things.

• • • • • • •

The train Steve was driving was rapidly gaining speed. We
had a second meeting with Dr. Smith. She referred Steve to an
endocrinologist to begin estrogen treatment. We learned about how
the estrogen would work, how quickly it would change Steve, and
what it would render irreversible. Probably within six months, the
estrogen would render him permanently sterile, and so, we talked
about sperm banking. We got a professional referral to another
doctor for a second opinion, which Steve agreed to attend at my
request. But the prescription was filled and bottles of hormones
were on his desk long before the appointment for the second opinion
was even made.

Most things could be reversed if and when he changed his mind
and decided to go back to being a guy. The part of me that still
thought about my son coming home to me was getting tired, getting
weaker, retreating. I felt like I'd done everything I could to be sure
the damage to Steven was minimal. In the end I'd learn that I
didn't need to do anything at all for Steven's sake; he was going to
transition no matter what. All I did, I did for me.

Banking his sperm was my idea, to keep the option of having

biological kids always open, no matter how one might go about doing that in the future. And sperm banking was the train's last stop before starting hormones—which were already filled in a bottle ready to go. In a whirlwind rush before my very eyes, Steve made five visits to Cryogenics of Birmingham, waiting the bare minimum 48 hours between each banking. "Can't you wait longer?" I asked, thinking this would enable greater sperm production (and perhaps even buy that extra time needed for him to change his mind). But he assured me each time, his specimens were healthy. In late August of 2009, he put 30 straws of the last vestiges of Steven deep into the eternity of liquid nitrogen vaults.

What stood between Steve and the two bottles of pills was the final visit to the bank. He didn't wait a single minute later, and with the first pill swallowed, he began the shift from son to daughter.

• • • • • • •

We kept really busy for the rest of the summer, and traveled around the country visiting family in other states. We spent August and September looking around for real estate Up North, a dream we've had for decades. With the Michigan economy in the tank, it was a buyer's market. And by October we had our dream vacation house on ten acres in the deeply secluded woods of northern Michigan.

This new little house was a perfect therapy session. Hunting for it and buying it, decorating it and fixing it up for the winter, was a great escape from summer into the late fall. It would be a good place to go to start over. We can say we have a daughter and a son when we meet new people there. They'd never need to know how much practice it took to learn to describe our children that way. It was part of my plan to start a new life, to have a place to go where the work of changing would not exist, where there were no memories with this son. I'd instantly be changed into the new person who had one daughter and one son. Here, I would begin to practice living this new life. The little house would be my getaway, my Walden Pond, my sanctuary.

• • • • • • •

Judy called me up one day in the middle of August and gave me a startling update on her friend, Alice, the other friend with a transsexual child. This young man had changed his mind about becoming a woman! Alice's approach had been to love her kid, but not pay for any transition related medical expenses, and now I was hearing that her approach had worked! Ear to the phone, eyes on the bottles of hormones, I sank into despair. Had my approach been the biggest mistake of my life? If I had withheld money instead of doling it out, it could have bought my kid the time needed to realize he was not transsexual. I had jumped the gun; I had made it too easy. I could have prevented this terrible mistake by blocking the means to transition. Instead I had made it easier.

Two weeks later I learned that Alice's child's attempt to suppress the dysphoria had failed. And in the next two years I would learn multiple times over that nothing can permanently suppress the gender dissonance of a transsexual person.

• • • • • • •

Even though we each traveled a different path to get through that first brutal year, and today we each remember it differently, we could not have worked harder to stick together as a family. Picking our daughter's new name is an example of our devotion to this end. Sarah's love for us, expressed by including us in this symbolic rite, did not go unnoticed. Throughout the year, from time to time, we'd have a team meeting to check in, to connect on some tangible level, and to toss out some name ideas. Although I understood, I was still disappointed that she didn't want a derivative of Steven, such as Stephanie. Such a bridge name would have been more natural for me, and kept me somewhat more connected with the child I raised, one who I felt I was already losing on so many other levels.

Disappointment notwithstanding, it was an honor to participate in the name selection, and with our fragile states, we approached discussion with respect and sensitivity. Sarah was Sarah's idea. I liked it well enough—it was simple, classic, and so common that it reminded me of no one else in particular. Sometime by late summer, we settled on the new name, Sarah Ann.

· · · · · · ·

In the fall of 2009 Sarah resumed classes at the University of Michigan for her Junior year. Sarah and her good friend Erin had signed up to lease an apartment together for the 2009-10 school year. They had signed the lease prior to Erin's learning about the transition and I was a little bit worried about how all that would pan out, but Sarah wasn't concerned at all. Erin had been actively involved in LGBT organizations, and was a liberal minded, kind hearted, extraordinarily generous and thoughtful friend.

I relaxed because I had figured that Sarah's senior year—still one year away—would be the biggest year of gender change for her, and that her privacy would be of the utmost importance then, but surely not this year, not so soon. Surely this gender change would take months or even years. Little did I know that with the onset of estrogen, the transition was already rapidly occurring. Within the next eight weeks, before our eyes and literally before Erin's eyes on a daily basis, Steven changed into Sarah.

Imagining that Sarah would have needed to live alone for her transition, I look back now and I thank my lucky stars that Sarah was blessed to travel through these days of her journey *not* alone, but with Erin as a roommate and companion. Erin provided unwavering acceptance, kindness and friendship, and someone to talk to and come home to every day of that transitional year. I hope Erin gained as much from the experience as she gave into it with her friendship. Until the day I die, I will be grateful to Erin, the wonderful person who stood beside my daughter during this extraordinary episode of life.

• • • • • • •

Ted and I often remarked on how the transition seemed to be moving way too fast. We had to keep up or we'd be left behind. My life became a disturbing mix of full-scale avoidance and startling, eye-opening reality checks as I emerged from the denial stage just barely in time to catch the train.

During the fall of 2009, Sarah started coming home from college for visits—in girl's clothes. I could tell she was working hard at getting us used to this gradually. But I didn't miss the subtle steps, and each one was a new knife in the chest. At first it was the tight-fitting jeans; I could tell they were tailored for girls, a misses fit, with fancy top stitching. Then came the tops, plain and solid colored, of a knit fabric that revealed every contour of Sarah's new and quickly developing body. I nearly passed out the first time she entered the house wearing a lipstick-red scoop neck sweater. Then I saw her pastel socks, then toe nail polish, then fancy purple razors replaced the black ones on the bathroom counter. One by one, then two at a time and faster and faster, changes were coming to my attention.

I have this image of chocolate candies traveling on a conveyer belt toward Lucille Ball in an *I Love Lucy* show from the 1960s. In this classic episode of the legendary comedy, Lucy is a candy wrapper at a factory.[3] At first the candies come, just one by one, several seconds apart, and she processes each candy with pride. Then faster and faster they start to come, two at a time, then ten, then twenty, and Lucy can't keep up. Anyone who has seen that show will be smiling now at the memory of Lucy, stomach filled, choking, cheeks bulging, eyes popping.

Sarah began to tell me stories of her androgynous look: many if not most people were already identifying her gender as female. People would greet her as "miss" at restaurants and stores. One time she went to a meeting on campus, and some women were already there when she arrived. But they wouldn't start the meeting because they were expecting another person, a guy, so they waited awhile for "the guy" to arrive, and Steve-Sarah had another story to tell because she was that guy. When Sarah called to tell me this story, it was just October 2009. She had only been on estrogen a few weeks, still dressed in boy clothes, still wearing boy glasses, but incidents like this began to occur regularly.

Sarah came home one weekend in November 2009 to attend the high school play with me. She had on a tight knit top; by now her changing shape was the first thing I saw, dominating her presence. I could barely hold conversations I was so distracted by "the developments on top." Her hair was long, eyebrows shaped and elegant, face was smooth and cleared of hair. I could not walk into the play with Sarah instead of Steve and pretend like not a thing was unusual about it—and I told her so. I asked her to dress as Steven for the November play, and again, one more time, for the Baker family Christmas party in December of 2009, and those would be the last two times I would ever be out in the world with my son Steven.

My child looked to me like a mix of Steve and Sarah nearly overnight, but to the outside world, she was already Sarah. She lived away from home during this early and most dramatic transformation period. The metamorphosis was difficult to absorb whether incrementally or in the larger chunks we got with each visit. Somewhere deep inside was the subtle, suppressed realization that I'd need to step in soon, and help this new girl with her changes.

The transsexual community might scoff at me for emphasizing the magnitude of the change I had to absorb. But in very simple terms, it is the converse of their own identity shift—the one they needed to make to escape the dissonance and present their true identity in the first place. Transsexual people who stay trapped for years trying to suppress their true gender already know how hard it is to adjust one's own reality to try to conform to expectations of others. Now that Sarah is finally free and aligned, I am the misaligned one instead. In my own reality, I always knew and aligned with a son, but today I struggle to conform to the existence of a daughter.

Sarah announced her intention of registering for January 2010 university classes as Sarah Ann Baker. January 1, 2010 would be the first day of what doctors call the "Real Life Experience." So in December we went to court and submitted a request for a hearing to legally change her name from Steven Andrew to Sarah Ann. By the end of Christmas of 2009, we had a daughter, Sarah. Ted and I knew we were on borrowed time now. She would not dress up to be a boy for us indefinitely; in fact, she would never do so again. A year into the journey, ready or not, we faced the next big step of the process: telling our extended family.

Trading Places

Chapter 8

Liberation
Telling the Family

One problem with writing this memoir over the course of the journey itself is that I've been constantly changing— and changing my mind about what to include. When I review my early journals, I hesitate to share some of them because today they seem too extreme, too sensitive, or just too dark. But to censor and soften the text and write from the perspective of a happy and healed parent would be a disservice to an interested reader who wants to know how it felt at the time—it would defeat the purpose of sharing this story at all.

During the year when we told most people about Sarah's gender transition, my journals about those conversations grew to be a hundred pages long. Many reactions that had seemed startling at the time have since softened and faded away, but many remain indelible.

● ● ● ● ● ● ●

Telling the people in our world about Sarah's transition was a huge undertaking. We spent months deciding how we would tell each family member and friend as we became ready. We spent a lot of emotional energy anticipating their reactions, and we braced ourselves for some casualties. A big part of my early despair was the anticipation of loss. During the darkest first months, my imagination was merciless and cynical. I was afraid everyone would abandon us.

Ted and I would not be ready to talk to our extended family for almost a whole year. We simply weren't strong enough at the start of this journey to talk about Sarah, much less convince others to support our child. It would have been impossible for me to ask for belief in something that I still denied. I was not convinced that Sarah's condition was legitimate and that her plan to transition would fix her inner dissonance. I could not allow anyone to see me in such a vulnerable state, to see me as a mother who doubted her child. I would not invite others into my questioning mind to agree with my resistance or to express cruel attitudes. I needed time and education before I would be able to present our story with confidence and dignity.

Waiting for Jeff to graduate bought us the time to gather this strength, and then Mom died in May as well. We handled the juxtaposition of two of life's great milestones, all the while carrying the heaviest secret we've ever had to bear. The secret began to dominate our life, and it got to a point where it took immense energy to push it aside so we could coherently interact with people.

In retrospect, I was given a unique opportunity to redirect this spirit-crushing energy into a glimmer of empathy. I can't help but think of how hard it would be to actually secretly live as a woman with a man's body instead of just someone who is secretly bearing the knowledge. In both situations, we experienced a sort of metamorphosis: as awareness and strength began to prevail, the need to keep our secrets was slowly replaced by the growing need to disclose them. So in the last weeks of 2009, Ted and I began our meticulously planned personal visits with close friends and family. We started by visiting isolated groups and the people least likely to judge anyone. We looked into the eyes and reached into the hearts of our people and asked them to join us in support of our child, because they also mattered in our lives. Throughout the next several months, we also sent a series of personal emails to larger extended family groups. A letter Sarah wrote, reprinted below, was an essential part of the delivery of this news.

• • • • • • •

December 2009

Dear family,

I am writing this note to explain an important change that is happening in my life. I wouldn't be showing it to you if I didn't care about you, respect you, and believe you to be fully capable of coming to terms with the information.

I am a woman with the misfortune to have been born in a masculine body. I have been painfully aware of this dissonance throughout my adult life, and I am finally taking steps to fix it.

Before I elaborate, I normally like to emphasize one thing which many people intuitively understand anyway: I remain the same person you all have variously known me to be. I still like to read and write, to play the piano, to talk about politics, music, literature, and countless other topics both conventional and bizarre. I still enjoy sarcasm and surreal humor. I still think a lot about ethics. I still hate it when people are mean to each other. And I am still a woman on the inside. The difference now is that you have one more piece of information.

Many people struggle to understand this concept because they have no analogous experiences: most people take it for granted that their sense of themselves as men or women is in harmony with the way others see them. It is almost impossible to imagine what it feels like for these two things to be in opposition without experiencing it yourself. I know that many people feel unsatisfied without some further reflection, though, so I often propose a thought experiment.

Imagine you wake up tomorrow morning and find that your body resembles those which are commonly associated with the opposite gender category. You would probably feel uncomfortable even before encountering other people. Now imagine you proceed with your everyday activities, and everyone interprets your gender based on your new appearance, determining the pronouns they use to refer to you, the bathrooms and clothing departments they expect you to use, the formal categories they place you in, the ways they interact with you, the sexual orientations and genders of potential romantic encounters. It stays this way the next day, the next week, and for the rest of your life. The feeling of being mislabeled becomes more and more jarring and less and less palatable as you have to withstand it for longer and longer, without any hope of ever being seen for who you are. And your body, of course, continues to feel alien, even if the surprise wears off with time. This analogy doesn't make perfect sense. It is certainly not a one-to-one parallel, nor does it cover the full range or intensity of emotions I have felt with respect to my gender. But I hope it hints at why gender identity is important, and at my profound unhappiness with the maleness that the world used to project onto me.

People sometimes ask, "How do you know that you are transgender?" Here is one response, and I mean it completely seriously: how do you know that you aren't? I believe that most people, when faced with this question, feel that they know, yet find it nearly impossible to explain why.

We are social beings, and we have a fundamental need for our inner identities to be reflected in our social experiences. As part of this process, labels are psychologically important. I was uncomfortable just knowing that everyone I met conceptualized me as a man. Even if there were someone who always treated men and women identically (which is probably never the case), this would still upset me. The label "man" is just wrong. It is incongruent with my sense of self. For more than seven years, I agonized over this incongruence in private moments and tried to hide it in public ones, feeling that something within me was broken.

Perhaps it makes sense, upon reflection, that gender identity is bimodal and linked to social perception, and that it doesn't correlate perfectly with genital development. Regardless of the clarity of the theory, though, my feelings, my sense of myself, and my innate knowledge that I am a woman are ineluctable. I tried for years and years to suppress these feelings, and the rest of the world unwittingly functioned as a powerful force against acknowledging them, but all of these efforts failed. My discontent with being perceived as a man, regardless of where I was or what I was doing, only grew more intense.

As a result, I have taken steps to change my body, including medications to bring my estrogen and testosterone to normal female levels. These hormones are producing gradual but dramatic changes in my body which will continue for many more months. Neurological evidence suggests that male and female brains, regardless of the physical characteristics of their bodies, possess receptor cites which "expect" particular ranges of hormone concentrations; hormone therapy has also helped to correct this chemical problem for me. I have legally changed my name to Sarah Ann Baker, and the people around me call me Sarah now.

I cannot begin to explain how much happier and more comfortable with myself I feel. On Christmas Day, I wrote a note to my parents that said, "I feel like I have finally attained a previously inconceivable degree of inner peace—like I've been holding my breath for years and I can finally exhale." It is a relief to leave my apartment every morning knowing that I do not have to pretend to be a boy anymore.

Thank you for taking the time to read my words. I understand that this information may require some time to process fully, and I want to encourage anyone who reads this note to ask questions in any way you feel comfortable, now or in the future.

– Sarah

• • • • • • •

Thus began the season of recovery and the most liberating part of the journey. We began to crave our visits with people as we grew stronger, more articulate, distinctly happier. A natural byproduct of this episode was the rich spectrum of reactions we got to this news. Every conversation brought something new to the table.

The Reactions

In this section, I describe the ways people reacted to the news of Sarah's transition, separating them into several different categories. As in the book as a whole, people's names and identifying details have been changed to protect their privacy.

Abundant Love and Support

The most common type of reaction was an outpouring of love and support. When Sarah came out to her private Facebook group of friends using an early version of her letter, she received nearly a hundred heartwarming responses immediately. Almost all the people we contacted in person also responded initially with love and support.

"I always liked Steven and he will be the same person to me, so nothing will change. I'll still love and admire Sarah because she is the same person as always," said one of Sarah's uncles, and one of her biggest fans.

"That's fabulous!" said Sarah's cousin who lives out of state and learned with a phone call. "I'm proud of her that she has the courage to be who she really is inside. Not a lot of people can do that."

"Well it's not going to matter, Sarah is still our family," said an aunt at another family meeting within seconds of the disclosure. We talked with this warm group of people for nearly five hours, but they began to use the name "Sarah" right away.

Courage and Bravery

"You are so brave. Sarah is really lucky to have parents like you."

Over and over again, people told me and Ted that we were good parents, and I *loved* it. I loved hearing about how strong we were and how lucky Sarah was to have us as parents. Indeed, I allowed the compliments to shape me, and began to feel proud at how well we handled the presentations, with such poise and dignity. I'd think to myself, "We are pretty amazing to be able to make this experience look almost easy." Getting this recognition actually fed into a self-fulfilling prophecy. It helped me build up and maintain this admired character, and it gave me the strength to keep going.

Never mind about Sarah yet, and the strength required of her brave soul. This experience was still quite a bit about me, taking egocentric but necessary steps in my process to eventually come to realize, in a sort of epiphany, who had been the strongest one of all.

Once in awhile, we did get a comment about Sarah's courage to come out as transsexual, although not nearly as often as the praise we got for being her parents. It was a little twisted, but in the beginning, when I'd hear about Sarah's courage instead of my own, I was surprised. I'd think, *What about how hard this is for me?* I was seeking reassurance and recognition for my own emotional efforts. It was a little like being in a turbulent airplane. I needed to get my own oxygen mask on first before helping anyone else—including Sarah. Was it selfish or natural to feel this way? At this point in my process it was maybe a little of both. This journey is a team effort; parents have to transition too.

Sarah appreciated the sentiment of being called courageous, but commented, "I do not think courage is the right word—it was necessity." Although transition may have been necessary, in my view, her journey did take courage. If I had cancer, and if someone said that if I walked a tightrope across the Grand Canyon then that act would cure my cancer, would the act be courageous or necessary?

Why Even Tell Us?

"Why did you tell us about this at all?" one relative asked us several months after receiving the disclosure via email.

If we weren't the ones to deliver this news, sooner or later someone else would have. This was our story, and we needed to be the ones to tell it with the respect and sensitivity it deserved. The news that a family member was "having a sex change" was sensational and difficult to contain. With each successive delivery of the story, a little bit more of the substance that we wished to express would have been lost, like dampening ripples in a wave. Our personal delivery put a human face on it from the beginning. This so-called "sex change" was happening to someone we knew who had a real story which deserved more than just a headline.

Even though this was a very private emotional family matter, it was at the same time the most publicly visible life-changing event imaginable. Many family issues are easy to keep secret, but this was clearly not one of them. To keep future interactions honest, everyone had to know.

The Need to Gossip

"Who else knows?" was a universal question. In virtually every case the question came up, often within the first five minutes of the conversation. "Who else knows about this?" or, "Who can I tell?" People sought permission to tell someone else almost immediately; sometimes they didn't even ask at all. The news is sensational, and it's human nature to want to be the one to deliver it. This was very hard for me in the early days, as I intensely wanted to control the flow—and content and integrity—of the news. We couldn't control the transition, but we still had a choice in how to deliver the news, and I desperately clung to that power. I believed that I could hold onto Steven vicariously through the spirits of those who still thought of him as such. I wanted to decide the timing of Steve's disappearance.

Struggling to come to terms with the concept of a transsexual child was a challenge for us, and sharing our emotions with others helped us cope. This therapeutic effect was one reason why we wanted to be the ones to deliver the news in the first place. But we knew at the starting line that this would be a race against time.

Human willpower has it's limits, and word of our story would leak quickly. My family was usually not the center of attention, and so it was odd and very difficult for me to suddenly be the subject of spreading news. I don't think about it at all today, but when we first came out about this, I felt very possessive, very concerned about how our news was delivered.

Why Doesn't Steve Do All the Talking?

"Why don't you make Steve do all the talking?" one friend suggested. "I learned that my nephew is gay and his parents are making him tell the family because it is his choice, his decision to be gay."

Of course, it is not a choice to be gay any more than it is to be straight—or transsexual—but I preserved the phrasing of the suggestion to illustrate this type of reaction. (I expand my take on "choosing who you are" in the next two chapters.)

Sarah had her own long list of close people to tell and she'd been doing plenty of talking about it for months. Sarah's biggest hurdle was already cleared: she had told us. Telling parents is often the most significant disclosure a transsexual child has to make. For Sarah, this was probably the critical turning point and most liberating milestone of her journey.

We deliberately planned to meet with many people *without* Sarah to assure a more open and uninhibited dialogue for us as well as the recipients. We talked about how difficult the transition had been for us and how hard I worked to resist it at first—words that helped many recipients accept the news but that would be cruel to say over and over again in front of Sarah. The private meetings were therapeutic for Ted and me, and a major factor contributing to the speed and success of our healing process. It was crucial that we come forward as champions for the cause of our child. We explained all that we had learned about the condition. We set the precedent of the support we wished for our child, and asked our friends and family to join us. Sarah is not doing anything "to us" such that we would need to express anger or vindication by punishing her, to throw her out to the sharks, to "make her do all the talking." It would have given the wrong message to force the burden on Sarah.

Medical Awareness

Occasionally we were bestowed with an intellectual gift of pre-existing medical knowledge about this condition.

"Well it can't be helped. It's biochemical," said one cousin, who is a wonderful mix of brain, warmth and sophistication. It was also refreshing that she did not confuse the concept of homosexuality with that of transsexualism.

A speech pathologist friend told us about a rewarding case he recently had helping a trans woman recondition her voice.

One of the most heartwarming responses came from someone who learned about Sarah from our email in March of 2010:

> I have read your letter with great care, compassion, and relief. I must comment that I feel thrilled for Sarah that she has found her new, true identity. One can only imagine the tortuous existence you must have felt being trapped in the body of a man.
>
> I have come to know the nature of gender dysphoria quite well over the past twenty years during my work at Hutzel Women's Hospital. It was here that the famous surgeon, Neil Wilson did his gender reassignment surgeries. As a [medical professional], I cared for the patients who were hospitalized for prolonged periods. ... They were the kindest, most misunderstood people I had ever met. Most were struggling with issues Sarah has had and many had lived in denial for years. I was most happy to discover that BCBS of MI covered this surgery, even in the mid 1980s as gender dysphoria is a true diagnosis. ... I cannot imagine being trapped inside of a gender opposite body. ... I can honestly tell you that no one in this house will judge you or say one negative thing about you.

Dismissive Oversimplifications: "Oh, is that all? You had me so worried!"

Some people really understood the complexity of our challenge, and expressed to us that they too felt overwhelmed by anguish when trying to step in our shoes. And some people oversimplified our struggle to the other extreme.

One person said, "So is that all you wanted to talk to me about?"

Another friend kept repeating, "Man, you really had me scared. I thought it was going to be something much worse."

A neighbor said, "I don't see anything sad about this at all!" I asked her how she would feel if her daughter came home with a double mastectomy, hysterectomy, permanently sterile, with a beard and a deep voice and announced out of the blue she would henceforth be a son. My friend replied, "Well if you put it that way!" And I wondered, "What other way is there?"

A business associate asked to see before and after pictures. A family friend who found out second hand actually giggled!

When the subject came up again after a few months went by we got comments like, "Oh that? That's old news!" or "I forgot all about that," sometimes accompanied by shrugs.

Although the simple and dismissive responses were not very therapeutic at the time, they brought a unique perspective to our growing body of support. These relaxed attitudes were in some ways more genuine than, say, one deeply emotional wellspring we encountered at first who then froze into an icicle months later.

References to Death and Dying

We got a number of variations of the following sentiment: "Oh, thank goodness! I thought someone was dying."

Death was the one comparison that often came up. Ironically, suicide is actually an alternative considered by some trans people who reach a point of "do or die." I'm sure our friends weren't thinking of it this way, but yes, some families *do* have to deal with death instead of transition. I could have replied, "Yes we know. We are so glad she chose to transition instead."

"It's not like he's actually dying," said a lot of people who simply cannot know what it *is* like at all.

While it is true that my child did not die, Steven does not exist anymore. As this memoir describes, we did have to mourn his loss in a unique way. Many parents, myself included, grieve our lost children, usually alone, because most people don't sympathize with, or even recognize the legitimacy of our experiences. Instead of rallying to support our grief, some even turn their backs on us. I've had backs turned on me both figuratively *and literally.*

Whatever Floats Your Boat

Many of the people who readily accepted Sarah's transition said, "As long as she is happy!"—which is first and foremost a kind-hearted response. But to me such a response implies that they don't really "get it," and although they may find transsexualism bizarre, they are fine with it. Most people want to be happy, but gender dissonant people transition to rectify a painful and debilitating condition. If I had cancer and a procedure was found to cure it, I'd pursue the cure as a matter of survival. Nobody would say to the hypothetical cancer patient seeking a cure, "as long as you're happy!" Ideally, happiness would follow (as it did for Sarah), but all the other conditions of life are still factors of overall happiness.

Humiliation

One friend had learned through the grapevine some time earlier in the season. When we arrived for our visit, he snapped, "I already know about this. I don't need to know the details. There's nothing to talk about."

Obliviousness

A few people got the news and seemed to remain totally, genuinely oblivious to it and its impact on our lives. In conversation, there was no trace of recognition that we were in the midst of an epic family tragedy. I could think of nothing else—the gender transition dominated my thoughts, my actions, my entire existence for a very long time. I had learned how much I was beginning to crave a listening ear by not getting one at all.

Unexpected Perspectives

When I mentioned that a part of my process included anger, one friend replied unexpectedly with, "I can imagine! It would be disappointing to be deprived of all the years of raising a daughter."

Another friend pointed out that Steven would lose his male privilege. But someone who is not male does not have male privilege to lose.

Life is Tough for Everyone

"You have to remember that everyone carries a bag of rocks," was one person's relentless message. He was almost obsessed with reminding me that there are many other challenges out there besides living through a gender transition.

I was alarmed and annoyed when one of the more popular primers on transsexualism advised parents to think about how much worse things could be, rather than acknowledging a parent's real emotional challenges in a gender transition. While this might work to nudge some parents out of their gloom, I found it to be a little bit patronizing especially considering the authors of that book never stood in the shoes of a trans person or a parent of one. In fact, this advice kind of highlights how isolated our struggle is from others that the mainstream will readily acknowledge and support.

Situations can be viewed two ways: relatively and absolutely. While comparisons to other challenges can put parents' pain in perspective, it does not take away from how they feel in absolute terms. When I go to bed at night feeling sad because I miss Steven, I don't suddenly feel better when I remind myself that he is not in a coma, or not a serial killer. These comparisons don't make me miss Steven any less. Though people mean well, this type of response would be like going up to a mom who lost a child to death and saying, "Things could be worse! You could have lost two children."

It is not my intent to discount other people's stories. I'm just telling mine.

I Always Knew Something Was Up With Him

"I'm not surprised" said a friend who had spent maybe a total of two hours with Steve in the last ten years. Her husband confirmed, almost proudly, "That's right, my wife wasn't surprised at all!" They shared with us what they had thought and predicted about our child. I still wonder, was this supposed to help?

A few people noticed something was up at Jeff's graduation party in June 2009, when Steve appeared with dramatically plucked and shaped eyebrows. This drew some attention and speculation. One guest at the party thought Steve was wearing makeup. Another just assumed that he was a transvestite. A third guest was certain this new androgynous look would ruin his future. When I later heard about these comments, I felt like my private space had been invaded since we had not disclosed the transition to anyone yet. There was a leak in the wall of my sanctuary.

One cousin relentlessly trumpeted for years that everyone detected our private nightmare at Jeff's party, and that it was awkward and awful. He reminded me of a kid with a magnifying glass held between the blazing hot sun and a tiny creature with no place to hide.

What Bathroom Will She Use?

When a neighbor asked us about bathrooms, we told him that Sarah would use the woman's room. He was mortified and declared that to be illegal.

Actually, it's perfectly legal for transitioning people to use the bathroom of their presenting gender in public places. Furthermore, it would be ludicrous to think it's better to force our gorgeous new daughter into a men's room.

More and more public places are showing sensitivity to gender variance and are offering unisex bathrooms as an option.

You Shouldn't Feel Guilty

The first time I heard this was the first time I wondered, "Why on earth would we feel guilty?"

When the book *True Selves* was published in the early 1990s, there was still speculation by many gender experts that transsexualism was caused by a combination of both nature and nurture.[1] While the authors of this book don't claim to support this theory, they give some examples of theories from the nurture camp:

> If a young boy is repeatedly dressed in girls' clothing, is positively reinforced for all feminine behaviors, or is rejected or punished for all behaviors that are considered to be typically male, chances are very good that eventually he will learn to behave in a feminine manner.[1]

But would such a child actually be a girl? The unfortunate case of David Reimer has been highly publicized and it spotlights the tragic flaw in this behavior modification strategy. When David was circumcised at birth, the laser tool accidentally sliced off his penis. Psychologist Dr. John Money confidently and pompously advised, "Just raise him as a girl!" which the parents did until puberty when the young person became tormented and sought to learn the truth. David worked for years to transition back to being the boy he was inside, and tried to live a normal life until age 38 when he committed suicide.[2,3]

No amount of behavior modification, electroshock, or talk therapy has ever changed someone's cognitive gender identity. It does not seem possible to convert a transsexual person to a cissexual person—or the other way around, like Money tried to do to David Reimer.

The Oldest Generation

Ted's parents, Sarah's grandparents, set an example of the deepest love and acceptance imaginable. Because they lived out of state, we had to tell them over the phone. We were uneasy about this, but word was leaking out in the family quicker than we had anticipated and we didn't want to risk that they learn about this news via the grapevine. With both of them in their mid-eighties, I was worried this news would shatter them. I have since learned that most old folks have a powerful sense of perspective when it comes to dealing with life's adversities.

Sarah's Grandpa thought for a minute after hearing the news and said, "Well that's what parenting is all about!" He then asked simply, "So do I understand that the counseling is saying we are not going to try to fight this, but instead, we are going to do what we can to work with it?"

We confirmed, "Yes that's correct. We can't change the gender of the mind, but we can change the body to match the mind."

Grandpa said, "It sounds like a great mental anguish has been lifted from her. We have to try to create a situation of acceptance." He continued, "We are a very special family. We have something in our family that not many other families get to have. This is not a burden; we have something extra for the world!"

Grandpa immediately pulled out his address book and asked us how to spell the new name: "S-a-r-a-h A-n-n." He double checked. "For years I've been telling people I have eight grandsons and nine granddaughters. Now my whole life is going to be turned around!" he laughed as he recorded the name change of his 14th grandchild into his phonebook.

Sarah's Grandma watched the Oprah Show the next day when a transsexual person was featured. She called me up afterwards and told me, almost puzzled, "You know, I don't seem to be having any problem accepting this. But Grandpa..." and then she paused a long time, while searching for the words. I started getting nervous. Did Grandpa lose his composure after absorbing the initial shock? I braced myself for a blow. She continued, "But Grandpa actually seems to be having an *easier* time with it than me." An easier time!

This excerpt is from *True Selves* by gender therapists Brown and Rounsley:

> Similarly, the reactions of other relatives such as siblings, aunts, uncles, and cousins can be equally diverse. The only exception I've found in my practice has been grandmothers. In almost every case, grandmothers have been supportive of their transsexual grandchild.[4]

In our case, *all* the octogenarian people we told accepted this news with exceptional grace and wisdom. Maybe they've seen so much that nothing fazes them anymore. Whatever it is, I hope to someday reach that level of inner peace.

Nothing

In March of 2010 we sent out the first email disclosure to an extended family group of about 30 people. We wanted to personally inform all the people in the family who would sooner or later find out through the grapevine. We worded the emotional and intimate letter such that there would be no pressure for anyone to respond. But it might have been our biggest mistake in this process to date, because that is the response we got the most often: Nothing.

The tendency for some people not to respond at all troubled me. In retrospect I think it was probably hard to compose a written response to news like this, but signs of support are important to a transitioning family. There are few journeys with this much risk of loss or abandonment. Yet to this soul-baring, personal and sensitive announcement, we received absolutely nothing in response from *most* of the recipients that were notified via email. Of the ones who did respond, however, their heartwarming words of love and kindness shined like bright beacons through a fog. We remain deeply grateful to those who sent even the simplest message. Through the overall journey, some people wrote to Sarah, others said they would write and then didn't, but most never contacted Sarah—or us—at all.

Fixation on Genital Surgery

"Is she going to have the surgery?" or "Is he going to have the surgery?"

This question came up often; sometimes it was the first question asked. It seemed to be based on a presumption that gender transition only "really" occurs at the exact moment of genital surgery—as if Sarah would become a woman only then, and only by a surgical procedure. So I ask rhetorically, "What brings people to this particular operating room in the first place?" People don't come here by accident.

Gender is a sense of self that comes from within. It is a complex system of hormones and brain chemistry. Gender dissonant people often suffer for years and even decades with painful, physiological disharmony. Also, because their bodies don't match their brains, the world cannot really see them. Trans people view the world from behind a troublesome shell—but the world interacts with the shell. Gender transition is a long, grueling process undertaken with two (oversimplified) purposes—to address personal physiological pain (usually with hormones) and to genuinely become a part of the world. Trans people can be freed from dissonance and truthfully present themselves to the world—and all this can be done without ever presenting their genitals.

Genital surgery can't change a person's gender. It can only change their genitals to match their gender. Sarah has always been female, and her gender will be female whether she has surgery or not.

You Have a Life Too

A friend called me in March of 2010, concerned that I was becoming too immersed in my daughter's transition. "You have a life too, you know," she said.

Sometimes I get to pick the things in my life, and sometimes they just happen to pick me. Ironically, way back in the early stage of the journey, this same friend had the sense to point out that we'd been given an extraordinary gift—a premature concept at the time. At month 15, I was still grappling with a lot of anguish. But when I stepped outside of the boundaries of my ever-expanding comfort zone, I found myself in the midst of a whole new dimension of life. I was finally beginning to appreciate the honor and the privilege of experiencing first hand this most fascinating corner of humanity.

Before I turn to the next page in my life, I have a precious window of time and opportunity to detail my unfolding story in a memoir. I can't seriously ignore Sarah's transition anyway, there is still much to be done in this journey. In fact, my future life, my new relationship with my daughter, with everyone in our world, and my chance at peace and happiness are all based on how we handle this transition.

Why Did We Let Him Do It?

I heard that a mother of another transgender child became upset, even contentious, that we presumably "let our child do this." A mutual friend relayed some of her questions to me: "Why did we support him so quickly? Why did we enable this transition with money?"

I'm guessing that by this point in the memoir it's pretty evident that I did my best to try to stop my child. But I also eventually figured out that this transition was not mine to stop. Steve—as he still was Steve to me—would be financially independent and economically equipped in the very near future. Either he would have our companionship through the journey or not, but the journey was going to occur. I took a look at him, and saw this person who was not yet bald and not yet broad shouldered, and thought, "Although the possibility seems remote to me, if he is right, then we should get him on hormones sooner rather than later."

My whole plan for the first half year was based on a finely tuned balancing act between the possibility that Steve was right and the hope that I could prove him wrong. So it seemed optimal to jump in and support him with very little risk at first. Most of what would

131

occur in the first couple of years would be reversible.

I knew I could not move forward psychologically into the final irreversible steps of this journey until I was convinced this was the right thing to do. Since those heartbreaking steps were still years away, if Steve was making a mistake, he'd figure it out before it was too late. But if Steve was right about being transgender, a younger transition is easier. I'd rather have a conventional-looking trans daughter who assimilates easily rather than a brawny one who might struggle with prejudice her whole life.

We didn't get to know that the gender change would make our child happy; nobody gets to see into the future. The only way to ever know was to take steps in that direction and assess the feel of the progress. *Was life getting better for our child?* In time we came to realize that the transition was something that had to occur. It eventually came to feel like we had, metaphorically speaking, found a cure for our blind child.

I'm sure the other mother who disagreed with our approach loves her child as much as we love ours. I am guessing she felt she was protecting him—like stopping a toddler from running out into the street. I had felt that way too at one time. Nobody can tell a mother what is the right or the wrong way to feel; not even another mother.

• • • • • • •

We were told many times how much it helped to learn about our struggle. Many people needed to hear about my resistance, my year-long plan to disqualify the diagnosis, and my hope that Steve would be cured without transitioning.

We detailed our investigation into the validity of the condition and our determination to understand it and make peace with it. We found common ground with people who start out with no knowledge of transsexualism. Only by starting at the beginning could we draw people into the story and work toward a level of understanding. To describe our journey without detailing the anguish would have made it seem too easy, even whimsical or deranged. Once our friends and family learned that I had not been convinced at first either, this information became the most powerful key to convincing them.

Every person brought something new and insightful to the table; not so much direct knowledge of transsexualism, but ways to cope with adversity in life, fresh insight and words of encouragement. After a year of conversations, not a lot had changed on the surface of our world. Among our friends and family there exists, I'm sure, a full spectrum of viewpoints. I believe some would be reacting to this issue quite a bit differently had it not been happening to the four of us, had we not made it personal. Our friends and family worked hard to learn about our transition, and in almost every case our support continued to grow. I won't pretend that some relationships aren't going to be a little different because of the transition. However, it might be hard to discern exactly who will be the one redefining those relationships at this point.

· · · · · · ·

As we move forward through the years, we still like talking about our transition, but from a healed and experienced perspective. These days, when I talk about it to other people, whether it be friends or family or the local pharmacist, I feel like the one in control, the one standing on the wiser side of the talk. Had we felt so vulnerable in the early days that we thought the rest of the world was wiser? Today we make a statement by example, exuding confidence, acceptance, and peace with our new reality. It is invigorating to finally describe our life as "having something extra" for the world.

Trading Places

Chapter 9

Making Peace with Religion

...but it does me no injury for my neighbor to say there are twenty gods or no God. It neither picks my pocket nor breaks my leg.

Thomas Jefferson, 1787[1]

I have a free thinking, intellectual perspective on spirituality, and I don't follow any organized religion. Although I was born and baptized Catholic in the 1950s, I was raised under no strict religious rule. I believed all religions had the same fundamental tenets—be good to yourself, be kind to one another, appreciate life and nature in all its glorious splendor. My parents led me by their example of a virtuous life. Our moral code was based on an equal mix of common sense, scientific intelligence, and respect for all of humanity. For example, there was a boy in our neighborhood who had some feminine mannerisms. I was never fed the dangerous ideology that this was a bad way to be, or, more oddly, that he may have chosen to be this way. I thank my parents for my accepting approach to people—and in an ironic sort of way I thank God. I feel lucky that I was spared the duplicitous message that it was right for me to judge others. After I grew up, I was surprised to learn that some people, claiming religious direction, judge gay people (and probably transgender people) to be immoral or sinful.

We know a lot of religious people of various denominations, and initially I was concerned about how some of them would handle the news about Sarah's transition. As it turned out, many of the most religious people we know have been our biggest supporters. I believe the people in our circle live in a comfortable place of balance between their religious beliefs, educated minds, and kind hearts. They walk through their lives with faith in God to support them through good times and bad. Most of them actually use their religion to help them accept people like Sarah who are different from themselves.

For some of our fundamentalist friends, Sarah's transition may have put their true convictions to the test. I hold in high esteem the people who have managed to rise above any trace of personal religious conflict to see with clarity the truth of the situation: a beloved person with a heart of gold and a passion for life is struggling to correct a painful medical condition. She is not a threat to anyone, but instead a gift to admire—a humble, gentle, and courageous soul who can teach us a lot about the will to be true to oneself. Observing the positive reactions of my most religious friends has revitalized my faith in our shared humanity. In fact, acceptance or intolerance of differences among people is not uniquely attributable to religious teaching. Like hate, love comes from within individuals, religious or not. Surely most would agree that living in truth is better than living a lie. I appreciate our friends and family, religious and otherwise, for their unbiased love and support throughout Sarah's transition.

Despite the fact that most of my own religious friends practice love and tolerance, religion is too often used as an excuse for intolerance in the broader world around me. Although religious ideology is not a part of my personal story, it is a part of the world I share with others, so it affects my life indirectly through its role in my cultural and political environment.

• • • • • • •

Religion is a deeply personal matter, and it can be a sensitive topic to discuss. Personal beliefs and moral convictions are sacrosanct, inalienable rights. So why do I dare tread on this sacred ground? Because when judges and law-makers inject their religious beliefs into decisions that affect our secular state and our public law, they are treading on *my* sacred ground. My beliefs and moral convictions are egregiously violated when government actions, ostensibly based in religion, cross the line and threaten me and my children.

The pretense of morality based on religion is likely the number one driving force behind many of the acts of discrimination, humiliation, and brutality that target those in the LGBTQI community. And people with this kind of hatred run for political office. There are zealots who want to mix their hate with our state and work with self serving purpose—using their misplaced religious views as an excuse—to push harmful and dangerous bills into law. An anti-bullying bill from my home state provides an example of this kind of intrusion. The events surrounding this bill felt personally relevant enough to compel me to include this chapter in my book.

In the Michigan Congress of 2011, two profoundly different anti-bully bills were proposed to protect our children in public schools from harassment and bullying. One bill enumerated protection for specific kids who have historically been targets of harassment such as gay and transsexual kids.[2] The other bill, sponsored by hard-line conservative Rick Jones, deliberately excluded enumeration.[3] Based on historical examples, it seemed clear that enumeration would heighten awareness of discrimination and lead to more effective enforcement of the policy; in contrast, a non-enumerated bill would send a message that it is OK to look the other way if gay or transsexual kids are harassed. Unfortunately, Rick Jones was the chair of the committee to decide which of the two bills would be brought to the senate floor, and he chose to bring the non-enumerated bill to the floor. Given the choice of trying to pass a bill that would be more effective at protecting *all* of our children, this senator, with all traces of logic eclipsed by hate, had chosen instead to pick the bill filled with the loopholes and cloaked protection—for the bullies instead of the victims. He never responded to my personal letter asking him to protect all of our children by supporting the stronger, enumerated bill.

In fact, Senator Jones became even nastier: he added a clause to specifically *allow* bullying in Michigan's public schools, if the bully claimed "sincerely held religious belief or moral conviction." With the addition of this clause, any student or teacher who thinks being gay or transgender "is wrong" would be free (and encouraged) to bully, harass, and torment LGBTQI classmates without any consequence whatsoever. This bill outlined how to legally sanction hate, bigotry, and bullying of children.[4,5] In November 2011, Michigan's Republican-controlled Senate passed this bill.

Fortunately this reactionary agenda received widespread media coverage, protest, and ridicule, and the senate revoked the clause exempting so-called religious kids from accountability. When this clause threatened to become law in my state, I felt compelled to write this chapter. Bigots' voices were being heard and I needed mine to be heard too. People voted Rick Jones into office. Did they really know who they voted for? A lot of people will not take responsibly for their own prejudice. They like to claim that it is God who hates people like Sarah; they hold up a biblical shield to defend or justify their own hate.

But their biblical justifications are transparently contrived. Take Leviticus, the Old Testament source of the infamous line so many homophobic people reference today as an excuse to hate gay people, and likely also transgender people: "If a man also lie with mankind, as he lieth with a woman, both of them have committed an abomination: they shall surely be put to death"—Leviticus 20:13,[6,7] (just a few verses after the universally ignored one about putting sassy kids to death, Leviticus 20:9[8]). Can it really be this one line in Leviticus that drives so many literalists to hate? Leviticus and Deuteronomy mercilessly and violently put people to death for *all kinds* of minor infractions![9] Modern followers of the Bible decide which passages are important today and which can be set aside. There is no reason to place Leviticus 20:13 in the former category.

And New Testament passages about LGBTQI issues are virtually non existent, or at least quite vague and questionable.[10-15]

The interpretations of the Bible have clearly evolved with the changing laws of people and governments over the eras, to keep pace with progress in science, philosophy, and culture. For example, in our modern world, we know that the earth is not flat.[16] Today, church leaders use cell phones, the internet, and satellite TV. People have walked on the moon and put a robot on Mars. The Vatican Council admitted to making egregious mistakes and pardoned Galileo—albeit 350 years too late—for implying the earth was not the center of the universe.[17] I don't know any people who beat their slaves with rods.[18] Although the Bible is rife with passages about how to brutally punish slaves, by 2012, slavery became outlawed everywhere on earth. Modern followers of the Bible might even concede that the idea of being put to death for working on Sunday is outdated.[19] Why is it that some of these same people cannot get past the outdated and erroneous notion that people born outside hetero cissexual parameters are somehow evil? This is even more perplexing to me since the Bible is robust with passages of honored same sex partnerships and gender variant individuals embraced by God.[6,20,21] Almost half of all species on earth exist outside the sexual binary.[22] Gender variance is not only natural, but much more common than the once feared—and now hardly mentioned—condition of leprosy.[23]

The only way I can make sense of modern organized religion is by observing that people just pick and choose what passages they want to follow. Some might even stop thinking for themselves and let others sort through this biblical material for them. They unquestioningly obey various *human* interpretations like commands delivered by God.[24] Some might just want an excuse to sanctimoniously judge people they don't understand.

The case of Gwen Araujo is a glaring example of vicious brutality grounded in categorical sanctimony. On October 3, 2002 four men beat California teen Gwen Araujo for hours with fists and shovels, choked her to death, hog-tied her and buried her body because she was transsexual. None of the men were convicted of a hate crime. One was given leniency because his lawyer argued that he had been tricked. Another was given leniency because he was shocked by and afraid of trans people, and he said he couldn't help but lash out physically. Only two of the four were convicted of second degree murder at all. On the day of Gwen's funeral, religious zealots assembled and held up signs proclaiming God's hatred for people like Gwen.[25-27]

Does anyone really believe that a benevolent God could endorse such cruelty and violence?

In Jasper, Texas, 1998, James Byrd, an African American man, was tied to a truck by white supremacists, dragged for three miles behind it, and decapitated. In Laramie, Wyoming, 1998, Matthew Shepard, a 21 year old gay man, was tortured and beaten then tied to a fence and left to die for 18 hours by two men who didn't like gay people. When the Matthew Shepard and James Byrd, Jr. Hate Crimes Prevention Act was brought to the floor of the US Congress in 2007, several right wing members of congress were opposed to this bill. The Act (officially passed in 2009) expands federal hate crime law to include acts of hate motivated by a victim's race or disability, as well as gender identity or sexual orientation. The socially conservative groups who opposed the Act said it would "muzzle people of faith" who dared to express themselves, implying, in spite of their actual religious teachings, that violence is an appropriate way to express one's faith.[28]

Some church leaders encourage hypocritical bigotry. Susan Stanton had been a very successful city manager of Largo, Florida for many years. But she was terminated from this position in 2007 when it was revealed that she was transsexual. "If Jesus was here tonight, and I'm very familiar with the Bible, I guarantee it, He'd want him terminated," said the Baptist minister at Stanton's public hearings before she was fired in a blatant violation of the First Amendment. The minister looked fierce; I actually thought he meant "termination" as in "summary execution." He continued, "I was disgusted, outraged ...of course it's against the scripture..."[29] Would this man of scripture predict the same fate for all people born with birth defects? Would he say that Jesus, divine minister of brotherly love, should fire someone using a wheelchair too? As contradictory as it seems, anyone who claims to follow every verse in every book of the Bible to the letter should indeed disfavor, even abhor all "defective" people, because Leviticus also has rules about them. *Anyone* with a blemish, a limp, or bad eyesight is "profane" and shall not "come nigh unto the alter."[30]

Some people with political, judicial and legal power will use their religion to justify harm to my child and others like her.[31-32] In 2010, Representative Paul Scott (R) ran for the position of Michigan Secretary of State on a platform of hate and bigotry. Scott declared in his platform, "I will make it a priority to ensure transgender individuals will not be allowed to change the sex on their driver's license in any circumstance."[32] When asked how this would benefit the economically distressed Michigan, he replied that it was about "values." He said it was about "preventing people who are males genetically from dressing as a woman and going into female bathrooms." Although he was aware that the American Medical Association declared Gender Dysphoria to be a legitimate medical condition (and that it is harmful to impede transition), he believed that by denying basic human rights to an already challenged group of individuals, he would solve Michigan's allegedly urgent problem of men sneaking into women's bathrooms.[32] Paul Scott revealed a total lack of knowledge on the heartbreaking condition of transsexualism as well as the state of affairs in Michigan. He didn't even seem to know that people can pee without any kind of driver's license at all.

Going all the way to the top, the 2011-12 presidential race for the Republican candidacy was absolutely loaded with politicians running on radical religious platforms. Most were vehement about their intention to reverse or eradicate many basic human rights of people in the LGBTQI community; a top issue for them if elected.[33-37] One candidate had even been a bully in high school. Former classmates recall cruel pranks on a gay student and a disabled teacher by a posse of bullies led by this candidate.[38]

· · · · · · ·

Bigots like to be heard and often they are in positions of power, but religious freedom is for everybody, not just the bigots. Trans people are as religiously diverse as people in any other cross section of society. Many progressive churches today welcome all of God's children. A progressive Catholic church in our community has initiated an outreach program to specifically encourage and welcome all people of any sexual preference or gender identity. St. John's (Episcopal) Church in Washington D.C. plans to ordain transgender priests.[39] Churches everywhere are replacing discrimination or uncertainty with welcome. Many religious leaders and ministers now challenge those who use the bible as an excuse to hate, denouncing hypocritical selection of its passages. In a groundbreaking statement in 2013, Pope Francis himself, the leader of a billion religious people worldwide, denounced the judgment of gay people. In her books, Christian author Joan Roughgarden highlights biblical evidence that gender diversity was embraced by Jesus and she references passages to that end.[40,41] Nowhere in the Bible does it say that a person cannot be who they are meant to be. In Acts 10, Peter baptized any believer. It is not up to a person to deny God's blessings to anyone, no matter how variant they may appear to be.[42]

I imagine some people come to a crossroads in their own ideological journey, where they must search their soul to ask, "Is it better to fill up with blind hatred or is it better to take a minute and think outside the lines, and try to understand the variety of people who live among us?" It is written in Romans 14:5, "Let every man be fully persuaded in his own mind"[43] — in other words, "think for yourself." This is one passage I would pick to follow if I was picking and choosing. It seems to me like there is room in the Bible to think and grow and still be a faithful person.

• • • • • • •

No one in our family has disavowed us to our face, although a few acted coldly for a while. The challenge may have been hard at first, but some of the most traditional-minded people have shown effort to think for themselves and learn a little more about the different kinds of people who live among us. Perhaps they see, like many religious people now see, that biblical justification for hatred is shaky at best.[40,41] The haters are going to be left behind as the modern world moves forward. I believe all of the people in our circle of friends and family want to live by their religion in only the most beautiful and generous way. Most seem to balance their religious beliefs with educated minds, common sense, and loving kindness. I don't know anyone who would shout maledictions at a funeral or condone legal torture of kids—but some of the people I know might have voted for the politicians discussed earlier in this chapter.

In examining the juxtaposition of religion and intolerance, I have learned more about both and I have made some peace with religion. Hate is a choice that comes from within individuals, not from God.

> "Difference of opinion is advantageous in religion. The several sects perform the office of a Censor morum over each other. Is uniformity attainable? Millions of innocent men, women, and children, since the introduction of Christianity, have been burnt, tortured, fined, imprisoned; yet we have not advanced one inch towards uniformity. What has been the effect of coercion? To make one half the world fools, and the other half hypocrites."[44]
> –Thomas Jefferson

Trading Places

Chapter 10

Queer Clarification

Reactions to our news about Sarah coming out as transsexual included many comparisons to homosexuality. Many people conflate gender identity with sexual attraction. This may be the most common area of confusion about transsexual people among the mainstream public today.

Some people expressed their support for Sarah by referencing homosexuality: "I'm fine with this. I even have a friend who is gay!" or "We invited a gay couple to our party!"

Another person said, "We attend a church which is very gay-friendly." He did admit that although their church embraces LGBTQI diversity, he had not yet knowingly met a trans person in attendance there. While knowing, accepting and befriending gay people is open-minded and "progressive," if not simply natural, this alone does not make one familiar with transsexualism.

Most cissexual heterosexual people living mainstream lives tend to clump all LGBTQI identities together, as the acronym rather encourages. But, simply put, sexual preference is defined by who you want to be with romantically, and gender identity is who you are. They are, in almost all ways, completely different concepts.

• • • • • • •

I am startled by the word "Queer." I guess it's a throwback to the days when the word had been derogatory. But today, some in the LGBTQIA community will wear the word like a badge, a symbol of pride for their courage and progress. The "Q" remains symbolically part of the acronym. At the start of my journey, I knew what the LGBTQIA acronym was all about. But I didn't know the difference between transgender and transsexual nor any of the words in trans-speak. So, as suggested by my friends, I will share my new understanding of some of the LGBTQIA terminology. In the second half of this chapter, I will share my perspective on some social and political topics that became relevant to me during our transition.

Sexual Orientation or Sexual Preference: Gay, Lesbian, Bisexual, Straight, Asexual

A bisexual person is one who is attracted to both men and women on a sexual level. Straight people are sexually attracted to people of the opposite sex. Homosexual people are attracted to people of their same sex. Gay is a term for anyone who is homosexual, but it is often used specifically with reference to gay men just as lesbian is specific to gay women. Asexual people do not experience sexual attraction to anyone. Although they have no interest in physical sex, many asexual people do want to fall in love and find a life partner.

Gender Identity

Gender identity is the fundamental sense of self as male, female, or something else. Gender identity is derived from within each individual and is separate from external perceptions and norms.[1,2] Most people are born with a gender identity that matches the sex of their body, but some are not. The physiological basis for gender identity is multidimensional and involves a complex system of hormones and brain chemistry.

Binary Gender Identity

This phrase describes people who identify as male or female. Most people, including most transsexual people, have binary gender iden-

146

tities, because they identify as male or female.

Non-binary Gender Identity

Some people's genders are not male or female. They may describe themselves as being both male and female, neither male nor female, in between male and female, or something else entirely. There are many different kinds of non-binary gender identities. A few examples of people who don't have binary gender identities include genderqueer, pangender, and two-spirit people. Some non-binary people identify as mix gendered, all gendered, or third gendered. Some have overlapping gender identities. Gender fluid people move between gender identities.[3,4] Many, but not all, people with non-binary gender identities dress androgynously in order to communicate their identities to the world around them. I don't pretend to know very much about every gender identity. But I have learned that there is great variance among us; gender identity is not limited to simply male or female.

Transsexual, Trans Woman, Trans Man

Transsexual is an adjective that describes someone whose cognitive gender identity is incongruent with the physical sex that was assigned to him or her at birth. Many transition or want to transition to a form of gender expression more in line with their identity. Most transsexual people identify as either men or women; they have a binary gender identity. They don't want to "cross-dress" or live one day as a man and the next as a woman. They aren't androgynous or genderqueer. They just had the misfortune of being born with the brain chemistry of one gender trapped in the body of the other gender. To eliminate this gender incongruence, some trans people change their bodies to match their brains and live out their lives as their brain-defined gender.

A trans woman or male to female transsexual woman or "MTF" is a woman who was born in a male body, like Sarah. A trans man or female to male transsexual man or "FTM" is a man born in a woman's body, like Jamison Green and Chaz Bono. The acronyms "MTF" and "FTM" are sometimes used, but some trans people view them as inappropriate because the acronyms give equal emphasis to "male" and "female" instead of focusing primarily on trans people's true gender identities.

Genital or Sex Reconstruction Surgery, or more descriptively, gender alignment surgery, is sometimes abbreviated to GRS or SRS. Many transsexual people don't have the means to have GRS and some simply don't want it. Genitals are irrelevant to nearly all everyday social situations. Usually with help from hormones alone, trans people can be freed from physiological dissonance and truthfully present themselves to the world—without ever presenting their genitals.

Some people use words like "post-op" and "pre-op" to describe transsexual people who have or have not had GRS. I think pre-op and post-op are among the most inappropriately used words in the trans-related lexicon.

Many cissexual people (new to the world of transsexualism) seem fixated on genital surgery as though having the surgery establishes the patient's gender only at that point in time. But the surgery doesn't change gender at all. It only changes genitals—to match the patient's gender.

Transgender

Transgender is an adjective and an umbrella term under which there are numerous subsets, including transsexual people and non-binary identified people. I interpret transgender to include the whole spectrum of people who are in touch with a gender variance within themselves. But some people use this word to refer only to certain sub groups. The scope of the meaning and use of the word "transgender" often incites debate in the trans community and its definition continues to evolve along with the trans movement.

Cross-Dresser or Transvestite

Cross-dressers fall under the transgender umbrella too, but they are not the same as transsexual people and are not usually transsexual. They are usually men who enjoy or get aroused by dressing in women's clothes. Some women who dress in men's clothes could be called cross-dressers too. Cross-dressers may be gay or straight people. They are typically happy with their genitalia, and have no intention of shifting their gender presentation permanently. "Transvestite" is an older word for the same concept, now viewed by some as derogatory. Most authors today use "cross-dresser."[5] Cross-dressing describes an activity anyone could engage in, whereas transsexual describes an intrinsic characteristic of a person.

Cissexual

Cissexual people are those whose bodies match the gender of their brains; most people are cissexual. They grow up and live life so comfortable with their brain-body congruence that it is usually difficult for them to understand the plight of transsexual people. Ironically, transsexual people seek the same congruence cissexual people experience without knowing it.[6]

Transsexual and Gay

It is possible for a transsexual person to also be homosexual. If a trans woman partners with a cissexual woman, they have a gay relationship or are lesbians. A trans woman who partners with a cissexual man is in a heterosexual relationship. The original sexual orientation of a transitioning person sometimes changes (and sometimes does not change) with the onset of hormone treatment.[7]

Queer

Queer is another umbrella term often applied to anyone who is anywhere along the gender or sexual continuum (except for straight cissexual people). Queer usually has a political implication—it implies that the person feels somehow separate from typical social norms about gender and sexuality, and wants to actively rebel against such norms.

Intersex

Intersex people are born with genitalia of both sexes evident externally and/or internally. An example would be an individual who looks like a woman externally, but has undescended testes. Sometimes genitalia are visibly ambiguous, and sometimes an intersex condition is found chromosomally, as in XX Males and XYY females. Last century, intersex people were known as "hermaphrodites" but this word is outdated.

LGBT, LGBTQIA, or even LGBTTQQIAA

These acronyms are used in activist groups because of alliances between the groups they include. The longest acronym represents the following people: Lesbian, Gay, Bisexual, Transgender, Transsexual, Queer, Questioning, Intersex, Asexual, and Ally. Questioning people are those who are unsure of where they fit in the gender variant or sexual preference continuum. An Ally is a supporter of the LGBTQIA movement.

There is no official acronym, though I personally see the first two used much more often than the expanded one. The word "Queer" is becoming more popular to use to symbolize the entire list.

• • • • • • •

In the next few pages I will share general information and my perspective on a few LGBT topics that became personally relevant during the course of my journey.

The LGBT Movement and The Diagnostic and Statistical Manual of Mental Disorders

Because people who tend to hate gay people often hate transsexual people too, people represented by the LGBTQI acronym have one important thing in common: they are often targets of prejudice, discrimination and abuse from the same haters. But with power and safety in numbers, they can sometimes fight for rights together as a larger group.

The modern gay rights movement began in the late 1960s and is more than 20 years ahead of the transgender movement. By 1973, gay activists managed to get homosexuality removed from the list of mental disorders in the second edition of *The Diagnostic and Statistical Manual of Mental Disorders* (DSM-II). Its replacement, "Sexual Orientation Disturbance," was removed from the DSM-III in 1986.[8] Over 25 years later, by mid-2013, the Defense of Marriage Act has been repealed and fourteen states have legalized gay marriage.[9] In other words, gay people have made a lot of progress for themselves. Some gay people might even be tired of dragging all these other queer people along for the ride on their coattails. But if transgender people don't align themselves with the LGBTQI subculture, they might be left behind in the dust. It would be much harder for them as an individual group to reach certain goals such as the passing of hate crime laws and the passing of marital-partnership laws. These important missions are best achieved by sticking together.

The DSM-IV-TR (2000) still labeled transsexualism as "Gender Identity Disorder"[10,11] but trans activists have worked hard to change this stigmatizing label. For the 5th edition of the Manual (which came out in May 2013), the diagnosis Gender Identity Disorder has been renamed to Gender Dysphoria, eliminating the misleading word "Disorder" and emphasizing "Gender Incongruence" instead.[12,13,14] Gender Dysphoria now has its own classification and chapter in the DSM-5 and is no longer grouped with sexual dysfunctions, paraphilias, and malignancies such as pedophilia. The DSM-5 recognizes a wide variety of gender incongruent conditions and emphasizes the use of the word "gender" rather than "sex" in these diagnoses.[12,13,14]

Trans activists, lobbyists and the American Medical Association worked with The World Professional Association for Transgender

Health, or WPATH, to improve the standards of treatment for transsexual patients outlined in the DSM-5 and to more accurately depict their condition in the manual. But gender incongruence is due to a medical condition; it is not a psychiatric disorder—no more than being gay is. So the ultimate goal should be to remove the condition from this psychiatric manual altogether.

Identity and Sexual Preference are Not Choices

LGBTQI people have another important thing in common: they know what it's like not to choose who they are. Actually, we all have that in common, don't we? Most people understand that their core identities are not consciously chosen.

Their own self awareness notwithstanding, some people still think LGBTQI conditions are willfully chosen. I suspect that people who can actually conceive of "choosing who they are" must have personal experience with this concept. I've learned about why many trans people "choose" to stay trapped in the wrong body. Similarly, I think the only people who might "choose" their sexual preference would be those who are gay but feel pressured by our society to try to be straight. After all, heterosexual, cissexual married couples are regal: they are privileged with income tax breaks, shared pension plans and family health insurance coverage. Up until 2013, gay people (and most trans people who wanted life partners) were denied these equal rights as citizens. The gay rights milestones of 2013 are major victories in the battle for equal rights,[9] but gay marriage is still illegal in most states, and LGBTQI people are still targets of social discrimination and hatred everywhere. I can see why a gay person might "choose" or pretend to be straight. But some of the most outspoken, staunch opponents of gay people have eventually come out as gay themselves. This makes sense because they have personal experience with "choosing" to do something unnatural— that is, pretending to be straight when their natural inclination was to be gay.

Similar logic can be used to describe "gender choice." For

example, Sarah pretended to be a boy even though her intrinsic nature was female. Cissexual people are happy with their gender and would not "choose a sex change"—probably not even for ten million dollars.[15] Yet many trans people who are willing to pay everything they have are denied the right to exist as their natural gender. Cis people take their gender for granted—they know their gender was not willfully chosen. Trans people bear the burden of proving this.

To people who have been told that being gay or transgender is a choice, I ask, "When did *you* choose to be a boy or a girl? Was it in first or second grade? Do you recall looking around your classroom at the girls and at the boys, and picking the gender of your first crush? Or did these things just happen within you naturally?"

Being Gay vs. Being Transsexual: Just My Two Cents

Reactions to our news about Sarah coming out as transsexual included variations of this startling comment: "It's harder to be gay. I think it is easier to be transgender than gay."

One embellished the idea, "You know, a gay person has to live with being gay his whole life, but for a transgender person, once you transition, you're done!"

In the beginning of this journey, Ted and I would practically have given our lives for Steven to *just* be a gay man, because we initially conflated the concept of gender identity with sexual preference too. For us, at least at first, that would have been easier because we would not have had to mourn the loss of our son. The only people ultimately entitled to opine on this matter would be trans people who are also gay, and the people who love them. So much depends on individual and family circumstance. Probably most queer people living in San Francisco have easier lives than those who live in, say, Tulsa Oklahoma. And any queer person in a loving family is likely much happier than one who has been rejected.

If there is a queer pecking order, gay men seem to be squarely at the top. I visited the Castro District in San Francisco in 2010, and there it was clear that gay men dominate. A world famous bookstore on Market Street, touting LGBT books by the thousands, had only seven books total on transsexualism. Maybe the acronym should really be GLBT.

It's almost fashionable to be gay nowadays in some circles, such as academia or show business or in diverse, liberal metropolitan areas. There are openly gay people routinely and prominently featured in mainstream, Emmy nominated, day time and prime time television shows.[16,17] By now, most people probably know somebody who is gay. The former head of the *Republican* National Committee recently came out as gay.[18] Priests and Bishops come out as gay. In our upscale, intellectual and diverse community, many of the successful businesspeople are openly gay. Our school district (although still just one of few) hires openly gay people into positions in every level of the school system. By 2013, polls showed that 81% of people aged 18 to 29 are in favor of legalizing gay marriage.[19] As I was finishing this memoir, the Supreme Court struck down the federal Defense of Marriage Act and gay marriage became legal in several states. In fact many people don't consider gays to be quite so "queer" at all anymore.

People in my community are generally accepting of gay people, but seem much less familiar with transgender people. I was led to believe by a medical professional that Steven might end up to be gay (instead of transgender) after they evaluated him and figured out what was *really* wrong with him. My doctor mentioned that his friend's son had thought he was transsexual, but ended up living happily in a gay life. That prospect seemed so much easier to me! Nothing would really change, and for all intents and purposes, it would be nobody's business anyway. In retrospect, I do believe the story from my doctor was "slightly customized" out of compassion to give me hope that Steven might not transition. When I sat in his office and melted with grief, he was probably at a loss for words. But during the week after our talk, he spent some time researching, then sent me an article from a medical journal with real statistics:

"When a person declares they are transsexual, in almost all cases, they are already at the point of no return."[20]

This exemplifies how unfamiliar our society is with this condition, even within the medical community. As for me, after just two years of living in this new world, I now see that people in our society are quite familiar with gay people, but seem to know very little about trans people by comparison.

Our school district, which I previously described as progressive because of its gay-straight alliance programs, hosts curricular events featuring gay speakers and their parents in high school health classes. These speaking panels help to educate the students about gay issues and what it is like to be gay. When I offered to speak on one such LGBT panel in 2013, they swiftly turned me down: transgender people and their parents were not allowed to speak on these panels.

When Ted and I went to our first PFLAG[21] meeting, the room was populated almost exclusively with parents of gays and lesbians. And this was on a day when the guest speaker was transsexual! We sat alone, astonished, and speculated about the demographics of this audience and the lack of transgender representation. The gay movement is decades ahead; it has support—and more familiarity— within the mainstream community. Some trans people don't come out until they are older; transsexualism is still so ill received that they wait as long as they can. By then, their parents are elderly or dead and unlikely to come to PFLAG meetings. Many trans people simply don't come out, and their families never have to deal with it. I didn't even go to meetings like this until I was so comfortable with my child's transition that I almost could have run the meeting myself.

Cissexual people—gay or straight—have brain/body congruence and don't need to do anything to appear to the world as they do to themselves. But on a physical level, transsexual people must endure one of the hardest journeys imaginable just to be able to live as their true selves. Transition can be painful, both emotionally and physically; and the financial cost is staggering.

A trans woman may undergo several major surgeries including facial feminization surgery, a trachea shave, breast augmentation, and genital surgery—which sometimes requires two surgeries. Some spend hundreds of hours and tens of thousands of dollars over years of time just enduring the painful process of facial hair removal by electrolysis. Trans men have at least as many procedures of their own. Most trans people are on a hormone regimen for life. Health Insurance policies often *specifically exclude* treatment for the condition. Medications and therapy to ease gender dissonance are often not covered. Many trans people routinely get interrogated, sometimes by strangers, about their genitals. Nothing can be more public, or more of a curiosity, than coming out as trans. Not everyone assimilates easily, and those that don't are at particularly high risk for ridicule, humiliation, even brutal hate crimes. It is still legal in most states for employers to fire workers just for being transsexual.[22,23] Churches oust transgender parishioners. Friends and families disavow them. Parents disown them. Transsexualism is misunderstood and often viewed as freakish or deranged.

Of course, gay men and lesbians also experience bigotry and hatred. But it seems naïve to assert that trans people have it easier than gay people.

I'll never know how hard it is to be either gay or transsexual. Most people, no matter who they are, just want to come out and find a safe place to live in a sometimes hostile world. Many LGBTQI people still encounter discrimination, cruelty and violence. But in the few years I was writing this memoir, attitudes started to change.

We are in the midst of a very rapid cultural shift to acknowledge the gender and sexual diversity among people in our world. I thank my lucky stars to be witnessing such healthy progress in my lifetime, especially with our personal lives so involved. Soon the terminology defined in this chapter will become common knowledge. Hopefully this chapter in my memoir will help to make itself outdated.

Chapter 11

Merry Christmas 2009
Turning the Corner

Find a place inside where there's joy, and the joy will burn out the pain.

Joseph Campbell

Winter arrived in December 2009, and a blanket of snow covered Michigan. Sarah came home one day and stood in the kitchen shivering and laughing, "Both my tits *and* my balls are frozen!" I laughed too, and for the first time in many months, for just a minute or two, my spirit lifted. It was a genuinely humorous moment. I thought about how interesting it must be to experience gender transition. My second hand experience could be interesting too, once I shook off the melancholy and worked up the conviction to be happier.

The bodily changes in Sarah were becoming more and more apparent. She announced that come January of 2010, she would begin to live life as a woman. She planned to register for Winter classes at the University of Michigan as Sarah. And so it was that around this time I arrived at the next station in my journey.

I had to get my bearings and analyze the situation rationally. Would I have one more Christmas with Steve? Or were we already too late? It flooded in, the flurry of possibilities of how to handle this Christmas, and I weighed the pros and cons of each scenario. We could have asked Steve to be present for one last Christmas, but it was almost easier to let Sarah be free, to give her that welcome as the ultimate Christmas gift. Why put ourselves through an emotional good-bye, when the opportunity to skip that and move forward was beckoning? The time to turn the corner had arrived, but I needed a nudge.

One day it just suddenly hit me. I realized she would be needing an absolute ton of girl stuff: sweaters and slacks, coats and hats, shoes and boots, hair products, makeup, accessories, and countless other items. All things considered, the timing seemed perfect for her to become Sarah. That Christmas, I would go on a shopping spree.

Christmas or not, she was going to need a bra without further delay. By November she had started to bud out, and would come home wearing tight knit tops that revealed the progress. This made me uncomfortable and even a little flustered. I was still on shifting sand and I needed to build a foundation before I could address the issue of my child's growing breasts. She was still willing to dress as a boy for me when we went out in public. But when she went out alone, she'd wear those tight, revealing knit tops, and seemed oblivious, or unconcerned, or maybe even proud of this new transitioning look. As hard as all of this was, the thought of letting her try to figure out how to buy a bra on her own, maybe still looking just a little like a guy, was unimaginably cruel. Like it or not, I used this impetus to focus on getting my rapidly changing 20 year old child her first bra.

Not knowing where to begin, I bought about ten different sizes of padded, A-cup bras, and brought them home for Sarah to try on in private. But all of those were still a bit too big in the cup for my developing daughter. So I went back out, this time accompanied by Sarah, and we shopped together. We could pretend, if need be, that I was the one who needed a bra. We decided to try the preteen girls department, in hopes of finding smaller cup sizes such as AA. The bras in the preteen area were adorable. Many of them were in bright, fun colors, or polka dotted, or flowered, and most of them had a near perfect size cup for my new girl; except that my girl had the torso of a 20 year old woman. We bought a bunch of these preteen sizes anyway. Then I went to work at the sewing machine adding inches of elastic to shoulder strap and torso dimensions, and with the pre-teen cups still intact, I created her first real bra. "Try it on!" I said to Sarah, hoping my creation would symbolize her mother's loving arms around her and the story would be done.

But she kept coming back, "It's still too tight, now too loose, this itches, this is poking me," and I kept modifying and customizing it. And, at night, she'd take it off and be free of the constriction.

"Welcome aboard!" I chuckled to myself. "Are you sure you want to live as a woman?" I thought about all the work that women put upon themselves. I thought about the many discomforts that women endure.

• • • • • • •

In early December, I headed to Kohl's department store, fairly excited about having this valid excuse to load up the shopping cart with tons of new clothes. The primary mission was to come home with a new coat for Sarah, but once there, I took one look at all the fashions on display, and I gave myself carte blanche. It had come to my attention that at that very moment, I stood in the midst of some outrageous 60% off "madness" sale that was to end within the hour. With this in mind, and the fact that I had no idea what sizes to get, I was literally scraping clothes off the racks into my buggy. In a matter of minutes, clothes began to spill out over the top of the buggy making it almost too heavy to push. Being only five feet tall, I could barely see over the top. I wondered if the scene looked comical to other shoppers—I had to work so hard to stifle my own laughter that my eyes were watering.

I'd never said the "d" word out loud yet. This was a perfect time to experiment and practice with all these strangers. I stood in line with my overloaded buggy, and held up a sweater and played the game. "What do you think of this for my 20 year old ... d-d-d-d-daughter?" I forced it out, wondering if the people would know that I never had a birth daughter, or detect that having a grown up daughter was somehow new to me. Would I be discovered as delusional or fake? It didn't come easier the second time; it was hard work all day. Sometimes I gave myself a break, and just said "niece," but I knew, saying niece, that this was not good progress. "I am hoping this cute one will fit my d-d-daughter." Over and over I practiced, pretended, whatever it took to recondition my brain such that pretending to have a daughter could eventually turn into the concept of actually having a daughter.

Our Christmas tree was already up. My shopping trip had been wildly exciting and I came home with a million coats and sweaters in various sizes and colors. The bounty under the tree would appear even more robust than usual, since I decided to wrap everything I bought in *all* the different sizes, postponing the inevitable returns until after Christmas. Next I had to inscribe the new name, "Sarah," onto the gift tags. The first tag took nearly an hour. I got the "S" part right away, S—just like Steven. But I was surprised at how reluctant I was to write the rest of her name. Labeling the presents to my daughter was harder than shopping for her. It felt oddly symbolic of "replacing" my child with someone else as though Steven had never existed, or would never exist again from that point on. So many ornaments hung on the tree from years past: "Jeff, 1998"; "Steven, 1995"; "Baby's first Christmas 1989 - Steven Andrew Baker." These names were engraved on ornaments here and there and scribbled on the cherished hand-made ones of preschool days. The first personalized "Sarah" ornament was to be a gift for 2009. In years to come, it would sometimes seem like we had ornaments from three different kids adorning our tree.

• • • • • • •

Hair styling products were also among the new presents I bought for my daughter. Would I be able to take a flat iron to my new daughter's hair? I actually quite eagerly anticipated this event. I knew it would be tough, weird as hell in fact, but she needed some help getting started with her hair. It would simply be an exercise, like physical therapy, and besides, how much harder could it be than the bra? It turned out to be psychologically difficult but also, not surprisingly, a key factor in Sarah's physical transformation.

On Christmas Eve 2009, Sarah opened her new flat iron, and we went upstairs together. She sat on a bench in the bathroom, facing the mirror as the iron heated up. I looked at the curly mop before me and thought of my Stevie and his trademark messy look. It had always seemed to need a cut. I often wonder today, if his lack of interest in keeping a neater look was due to the lack of interest in being Steven at all. The flat iron beeped and I took the handle and began to sweep through, lock after lock.

And as I swept, I peeled off Steven and uncovered Sarah. Out of the awkward gangly shell of a male emerged an elegant, beautiful, natural woman. Just like magic she went from a duck to a swan. It was startling how much better she seemed to look as a woman.

• • • • • • • •

Christmas that year was positioned right at the top of the emotional scale for Ted and me. As we grew tired of despair we seemed ready and eager to let the joy begin to weigh in. Sarah looked good in all her new clothes and the positive feedback from body and soul was palpable. I probably took a thousand pictures that very first Christmas with Sarah. I wanted her to keep all the new coats even though I bought four different styles, and two sizes of each. She modeled them all for the clicking camera. I had to laugh at the moment I first felt a tinge of envy: at her age, I swear I never looked as good as she did. We were turning a corner and the tone and rhythm of the journey was changing. This was a phase of blended emotion, morphing perception, mixed pronouns. Quite often Ted and I would mix "Steven" and "she" or "Sarah" and "he" multiple times in a conversation and even within the same sentence. This made us smile; we were starting to have a little fun with our challenge.

• • • • • • •

Through the first twenty years of raising two boys, I often wondered how hard it would have been to raise a daughter. With the notable exception of that shopping spree at Kohl's, I had never really liked shopping for clothes. I had no sense of or concern for style. I would have needed help then, and obviously needed help now, so I turned to my friend Judy, who had a great eye for fashion.

Around New Years Eve 2009, we arranged our first all-day shopping trip with Judy and her two daughters, Kelly and Kate. This was Sarah's public shopping debut as a woman, and a milestone event—for all five of us girls. The highlight of the day was to get Sarah's ears pierced at Claire's jewelry store, which offered a piercing service. I must admit I was nervous in the store standing next to my new daughter as we looked through the racks of jewelry. Would someone figure us out? When Sarah talked, did her voice draw attention? I kept looking around, wondering who might be staring at us, but no one ever did. It was going perfectly smooth until we got in line to wait for the ear piercing. The piercing technician asked Sarah for her driver's license to prove she was over 18 to sign for the procedure. Oh dear! It had been so fun and reassuring to skate through this event undetected.

Sarah sheepishly handed it over, warning the technician that she didn't look the same anymore. After all, the picture was taken when she was 16, not to mention when she was a 16 year old boy. But, the lady didn't even blink. She jotted down the data and handed back the license. Within a few minutes Sarah was on the bench grimacing as the tech cocked the trigger on the piercing gun, now clamped on Sarah's ear lobe. Kelly and Kate made a comforting remark, and started to chatter about how good "he" would look, then realizing the accident, quickly switched to the "she" pronoun mid-sentence. Undeterred, the technician kept working. We all snickered and tried to make light of it. The tech had seen the license and knew what was going on, but kept a straight face. We chattered away, the tech finished up, then turned and looked at me and said, "It's cool, you know. I get about one every month." She was referring, of course, to transsexual customers. What an interesting statistic—from just this one store! The tech had a composed, almost tough exterior, but said she thought we were pretty cool customers, and that we made her day. In fact, she made ours, too.

After buying Sarah some jeans, a scarf and a purse, we stopped for hot pretzels and sat on a bench in the middle of the mall to eat them. The place was crowded, teeming with shoppers looking for after-Christmas sales. A guy walked by and ogled Sarah with his bold eyes and body language. I was cynical, and thought he had clocked her as transsexual, and that must have been why he had stared at her. But the three younger women said the message was clear: the guy was hitting on Sarah. They thought it was creepy; unsolicited sexual advances aren't necessarily a welcome or positive thing. But to me this one incident was oddly comforting. Creepiness notwithstanding, I was thrilled by the affirmation that Sarah was viewed as a woman.

The camaraderie of five women shopping was a memorable gift to Sarah. The day was fun, productive, and very positive. On her first day out—the debut of her real life experience—a guy hit on her. It was encouraging to see how easily Sarah morphed into a woman. One by one my great worries were falling like dominoes. Wouldn't it be wonderful to just "go with it" and enjoy the success of the transition? In the months to come this concept would have a snowball effect, and the need to heal would become greater than the need to stay depressed. I longed for the happiness in life to return, and at this point it began to seem possible. I often asked Sarah if she had second thoughts, if she would ever go back to being a boy, and her response was always "absolutely not." We had to move forward, but the process was easier said than done.

• • • • • • •

I still had dreams, but I hadn't had one of dead Steve for quite some time. Maybe the neurons in my brain had started to connect—to conceive that my son Steve and my daughter Sarah were in fact, at the core, the same person.

I saw it once in real life, the last day that Steven popped out of Sarah. Sarah had been gradually dressing in women's clothes throughout the latter part of the fall; piece by piece she was changing her image. She wore pink socks. She wore girls' blue jeans. She pulled her hair back in a high pony tail and started to use barrettes and scrunchies. But at Christmastime, we asked Sarah to dress in boy clothes one last time to attend the Baker family Christmas party because this side of the family had not yet been told about the transition. Sarah's changes had been gradual but steady throughout the fall, so I was taken aback when she emerged from her bedroom as Steve, the person I once knew—Stevie, my child, and one of the greatest loves of my life. I was momentarily stunned, shocked by the reminder of what I had lost, or what I thought I had lost. Yet, I could see for myself, that the Steve I once knew was still standing before me. Although it wasn't a dream, it was extraordinarily surreal. I was overcome with grief still buried deep within me. And then I healed a little bit more because I saw Steven really was still in there. I was getting closer to merging the "two people."

I thought about asking her to throw me a fish from time to time, to dress in Steve's old clothes, tie her hair back, and let me see that my child was still there, and that my lost child and my found child are one and the same. It's funny how that would work out. In the past, it was Steve that had to dress up to show himself that he could be whole—she could be the girl that she really was inside. Now that I've traded places, I crave a similar therapy to give my tormented brain some respite. To see Sarah dressed up—not so much as a boy, but as my Steve—would show me that the child I once had is still alive in there (and is very much a part of who Sarah is). This physical manifestation of concept could be used as a tool to help me comprehend the incomprehensible. But that unforgettable day during Christmastime 2009 was the last time I ever saw Steven.

When I saw the embodiment of Steven at Christmas, I was assured that he was still in there. The irony is that for the past 21 years, whenever I looked at Steve, Sarah was the one actually in there.

I would someday learn that for her, pretending to be a boy again, even for a moment, and especially so soon after the trauma of doing it for so many years, would be torture. Besides, it would not be long before her face and body changed enough that it would be impossible for her to present as a man. But I was tortured too, as the mother of a long lost child named Steven. I only wanted a sign that our child was still in there. I was not consciously looking for a way to think of Sarah as a boy, I was just looking for my familiar child. When Sarah emerged out of Steven, she did not merely redefine the gender presentation of our child, she seemed to replace Steven entirely.

• • • • • • •

I still had dreams, but my dreams were getting better. They were much less brutal and far more healing. In the middle of the night, January 25, 2010, I found myself in an elementary school classroom with a couple of little kids sitting at a table making crafts. One of the children was mine. The father of the other child came into the room, a tall man with a soft round face and friendly spirit. We talked a bit about the crafts the students were making, and then he shook my hand. His hand was small, soft and gentle. The nice man left. I asked his child, "Is your dad transgender?"

The child looked up and had to think for a minute, and said, "Oh yeah, he's transgender," as though I was asking about the weather. The child went back to the craft, and I stood there thinking about how this was not an issue for the kid, but only a second thought.

When I woke up, I was startled by my own creativity within that dream. I had actually created a plot with a twist that I didn't even see coming! It was as though I had different levels of consciousness spinning gears in my brain that didn't seem to know about each other. I felt a little like Sybil.[1]

165

This dream told me several things: First, I was beginning to look at the positive aspects of my journey. The next generation is going to be more tolerant and open minded about the range of our human experience. As my son Jeff had once told me, they actually "get it." They are more advanced than the generations before them and are able to think outside the rigid box. Second, I was transitioning into a better stage; the image of my dead son was waning. Third, the concept was so complex for me that only through a dream did I discover these new levels of my own consciousness. Even my dreams were affected by compartmentalization. The complexity of my own struggle was helping me sympathize with Sarah's complex struggle as well.

• • • • • • •

One day in January 2010, Sarah and I went shopping for new dress shoes. Later in the month she would be appearing before a judge to ask for a legal name change, and she needed to look good. She picked out several pairs and found a bench on which to sit and try them on. She had worn thick sport socks to the shoe store, and suggested they might give the shoes the wrong fit. "Yeah," I said, "We'll just get you a pair of disposable nylon Footies. They supply them in dispensers around shoe stores." I still had a chance to show my daughter a few things about life in the world as a woman. She tried the first pair of shoes on, stood up and walked a few steps. The boxes were opened up all around her, shoes strewn about on the floor. They kept collecting there on the floor, outside of their boxes, and eventually they began to crowd the area. Sarah used her foot to nudge a few of the boxes out of the way, and some of them fell over. While a lot of girls might pick up the loose shoes and replace them into their boxes, gently stacking them aside, the way she pushed them seemed masculine to me. I whispered, "We need to teach you how to be a girl" and although I thought it was a little bit funny, she only barely cracked a smile. Maybe she thought we should be getting past this; it had been over a year since her disclosure to us, and eight years since she'd figured out her gender. Indeed I would learn in the years to come how frustrated Sarah had been with me during these first weeks of the new year. She grew tired of me framing her normal behavior as masculine. But from my point of view, it had only been a few weeks since the start of *my* life with a daughter. I still had a morphing perception of my changing child. In the first weeks of the new life, this girl was still a little like a guy, or so it occasionally looked to me, as I continued to view the layers of this person through the eyes of a mom who was trying to process them all. Like mirages in a dessert, waves of one layer would morph into another, taking turns to be present, whether it be in personality or behavior. Someday I'd have the clarity to imagine that if I'd raised her as a girl all along, she'd likely still have nudged the shoes, and I would not have given it a second thought. But at that moment, the whole experience was brand new to me.

· · · · · · ·

When I go out to run errands in the community, I frequently run into people I know. One time in early winter, I absentmindedly found myself inside the local Costco with Sarah. I suddenly realized that I might have put myself into a tight corner as I was not yet prepared for any chance encounters with neighbors. It was getting to be pretty easy to go out and about with her, but so far we had not wandered quite so close to home. We sped through the store, and I sent Sarah off fetching various grocery items to expedite the visit. I panicked as I imagined the predicament we'd be in should we bump into a neighbor. At that time, we had barely started to come out publicly, had only started to tell the family about Sarah, and so I knew I was not yet ready to meet a neighbor at Costco. We got out of the store unscathed, but I had some things to think about. I wanted to be graceful about this, not awkward. I didn't want to introduce our new family situation with any sense of weakness or sadness.

In mid January, I thought I had become a little more comfortable, more confident. Sarah needed new pants for her upcoming court appearance for her legal name change. We drove to the nearby Kohl's department store, and when we walked in, I immediately spotted a woman I knew (before she spotted me), and I couldn't continue into the store. I didn't know why right at that moment, but I still wasn't ready to face the community.

This brought it to my attention that I'd be at a total loss for words in an impromptu disclosure. I tried to imagine the possible scenarios. "Oh you remember my daughter Sarah...." How could that be true? In most cases, the acquaintance would remember that we had raised two boys. What if I said, "I'd like you to meet Sarah," to someone who had known Steve for 20 years already? Or, I could just say, "Hello, how are you?" and nothing else, ignoring any introductions or explanations altogether, and just let them wonder if the person I was with looked familiar. Would they ask? Who would ask a beautiful young woman, however mysterious she may be, "Did you used to be a guy?" Should I just pretend that Sarah is not even there? It would be awkward. I needed to be equipped with something to say with poise and class if faced with presenting Sarah on the spot.

Sarah and I laughed at the scenarios I thought of and discussed my lack of readiness to handle encounters like them, then we drove 30 minutes to a Kohl's on the other side of town. One might think this was a shameful act, but it was just the opposite. Those traces of anguish, resistance, hopelessness, uncertainty must be extinguished, or well under control, before any impromptu encounter. I needed to make my peace, hold my head high, and be ready to face the community as a proud and supportive parent must do. It is important to remember that this journey is more complicated and layered for a parent than it might seem to be through the eyes of an academic reader, or even through the eyes of a transgender reader. My real life experience as a mother with a new daughter was still less than one month old.

By March 3, 2010, the feeling that we had turned a corner was evident. I finally decided I could handle the local Kohl's that day. Sarah and I went to check out the jewelry sale; something I would have enjoyed through the years had I been given the chance to actually raise her as a daughter. I told her that Christmas shopping would be so easy from now on. If we ran into a neighbor, I would simply say, "As you can see, we've been going through some changes in our family. You used to know my daughter as Steve, but she is called Sarah now."

Trading Places

Chapter 12

The Yin-Yang Milestones
I Miss You Steve

Yin and yang may be loosely described as opposite forces that must coexist to form a whole entity or system. In this case the entity is our family unit, and the forces of transition from Steve to Sarah within it. I see a similarity with Newton's third law: for every action there is an equal and opposite reaction. Every gain the trans person makes results in a loss for the loved ones left behind.

For Sarah to exist, Steven could not. Steven began to vanish as Sarah slowly emerged, and I watched my son fade away. As my child became happier, I became more dissonant, so little by little, throughout 2009, Steve and I began to trade places. It was necessary for incremental changes to take effect for Steve to transition to Sarah. Once in a while, an incidental event or change would strike me quite hard, and I called these moments the yin-yang milestones.

· · · · · · ·

"All Rise!" the officer called. "The Honorable Judge Ann Marie Brent presiding." The judge took her seat.

"The court calls the case of Steven Andrew Baker in the matter of the petition for name change from Steven Andrew Baker to Sarah Ann Baker, and to request a new birth certificate."

"Thank goodness," I thought, "We are the first case of the day." I wondered if the court officer had deliberately put us first on the docket. Cases like this are probably quite interesting.

When we first arrived in the court room an hour earlier, Sarah checked in with this officer, and presented the notice to appear. The officer read the notice then looked up and questioned, "So how are you related to Steven?"

Sarah replied, "I am Steven! I am here today to change my name to Sarah." The officer, a kind looking relaxed woman, gave her a second look—not just surprised but impressed with the apparent situation of the elegant and confident young creature before her.

When Sarah was called to the podium, I could feel a few sets of eyes on us both, and it was fun. The people in the court were probably getting a buzz of shock to be hearing the details of the matter before them. "Are you serious?" Quizzical brain waves were zinging about the room. "That person up there was born a guy?"

The judge was a wonderful woman with a round happy face. She was one of those people profuse with inclination to talk and smile at the same time "Do you solemnly swear the testimony you are about to give is the truth, the whole truth, and nothing but the truth?" She asked, smiling. Sarah promised.

"And the reason for the request is not made for fraudulent purposes?" the judge asked further. Sarah confirmed.

"And the reason you are requesting the name change is to more accurately reflect who you are?" The judge beamed with a gigantic smile, possibly wondering how this lovely young woman could have been living with a boy's name in the first place.

"And the spelling of the name is as follows: S A R A H ... because once I sign it, it's official." She verified with Sarah.

"I see you are keeping your initials!" They shared a touching moment. This judge was great.

"I am granting your request for the name change. Please see the officer for instructions for filing. And, congratulations!"

Her final word nearly brought tears to my eyes—my robot eyes—as I sat there at the mercy of Yin and Yang, for one of the very last times.

We were lucky to be assigned to this particular judge, not so much because she granted the request, but because she was so compassionate about it. I think Sarah and I both expected this event to be much harder than it actually was.

A year prior, I could not have imagined surviving this day. I loved the name Steven. I miss calling him Steve. I miss telling our cat that his "Stevie is coming home." I still have fleeting moments of sadness. On that cold day of January 25, 2010, one full year into our transition, I experienced the yin-yang equivalent of the funeral dream. It could only get better from here.

When the proceeding was done, the court order filed, the excitement all over, a now legal Sarah drove back to school in Ann Arbor, Michigan. Back home, all alone, I tried to regroup, but no part of me could help any other. I could not find strength in my mind or my body or my spirit. Few things in life have ever depleted the whole essence of me to this degree. I didn't even make it to the couch. I laid down on the hard kitchen floor next to our cat by the heater, and instantly went to sleep.

21 years ago, on March 10, 1989, Ted and I rushed to Sinai Hospital at 4 o'clock in the morning. We had no girl name picked out because I was sure I was having a boy—truly a mother's intuition. We had decided on the name "Steven," because we both loved the name. He traveled through life touching souls he met in so many ways, Stevie, Steve, Steven Andrew Baker ...

• • • • • • •

Through the first years of my transition, feelings of sadness and loss were easily triggered by these yin-yang milestones. The events were small at first, much smaller in magnitude than the name change. But the early ones affected me the most, because we started out with absolutely zero indicators of a female presence in our child. Any quantity or substance, no matter how small, is infinitely greater than nothing at all.

Earlier, I described myself pushing a shopping cart through

Meijer in a stunned, surreal stupor, pretending to shop for a daughter. My very first exercise that day in January of 2009 was to buy Steve a package of pony-tail scrunchies. In that first month of my transition, it was meant to be a silent but clear message of support. When I presented her with the little $4 gift, it delighted her and she gave me a big, emotional hug; she understood the message that I would try, and that I would be capable of baby steps. The next time I saw her, later that same day, she had pulled her long hair back into a pony tail. It was not at the nape of the neck like the kind of pony tail one might see on a hippie guy, but instead, the high up kind of style worn by girls. When I bought the scrunchie, I had only been pretending to shop for a daughter. I never thought Steve would actually wear it! When I saw this new look, my first yin-yang moment was to trade a little pretending for a little reality.

The feminine presence inched in throughout that first year, very slowly at first, in tiny but jarring increments. Early in the year, when Steven was home from school for spring break, there appeared on her bathroom counter, along with the teenage male shaving stuff, a bottle of feminine foundation makeup. I wondered if Steve had left the makeup out on purpose, for me to discover, for me to get used to, encouraging me to take another baby step. The shaving stuff was there too, so my son was not nearly a ghost yet, but a daughter was beginning to emerge. The tiny bottle of foundation sat there in defiance shouting, "ready or not, here I come!" I viewed the juxtaposition of these personal toiletries as tangible representations of gain and loss in the same snapshot.

Facial hair removal, although relatively benign, was the first step toward permanent, irreversible erasure of a universal hallmark of manhood. I remember the early teen years when Steve first displayed a peach fuzz mustache, and how exciting it had been to watch my boy turn into a young man. Seven years later, in March of 2009, I learned that Steve had begun laser facial-hair removal treatments: the permanent obliteration of masculine traits had begun. At this milestone, my son started to fade away physically. We also traded unshared history: many years ago when I had perceived the onset of his future as a man, she had begun to realize at that same time, the concept that she was not a man.

Another milestone was the unexpected discovery, in May 2009, that the therapist and Steve had been waiting for me and Ted to join them in a session. When I noticed that he stopped going to therapy I allowed myself to feel immense relief, as if my wish had come true and the therapy had cured Steve of gender dissonance. Instead, I learned that the sessions were suspended because it was time for Steve to start hormone treatment, and they wanted to bring me and Ted on board. At this moment, the epitome of yin and yang, we traded hope. As I desperately clung to the last ray of hope that my son would return to me, Sarah waited, anxiously hoping to begin her life as my daughter.

In the early fall, Sarah started coming home from college wearing one or two new articles of girls clothing each time she visited. By this time, Sarah had started hormone treatment. The estrogen had started to work its magic on her features in a matter of weeks. The rapid and dramatic changes in her look from one visit to the next were a constant challenge to my concept of the time it would take for the transition to move forward. Just when I thought we could stay at one station awhile longer, we'd suddenly be light years ahead.

The stories of Sarah being identified as a woman throughout the fall of '09 were a yin-yang experience of a different sort. For the first time I was trading my loss for *my own* gain. Still wearing a man's coat, shoes, and glasses, with boy-like messy, long hair, and only a few weeks on estrogen, people were already identifying her as a woman. At the stores and restaurants, they called her "Miss." The bank was befuddled by Steve's driver's license and didn't want to cash her check. These were very encouraging gains for her, and a pleasant surprise and relief for me.

By Christmas 2009, she looked and dressed so much like a girl, we had to ask her to dress as a boy one more time in order to attend the Baker Christmas party. There were to be 50 people there, none of whom would be informed of the transition until the weeks after Christmas. So Steve dressed for the party in his old favorite big black sweater, blue jeans, and tennis shoes, and he left his hair messy like a long-haired guy. When he emerged from the bedroom, it was as though a ghost had come back from the dead. I saw my son Steve once again by this simple act of dressing in an old outfit. I had not realized just how much my child had been changing into the look and shape of a woman: the changes were so dramatic that my son had almost completely disappeared by that time. My heart became heavy with the familiar ache of loss. While I longed for the presence of my lost child, Sarah hated presenting as such. This surreal milestone moment remains at the heart of the transition for me: I traded a dead child for a living one.

After the legal name change in January of 2010, we had the court order to obtain a new birth certificate. This milestone would result in the permanent elimination of the official record of the birth of our son, Steven Andrew. I had obvious mixed feelings about the real possibility that Sarah would choose to permanently seal off her original record of birth. She had the option of leaving the original data intact, like perhaps a newly married woman might do when taking on a new husband's surname. But in Sarah's case, the old data should be sealed, and the original documentation of the birth of Steven, gender M, should be deleted from the birth certificate. The new one issued will show only Sarah Ann, and in Michigan, with a specific doctor's letter, the gender marker on the certificate will eventually be changed to F. When this occurs, it will drive the final nail into the coffin to permanently exterminate the record of the birth of my first child, Steven.

As Steven, he wrote a letter to me at the start of this journey in which he said he would always be my son, but also my daughter. In retrospect, this outcome would have been impossible to predict. Today I feel that for Sarah to exist, Steven must not.

· · · · · · ·

To this day, I still miss Steve so much I can hardly breathe. At first logic tells me that Sarah is the same person now as she was back then. But if Steve and Sarah are the same, why did Steve need to change into the personification of Sarah at all? The more logical I try to get, the more paradoxical it seems to be. What defines a person? What defines a person's identity? Can one really stay the same person while becoming a different person?

Identity: "The individual characteristics by which a person is recognized or known,"[1] or "sameness in all that constitutes the objective reality"[2] of a person, or "the condition or fact that a person or thing is itself and is not something else."[3] Gender is likely the first thing most people identify about another person. It is so fundamental to our identification, our existence, that it should be easy to understand why a gender dissonant existence would be torturous. If you change your perceived identity by changing your projected gender, then do you change the person that you are? In a way, you do: you are a different person *to those of us who had perceived you as the other gender before.*

For every action, there is an equal and opposite reaction, but after each step back I regain momentum and continue to forge ahead. I wrote most of this section of the memoir around month 13 (the time of the name change), when I was immersed in helping my new daughter get outfitted in a thousand ways. Just to get ready for court, Sarah needed dress clothes, new shoes and myriad other accessories most 21 year old women would already have in a wardrobe. We had to keep working to make up for lost time. I tried to stop struggling and resisting and instead shifted my energy into the monumental task of helping with the transition. I was getting to the point of enjoying it a lot more than I felt sad about it.

For every gain, there is a loss. But parenting is complex. As Sarah gained, despite my loss, I also felt the joy of her gain. Allowing myself to feel the joy would someday make a lot more sense than letting that feeling of loss continue to linger. I am trying to learn how to merge these two people together, like Sybil and her multiple personalities. I am not quite there yet, but I keep taking baby steps forward. The human mind is remarkably adaptable.

Chapter 13

Conceptualizing Gender Dissonance

Many people may not consciously realize how much they are defined and identified by their gender. I raised my boys to be people first: I believed that their genders would therefore be second or third or somewhere less significant in their identities. I believed my philosophy to be natural and fundamental, but I was forced to face my own self deception as I watched my child's outer gender change: it was as though the whole person of my child had faded away and had been replaced by an entirely new person. I discovered that my touted "person first" idea was built on sand, because underneath the sand I uncovered a rock solid innate sense that a person may be defined by gender on a very primal level. I never knew that instinct was so powerful, at least within me. Inasmuch as it has been established by biology and enabled by human cultures, gender is an undeniably important part of identity.

Early on, I asked Steven, "Why can't you just live as a person first?" And I recall a response much like this: "Because I am not seen as a person first, I am seen as a man first. I am a woman, I have a woman's brain, and when I am seen as a man, I am not seen as the person who I am." In other words, she lived a life projecting a persona that did not reflect who she was inside. She essentially did not exist in the eyes of the world.

This concept helped me understand why transsexual people must change their outer shells. If I had known a woman as a man all this time, then I knew the wrong identity of that person. The only way that misaligned people can be known as themselves by me or anyone else is by allowing us to view them as they are.

Even the most open minded people who believe they are gender-blind may have to work through deep levels of reasoning within themselves to make sense of a transitioning loved one. If I want to resume espousing that a person is a person first, I must find that my child somehow still exists in the human being before me. I think we parents and other loved ones are given a rare opportunity to examine and redefine our own philosophies. When I see someone who looks androgynous, I become distracted and determined to put that person in one of the binary categories, observing almost nothing else about the person until I do.

• • • • • • •

To imagine the magnitude of the complexity of this condition, having the brain of one gender trapped in the body of the other gender, is not an easy task. Unless you really have to, like a loving parent has to, or unless you really want to, like a gender therapist might want to, it is a task that few are willing or able to undertake. You have to hammer away at it, determinedly. In my case, I tried to come as close as possible to understanding the feeling (the agony) of a gender dissonant existence. These are five of the mental exercises that I regularly employ.

Exercise 1: Rational Thought

Being gender dissonant is nearly impossible for a cissexual person to conceive. We cissexuals are subconsciously comfortable with the gender aspect of our identity, and most of us never even think to question it. We take for granted our innate harmony. We probably never think much about the extensive biochemical, neurological, and hormonal systems linking together all the parts of ourselves that substantiate our gender.

Most people with gender congruence, or unity of mind, body, and spirit, would never think to alter the sex characteristics of their body. The thought of this is so horrifying to many people, it is natural to avoid thinking about it at all. Some extremists and sanctimonious people find the idea so troubling, they simply tag it as "wrong" or controversial or even sinful. But even people who don't judge others find it almost impossible to imagine changing their own gender. To grasp the concept, one must examine why a person would go to such extraordinary measures to change their identity, risking the loss of friends, family, and livelihood. Transsexual people will actually pay tens of thousands of dollars *in addition* to facing these risks. They endure excruciating pain. They risk ridicule, alienation and hate. So why would they transition rather than just stay the way they are? Because that is what they must do to achieve gender congruence, too.

In her book *Whipping Girl*, Julia Serano describes an exercise in logic to help people think about being transsexual. Simply consider an offer to take ten million dollars to change the gender of your body and live the rest of your life in it.[1] It is unlikely that any cissexual person would ever make this trade if they thought seriously about it. If, however, by some act of nature, you were suddenly *forced* to inhabit the body of the opposite gender, what would you do to switch back? Transsexual people actually live that nightmare—by some act of nature, their bodies were traded before birth. Many of them do whatever they can to trade it back.

The repulsive idea of forcing a cissexual person to live life as the wrong gender is the same as forcing a transsexual person not to transition. Once a trans person's body congruence is established, they too would probably not be willing to change back, not even for ten million dollars.

· · · · · · ·

Patty Duke won an Academy Award for her role as Helen Keller in the 1962 Movie "The Miracle Worker."[2] The epiphanous moment in this true story was the scene at the water spigot. Anne Sullivan, the devoted and perseverant teacher, signed the word 'w-a-t-e-r' to Helen once again, as she had done a million times before to no avail. But at that breakthrough moment, the window to a whole new world suddenly opened, wherein Helen finally and instantly became cognizant of a totally new concept—in her case the concept of language. To this day I view that scene as the most perfect manifestation of a true cognitive paradigm shift ever put to film.

A cissexual person who is truly trying to grasp the concept of transsexualism must have an epiphany of similar magnitude. Such a person must be willing to think about it patiently, with pure, unbiased, unobstructed logic.

It's easy for the average cissexual person to ignore the plight of transsexual people and go about life never having to think much about them and their dissonant identities at all. This is all that the average transsexual person wants and deserves as well—to live a comfortable life and never have to think about gender dissonance again.

Exercise 2: How Do We "Know" Our Gender?

I came up with another exercise when I asked Sarah early on, "How do you know you are transsexual?" and she replied, "How do you know that you are not?"

My maternal grandparents were Sicilian-Italian, and I have olive skin and dark hair. I grew up in a very White-Anglo-Saxon-Protestant community, and my look was in the minority at that time. Throughout puberty, dark hair grew all over my petite body, and a faint peach fuzz mustache appeared on my face. I have vivid, humiliating, self-loathing memories of 7th and 8th grade directly related to this hairy issue. One time a mean boy made fun of my mustache as I sat down for class, and 45 years later, I still remember the look of the boy and the position of his desk behind mine. My self esteem sunk and my self-image was shattered; I was consumed by the shame and embarrassment of being a hairy girl. Only boys were supposed to have facial hair! Except for me—I was stuck with this unfortunate, defective appearance. I was a slow-to-develop, flat-chested girl *with a mustache.*

Years later I finally did bloom. Electrolysis removed my peach fuzz, and with shaved legs, pierced ears, makeup and high heels, I became a sexy young woman. Life became fun; all was right with the world.

I asked Sarah, "How do you know you are transsexual?" And she replied, "How do you know that you are not?" 45 years post-adolescence, I can say, "because I did *not* want the mustache, and I most definitely *did* want the bra."

All of this emotional cacophony came from my brain. I wasn't thinking about genitalia or having sex at age 13. I didn't even know what a penis looked like. I was simply being me, navigating the perilous waters of adolescence. Even the most stubborn naysayers can relate to adolescence without much strenuous thought. This turbulent, hormonal period of life is a common ground, and can offer tangible examples of how to conceive of gender dysphoria. No 13 year old girl wants a mustache. If a 13 year old wants a mustache, he is almost certainly a guy, even if he is trapped in a girl's body. At age 13, even ten million dollars would not have made me any happier about having a mustache.

Exercise 3: Empathize with the Feeling of Dissonance

As my child became whole, I became the fragmented one instead. The challenge of dealing with the incongruence gradually changed hands: I was the one with the dissonance now as I struggled to conjoin the "two people." I had a perception of *him*, who was an unperceived *her*, and I had an emerging perception of *her* that was in the fading body of *him*. I woke up every day thinking one way and thinking the other way at the same time. I fit Leon Festinger's "cognitive dissonance" definition exactly.[3] Could it be that my experience was in some way similar to what Steve had been feeling his whole adolescent life up to that point?

Wrestling to suppress dissonance is exhausting and futile. But in my moments of struggle, I have an opportunity to empathize. I have an abstract sense of what my child might have been dealing with before transitioning and realize that my dissonance can be rectified much easier by comparison. Yet I would do almost anything to have a sense of unity once again: I understand, on some small level, the driving force behind gender transition.[4]

Exercise 4: Sarah Was In There All Along

Another therapeutic way for me to think about Sarah's transition was to consider that the person we brought up had been Sarah all along. The mind and soul of Sarah was living inside the body of Steve for almost 21 years. Though I try to search for the mind and soul of (my lost child) Steven residing inside the body of Sarah today, it had in fact been the other way around for the first 21 years. And as difficult as it is for me to grasp that they are one and the same person, it must have been at least that difficult for Sarah when things were the other way around, when Sarah was the only one who knew that the identity visible to the outside world was not the same as the one residing within.

Sarah once said, "Everybody changes when they grow up. Jeff doesn't look the same as he did at 14 either." If I can't imagine my young child as Sarah, maybe I'll just keep my memory of Steve, who simply changed quite a bit more than usual while growing up.

Exercise 5: Learn from External Sources

Studying was (and still is) an important exercise for me. Reading books and memoirs written by trans people humanized the condition for me. Their personal stories were enlightening and inspiring and easy to read. Some were funny and reached out through the humor and some were so brilliantly written I've come to associate trans people with geniuses and heroes. Political commentaries on transgender societal challenges and legal issues filled in the blanks much later in my journey. Gender studies texts on transsexualism and research in the science behind gender identity are works that also appealed to me. Today, as I am more immersed in the subculture, I am meeting many more people like Sarah. They are kind-hearted, regular, gentle people, like you and me, like the person next door, but with a tragic biochemical misfortune. I have developed enormous admiration for these courageous souls. I continue to learn more about gender dissonance and what trans people have to go through just to have something most of us had been granted at birth.

Trading Places

Chapter 14

Affirmation

On her 21st birthday, Sarah went to the Secretary of State to renew her driver's license and to update it with the recent name change. She left the gender box on the form blank, hoping the desk clerk would simply fill in the obvious "F" thinking Sarah had missed it. But the clerk reviewed the previous license picture, digitally recorded in the State's data base, and noticed that Steven at 16 was male. Although the clerk was sympathetic, it's illegal in Michigan to knowingly change the gender marker from "M" to "F" on the license until one has had a qualifying trans related surgery. It was an oddly defining moment for me to be so utterly disappointed that Sarah was stuck with that "M" on her license, because a year ago, that would have made me happy. Instead, I found myself thinking about ways to beat the system. Some states will change the gender marker with much less hassle. While I was happy for trans people living in those progressive states, I felt unlucky to be in the jurisdiction of one that was not so progressive.

More and more often I'd startle myself by my own cognitive adaptation to this transition. I was beginning to settle into a "new natural" state of existence. It was an honest reaction to feel upset about the license stuck with the "M" male marker. It was becoming more natural to say "Sarah" by now, and a bit of a struggle to say "Steven." And most amazingly, it was becoming second nature to see a trans woman, not just as a woman, but only as a woman, and not give a thought at all to who this person had been before, or how others may see her as ambiguous.

Dr. Marci Bowers is one of the world's leading genital reconstruction surgeons. To my knowledge, she holds the unique position of being the only such surgeon who has experienced genital reconstruction surgery herself. Marci, a beautiful and successful career woman, is also a transsexual woman. She is the doctor in the TV series "Sex Change Hospital"[1] and was featured in a documentary called "Switching Sexes: The Aftermath."[2] At one point in the documentary story, Marci talked about her kids, and how she wished she could see them more often. She was divorced, she didn't appear to have custody of them, and they lived in another state. I thought it was a little bit odd that she didn't have a better custody sharing arrangement, like most mothers usually do. I pondered this a minute and decided that the courts probably gave custody of the kids to the dad instead of to Marci, the mom, because she is such a busy surgeon. This is what I concluded *while watching a documentary about transsexual experiences*. It took me several minutes to realize that Marci was, in fact, the "dad."

I experienced this phenomenon again and more personally in Boston where we took Sarah for her trachea shave surgery. She was put in an expensive private hospital room for her overnight stay, without our request or consent, and I wondered why they would have taken the liberty to do that. Eventually I just figured it was because we had paid a lot of money out of pocket for the pricey procedure and this was simply a fringe benefit. I had apparently progressed to the point where I completely forgot about Sarah's transsexual body. Sarah's medical staff, however, was aware of it, and the private room was because of the possibility of a negative reaction from a cissexual female roommate. It was days later when I finally realized that this was why Sarah was given a private room. The reality of the situation never occurred to me at first, but when it did, I laughed. I felt a sense of affirmation in my new-natural state of mind.

· · · · · · ·

Along with the affirmation came a sudden realization of how much I'd grown from having lived through this experience. My new wisdom and sure-footedness gave me the upper hand in situations regarding this issue both externally and internally. I was no longer shaken by the riot of reactions positive transsexual stories in the media sometimes incite. The people who comment rudely about trans related news articles on the internet (and elsewhere) no longer seemed to bother me. Such people weren't scary or threatening anymore; now they just appeared simple-minded, like baser life forms.

I, on the other hand, had entered the realm of a vast new dimension of humanity: a beautiful world filled with countless rich stories of courage and strength. Throughout this transition I had come to know quite a few of them. At one of our stops along this journey, we shared a hospital stay with numerous other patients undergoing trans-related treatments. One vivacious and talkative young woman had just turned 18 and was therefore emancipated from the stranglehold of her transphobic father. She embodied the soul of a child who grew up in a small Texas town, once stuffed into a locker at school for being "different." Yet her spirit utterly glowed with unchained joy to be on this road to transition. She was accompanied by her mom, her grandma, her aunt and by Jesus, as her family lovingly assured. They carried her through this journey—embracing, protecting, and encouraging her. When our paths crossed along the way, they inspired us too.

Another patient was 80 years old, quiet and dignified. She was too late to live out most of her life as a woman, but not too late to die and be buried as one. It touched me deeply to witness this brave woman finally reaching her dream to be freed from a lifetime of entrapment and pain. I wondered what she thought of the rest of us there: the bubbly teen, the grad student, the young professionals. Did she feel a bit of sadness, perhaps envy that the path to transition had not looked so promising for people of her generation? Did she also feel lucky to witness—at long last—the dawning of hope and great strides of progress for people like her? I imagined a tired soul filled with peace at last, and a reserved exuberance similar to that expressed so unabashedly by the teen. I've learned stories of heartbreaking pain and loneliness and I've witnessed great moments of love. Inspirational stories of transgender lives come from every corner of the world, and have existed throughout human history, and now our story is among them.

• • • • • • •

One night about 15 months into the journey, Ted and I were talking about how happy we were with the progress made to date, referring not just to Sarah's transition but to ours as well. He said, "I can't even begin to imagine how much progress is still ahead."

I agreed. "Even if we stop right here, it seems good enough for me. I feel happy most of the time and I didn't think I'd ever be happy again." Little by little we had crossed off the items on the list of things that could have gone wrong but did not. The world had not come to an end.

One year earlier, it seemed impossible to even think about telling friends and family. That ended up to be a liberating stretch of the journey, and the reactions were overwhelmingly supportive. One year earlier, neither one of us thought that our child could ever look good as a woman. We had only known the face of Steven, a guy. We worried for his safety, that he'd end up lonely, his future in ruins. Instead, Sarah turned out to be a strikingly beautiful woman without any cosmetic changes other than her neck. A year earlier it was my belief that this was a catastrophic mistake. Ted and I talked about our initial expectations that Steve would turn back and stay a guy. After a year of trying to figure out what was "really wrong" with him, we came up empty, exhausted, but much more educated about this condition and how to really fix it. Accepting that there was no chance of turning back and surrendering the battle relieved an enormous source of anxiety, and cleared a path in my mind for more positive thinking.

Witnessing Sarah becoming a happier person finally affirmed that transition was the right thing to do. Ted could see a light in Sarah's eyes. A friend thought she got taller. For the first time, she seemed interested in her appearance. Her social life picked up. She had more dates in her first few months as a woman than she'd ever had in all the years before. The irony is that Steve probably would have spent his life lonely and unhappy on many levels. I am now convinced that Sarah has a better chance at happiness than Steven ever would have had. As a child, Steve used to stand back like an outsider, and observe the people of the world; now Sarah is actually one of them.

Trading Places

Chapter 15

The Year Long Test
Finding Equilibrium

We are not the same persons this year as last; nor are those we love. It is a happy chance if we, changing, continue to love a changed person.

W. Somerset Maugham

The year 2010 was what some medical professionals call the year of "The Real Life Test." Sarah refers to this as the time when she could finally stop pretending to be a boy. She considers the word "test" to be a misnomer: she didn't need to test her gender—she already knew she was a woman. Instead, Sarah shed the shell of Steven and all the energy that had been trapped inside was set free, like a butterfly emerging from her chrysalis. At long last, she could begin her experience navigating life in a world which perceived her as a woman. As the year progressed, we witnessed our child become much happier and more alive in ways we had never previously imagined. Regardless of what the experience was about, most surgeons today would require Sarah to live as a woman for a year to be eligible for genital reconstruction surgery.

The year was perhaps more of a test for me. My relationships with both Sarah and Ted as well as my dealings with the rest of the world were repeatedly tested. When we turned the corner at Christmas 2009, I had thought life in transition would be an easier road from that point on and I relaxed and started to get comfortable. But obstacles reared up time and again, catching me off guard, veering me off course and I learned I still had a lot of emotional issues to process. I'd regroup, overshoot, then crash back down again. A year earlier I established an alter ego to cushion this process and to prepare for the remote possibility of transition. By now of course, my alter ego and I shared equal time in the driver's seat, which explains why the path was like that of a roller coaster, and why I recount it that way in this chapter.

• • • • • • •

Sarah was only about three months into the real life test, going out in the world as a young woman, when guys began to come out of nowhere to line up for dates with her. For the first time in her life, she experienced romance, the chemistry of a soulful connection, the euphoria of a physical embrace. It was a joy and a relief to see our child so comfortable and so happy as a woman. Steven lived nearly 21 years and he never even had so much as a best friend. Yet just three months as Sarah and it seemed certain that she would dance in life's bubbles like those newlyweds in Maine. Ted and I were startled by how quickly this was happening. This was yet another part of the process that seemed to be moving a lot faster than we expected. Still rushing to keep up with her, my accompanying emotions began to expand. This journey was starting to get *really interesting.* All the dates she had in the beginning of her experience as a woman never had a clue that her name had been Steven just three months before.

"I feel like I'm deceiving him" Sarah said to me one spring evening after coming home from a date with her new friend Jake. "I feel like I'm deceiving him because I'm still in love with Sean."

I thought for a minute about how new she was to the dating scene. By the age of 21, virtually all of Sarah's friends had been dating for years. Our own Jeff seemed to have his arm around a girl since first grade, and by age 16 he was a seasoned charmer. But Sarah had missed out on all the teenage coming of age years and accompanying awkward dating experiences. Teens learn a lot in those years: the art of flirting, the first crush, the first kiss, the pain of rejection and heartbreak and how to bounce back afterwards.

"People do that sort of thing all the time," I replied to her concern about dating Jake on the rebound. I said, "If it's not going to work out with Sean, you need to move on sooner or later anyway. You will know if it starts to get too serious with Jake, and you will know when to tell him about Sean."

I wondered for a minute about Sarah's other secret, and why that did not seem to be of concern to her at all. I said, "You know, if it starts to get more serious with Jake, you'll have to tell him about the other stuff too."

"What other stuff?" she asked, to my bewilderment. It was as though she sometimes seemed to lose sight of the fact that she was still in a transitioning body.

"Jake assumes you have a vagina," I said, getting right to the point. "One of these days he's going to start thinking about poking it."

She replied quite tartly, "It's not my fault if he assumes I'm cissexual." She argued that it is not her responsibility to inform people that she is trans.

I countered, "OK then, so you'll want to remain celibate?"

She explained that the difference between her secret about still loving another man and her secret about being transsexual, is that keeping the secret about Sean is her choice, something she considers genuinely deceptive.

I was going to put this story in the next chapter about differences of opinions, except in this case and at this time in my journey, I see her point. It can be tough to figure out how to navigate the dating scene as a transsexual woman. She can't tell someone right away or they may not bother to get to know her. She can't wait until things get too serious either, for obvious reasons. So just when does a transsexual woman tell her date that she was born in a male body? There's no protocol on how to handle this situation. At this point, most new people in Sarah's life don't need to know her history. I worry about what can happen when a date finds out that she is transsexual. Some trans women are met with brutality at that point.

· · · · · · ·

Some believe that even when a woman transitions at 50, she will go through a brief period of "female puberty" as estrogen is introduced and her body chemistry changes. Some trans women say that a thick fog lifts, colors get brighter, emotions become more intense. Sarah was 21 when this happened to her and by this time I was her friend as much as I was her mom. She privileged me with some of her most intimate personal experiences as a new and attractive young woman. She shared stories of her first dance, her first kiss with a hot guy; I bet this would have been too much information for a typical 14 year old adolescent girl to share with her mom. For a brief time I got a glimpse into a world that others may not usually see. These exciting and normal human experiences further validated the condition in my eyes and illustrated how necessary it was for Sarah to transition to finally become a whole person. The enigmatic loneliness I had always sensed in my child as he was growing up had vanished completely from her.

· · · · · · ·

Sarah inherited a prominent Adam's apple. When she was a young man, it was fun to watch it slide up and down every time he laughed, but this was not a very becoming look for a woman. This telltale sign of former masculinity was scheduled for removal that coming May. The trachea shave, as it is called, is one of a few common feminization surgeries that trans women may undergo. Sarah was lucky to be transitioning at age 21. Because of her youth and her slender build, she didn't need anything else done. She never developed a rugged chin, nor a bossing brow, but maybe she would have if she had been exposed to testosterone for ten more years. I began to appreciate the many advantages of transitioning young.

By spring 2010 in Michigan, the weather was too warm for Sarah to wear the heavy turtleneck sweaters we gave her at Christmas. Since we had five weeks to go before the trachea shave, I made a bunch of silk scarves for her to wear around her neck in the warm seasons to help cover the apple. When Sarah came to visit, she was greeted by a stack of scarves and matching tops in every color of the rainbow. "You're amazing!" she exclaimed, as she looked through the new outfits. "You have all these new things for me to wear just when I needed them!" I wondered if she was just trying to assure me that she will always need me to be her mom. Indeed interactions like this one of reciprocated positive feedback, reminded me of how important it was to nurture our bond and keep it strong. The scenario was a symbolic gesture on both our parts; not only do we still need core aspects of our old relationship, we can also have fun with our new one.

I was pleasantly surprised at how lovely and elegant Sarah was as a woman. We were once told that it was a shame to waste those spectacular blue eyes on a man. Strangely out of place on Steve, they fit Sarah tailor-made, like a glove. That spring we played with Photoshop, drawing new noses, reshaping her chin, in case we decided to tack those procedures onto the upcoming surgical plan. We could very easily have made her stunning if that was the intent. Making Sarah's nose more petite would make her prettier by some standards, but not any more of a woman. In fact, she resisted the idea of changing any more than her neck, as it would erase too much of her former look. As it was, much of her appearance would be modified by hormones alone.

Some years ago I'd watched the Adam's apple develop along with the facial hair and the deepening voice, as my boy morphed into an adolescent young man. A year ago the thought of its future removal had deeply depressed me and I had expected this to be a traumatic milestone event. But finding the bottle of makeup in the bathroom a year earlier had actually been much harder on me. The intensity of these milestones weakened as I witnessed Sarah's quality of life improve with each one. By now I was having a lot of happy days. "This isn't so hard anymore," I'd been starting to think more often. "We're going to get through this just fine."

· · · · · · ·

Life had been so hard the first year that when the first signs of hope and happiness began to trickle in, I was quick to latch on. I overcompensated for the first year of sadness. Sarah was looking great, and we had a lot of fun building a new wardrobe. Transforming our duckling into a beautiful swan kept us busy. It was uplifting to get kudos from the name changing judge. It was oddly reassuring to watch guys ogle Sarah when we went out shopping together. The drive to Boston was a good time for family bonding and the neck surgery went well. We began to see remarkable changes in Sarah's happiness and self confidence. All the bad stuff that I feared could happen did not happen at all. On the contrary, and most unexpectedly, some of best things in life were happening to Sarah instead. I was excited about our role in these changes. We'd be positive examples to society, we could help educate, we could help the world become a better place! I had convinced myself that my emotional adjustment wasn't so hard anymore. It was even a little fun as the mom of a new daughter. But like a bubble of exuberance in an overbought stock market, it stretched too full, and then one day it suddenly burst.

After all the joy and success, what remains the same at the end of the day is that Sarah is not the same person as Steve. Hormones are among the most powerful forces in the human body. They have changed her attitude, her confidence, and her physical appearance dramatically; they have changed her gender and her whole identity— at least in the eye of the beholder. Our relationship has changed. Sometimes it seems like all our conversations are like mini-arguments. Although I think I talk to Sarah like I talked to Steve, Sarah's replies are different than Steve's would have been. They are often abrupt, argumentative, occasionally sarcastic, snippety and terse. Her emotions and mine are now both right at the surface. She comes home to visit and acts like a girl, laughs like a girl, as new, unexpected, and unfamiliar dimensions to her personality are emerging. It is as though these attributes of her character had been held prisoner right along with her gender for twenty years, bundled and trapped within the complicated, stifled, dissonant existence of the soul *we* had known as Steven. Finally set free, they are visible to me for the first time, blossoming to fruition without any delay. The changes in look and personality are so dramatic that nearly every aspect of the old Steven is being eclipsed or replaced by them. The compliant, soft, gentle soul who used to be Steven is nowhere around. At times I feel I don't know Sarah very much at all, and I think, "Who are you and what have you done with my child?" Now she is off on her own in the world; the days of growing up with Mom and Dad have passed. I had 20 years with Steven, but I never had the chance to get to know Sarah. Sarah is not the same person that Steven was—if they were the same, there would have been no need for a transition. It's been a very long time since I last saw my Steve, but I just saw Sarah last week.

I wonder if Sarah views me differently now too, through those powerful estrogen lenses. She has said that although Steve never verbalized his opinions of things about me that annoyed him, he had always wanted to do so. I guess from the inside looking out, she is the only one who can actually feel that she is still the same person.

Ted and I get teased when we tell friends about my initial difficulty with our new daughter's personality and the strain this put on our relationship during the second and into the third year of transition. The people who raised little girls from birth assure me that all little girls change dramatically at puberty. I know they mean well, but our situation is different. We don't wonder what happened to our little girl.

When I shop the stores for pretty new clothes, I smile to think how good Sarah will look in sparkles and lace. Then I pass the young men's department with navy blue suits and purple striped ties on display and I try to ignore this chamber of reminders of who we have lost. Still smiling on the outside, my soul fills with sadness as I rush past the racks of suits hanging empty, like skeletons, symbols of my anguish. I had another son once, but he has gone away. I used to shop in this department for him.

I thought it was strange that it only took me a year to get so comfortable with our new reality. Now I know that I'm really not there yet. I'm still oscillating around a new equilibrium—sometimes too exuberant, sometimes deeply missing the son I once had. This journey might be more than a marathon. It might be lifelong, a rambling road with ups and downs, bumps and circles, and roadblocks. Sometimes I even go backwards.

• • • • • • •

The fanfare waned throughout 2010. People who I had talked to only one time about the transition usually didn't want to discuss it again. Many seemed to exude the sentiment, "I've heard enough. Let's just get on with life. Can't you get over it?" I was left behind to fend for myself, to struggle silently as the rest of the world moved on.

One time in late May, I called my cousin Pam, and she seemed oddly (or perhaps predictably) more distant with regard to Sarah's transition. Six months prior, she had responded to our news with the greatest emotion, tears and compassion, but nowadays, she won't even reply to my emails. When I finally cornered her on the phone, she said, "Well, it is what it is and we aren't dwelling on it. We are all just getting on with our lives." After some silence, she continued, "It will be awkward, but we love Sarah and we won't abandon you." It was as though Pam was tired of hearing about this big deal transition hogging the spotlight and getting all the attention in the family.

I had sent out a letter in mid-May 2010 to update the family on how well Sarah was doing in spite of the challenges of transition. Pam had ignored the letter. When I mentioned the letter to Pam at this time, she said, "I know why you sent that. But it made me feel like I should send out a letter talking about all the great stuff my kids are doing too!"

For some, the enormity of our challenge had completely evaporated (if it even existed at all). I was relatively satisfied that the end result was blind acceptance. But if it was compassion I was looking for, or even someone to talk to, I did not find it here. The most troubling aspect of this realization is that little concern was ever expressed for Sarah. Few people acknowledged what Sarah might be going through on this extraordinarily difficult journey. Perhaps they were more comfortable ignoring it.

In any family tragedy, sympathizers initially give a lot of attention to the grief-stricken family, but eventually they move on. As others lost interest in lending an ear, we were on our own once again. When somebody asks how I'm doing these days, it's OK to say, "Doing great, yourself?" but unacceptable to say, "Depends on which one of me you're asking. Some days I miss Steven so much I can hardly breathe." Strangely, both statements are usually true. Like having kids in the first place, it's impossible to know just how life-changing this experience is unless it happens to you.

• • • • • • •

Driving through the fog of 2010, trying to find my way in this unfamiliar new world, I was not often able to see what was coming around the next bend. One event that triggered an unexpected setback for me occurred on April 21, 2010. Sarah gave her first public presentation to a gender studies class at the local Community College, and I was invited to attend. I didn't do much to contribute, but my presence was a message in itself. This was our first taste of family community involvement to help advance transgender awareness, and I was quite excited. But as the event unfolded, I was left feeling stunned and more distant from Sarah. She stood in front of a classroom of strangers and unabashedly revealed a lot of information and emotions that were new to me until right then and there.

I learned during the lecture that Sarah lost some friends after she came out as transsexual, and one was avoiding events where Sarah was present. I learned of a time when Sarah had blood drawn at a medical center and a chatty nurse stopped speaking and turned to ice after glancing at Sarah's chart. Hearing these things, I came to know that Sarah was experiencing some loss and some blatant discrimination, and I felt that this had been shielded from me. My comfort had been built on a porous foundation. These revelations were like little bombs dropping on me, but in this public setting surrounded by strangers, I was bound by social codes of conduct and composure, so I couldn't react.

I listened for pitfalls as Sarah described her childhood to the class, and to my relief she said it was good, she was a happy child, and she was happy and comfortable as a little boy. But she avoided talking too much about it; and of course never mentioned her birth name. It felt vacuous, the description of what I remember to be wonderful, magical years—the best years of my life. She went on to say, "I had figured I would transition during middle school and start high school as a girl," and at that point I nearly passed out. Wasn't I there during the middle school years? Was I so high up on top of the world that I was unable to see? Sixteen months earlier, she had told us that she began to feel gender dysphoric in middle school, but the thought of actually transitioning had seemed insurmountable, too hard, too much work. She had tried to suppress it, as many trans people do, and had hoped it would go away. It was jarring to hear this story told again, forthright and succinctly, and not in the tiny, soft chunks that I had thus far been trying to manage. I listened to Sarah talk openly about this part of her life that she kept from us for so many years. I lived those same years right alongside my kids, intricately and passionately involved in their lives, and never spotted a single hint of gender dissonance. I never knew that Steve was leading a split life: one as Sarah on the inside, and one as Steve for the rest of us on the outside. I still couldn't believe that Sarah's struggle with dissonance had been going on right under my nose. Surely this person at the front of the class was talking about someone else's past, and I thought, again, "Who are you and what have you done with my child?"

I discovered that day at the college, just 16 months into the journey, that I was not yet as comfortable with the transition as I had thought. For the next several days, I relapsed, sad and despondent, just like I had felt a year prior, as though no progress had been made. I felt alienated, disconnected, left behind in the dust as Sarah chugged ahead into her dream-come-true future. I struggled with this selfish attitude. What was happening to me? Was I strong or weak? Was I happy or sad? Did I really think I was having fun with this transition, or was I just pretending? *Isn't it true that I still wished it didn't have to be this way?*

In the years to come, we participated in many more public presentations and they were all quite rewarding, as I had first imagined such events would be. The first one was too, in retrospect, because it gave me another perspective into my own complicated mind and allowed me to address a few more repressed issues about the transition. At the time it seemed like I took a step backwards, but in truth I had to step on this essential stone from which I would eventually move forward.

· · · · · · ·

Throughout the spring and summer of 2010, Sarah had a lot of dates. Many of them came and went without ever knowing that Sarah was transsexual. But once in a while she reached a point where she wanted to tell the guy about it. She always did so in a public place where there were plenty of other people nearby, in case the guy got upset and she needed help. With the kinds of people she picked as friends, this was an unlikely scenario, but it was better to be safe than sorry. Every single person she told was shocked and incredulous, but also very kind and respectful. In fact, her one boyfriend Sean worked very hard to get past Sarah's history because he adored her and didn't want to let her go. Though they eventually parted ways romantically, I've heard they're still friends to this day. Things would only get better as Sarah continued transitioning. I never thought I'd see the day where I'd be anxious for her to have genital surgery. But I still figured that finding a soul mate and someone to love would never work out for someone with such a complicated history.

One day in the summer of 2010, Sarah met Nathan through an online dating service. She was not particularly anxious to go out with him. She had guys lined up for weeks to come, and still had some feelings for Sean. She decided to tell Nathan that she was transsexual straightaway, and figured he would then lose interest. But even after learning this information about her, Nathan still wanted to meet her. Of all the times I'd imagined Sarah breaking such news to a date, I had never once thought it would be *before* the first date. He walked into her life one Saturday afternoon in September of 2010, and he remains there to this day. Their souls connected instantly. They had a lot in common—kind hearts, big brains, gentle spirits. They spent their first day together talking, and when we called Sarah later that weekend to see how the date had gone, Nathan had not yet left. A lot of cissexual people travel through life and never have a weekend of bonding like this; many never find love at all. Yet my transsexual daughter, only nine months existent, had felt a hint of the magic of a dance in the bubbles.

· · · · · · ·

By late summer I felt like I'd just emerged from the dust of a yearlong hurricane. After the flurry of positive changes and exciting activities of the first half of the year, I finally had a chance to rest and retreat and get back to the business of being depressed. They say depression can come back to haunt you even years after a traumatic event. You can't always get better by going around this process. Sometimes you have to walk through the fire to get to the other side. It may seem strange to continue to talk about dealing with depression as our child became happier. We had to accept the fact that if our child had stayed the same as we knew him, there would have been no chance of the happiness we see in our new child today. It was depressing to grapple with the paradox that it was necessary to kill the child that we once had in order to bring life to the child we now have instead.

I did a lot of work on this memoir during these months. It was my catharsis, my focus, and my purpose. It was a stabilizing counterbalance to my otherwise discordant life; a dependable confidante at my side in a laptop, as I traveled from coast to coast that year. An in-law once asked, "Just how long is this story going to be? I thought it would have ended by now!" And I thought, "It will be as long as it needs to be to get me through this process." She seemed puzzled, almost disappointed that the story was not short and simple.

· · · · · · · ·

Ted and I managed to walk through the storm with the same desired destination. But we processed the transition in different ways, and experienced the stages of grief at different times. The space between us took on various shapes as we navigated our separate paths. Sometimes the space filled with rock, sometimes a glacier, and sometimes an empty, lifeless vacuum. And sometimes, perhaps just often enough, we shared the space together as parents, and filled it with rich, intimate, healthy conversation. The transition brought us both closer together and farther apart. With our sensitive natures and volatile levels of tolerance for each other's coping styles, it's easy for us to see why times of tragedy can sometimes split families apart.

It is just not possible to have a better husband than Ted. With thirty years of machine-like teamwork, and hundreds of thousands of shared happy times, we've built a wonderful life together. Very few situations ever threatened our steadiness, our harmony, or our resolve. So when spokes fell out of our near-perfect wheel, the gaps were quite glaring for a while. The threat of layoff in a bankrupt auto supply company was already weighing Ted down. So he worked long hours for months on end to remain valuable, or to escape his own demons, or maybe a mixture of both. Reflecting upon it, he told me one time, "I feel like we've had three children, not two." One day within the second year of our journey, he succumbed to anguish over the metaphorical death of his firstborn son, and mourned the loss of Steven. This was the place where I had been a year earlier when I shared my death dream with him—and when the first spoke came out of our wheel. For the first time in his life, Ted began wondering if he should be seeing a therapist.

What doesn't kill you makes you stronger. We continued moving forward together, Ted and I, some bonds stretched, some frayed, some broken forever. But for each bond that broke between us, like snapping a branch off a tree, two new shoots have since grown in place, creating new bonds that are stronger. We are, after all, the only two people in the world who really know what the other one knows. We only have each other for this.

On appearance, Jeff seems to be taking this change in his sibling in stride. He once said his girlfriend's brother could fill the now-available role of best man at their wedding someday, and Sarah could be maid of honor. The new generation sees a lot more of the world through their internet lenses. Us baby boomers learned "I'm OK, You're OK,"[1] then we raised our kids that way. Most of our kids seem to understand the importance of personal self discovery and being true to oneself. At least I know Jeff does. With his strong personality and belief in his new sister, he will make a real difference in how transsexualism is presented to the world.

• • • • • • •

I have an elephant with me wherever I go now. When I run

into friends out in the community, many of them know about what happened in our family, and we talk with the elephant present. Others may not know yet, so I try to have the energy in store to talk about Sarah's transition if there is a sensible opening. Sometimes I waffle: most of the time it's really none of their business. But continuing to keep the secret has become as taxing as sharing it can sometimes still be. It's almost worse to talk about Steve like he is still male, like he is still around at all.

I was pleasantly surprised by the fact that almost everyone in our world was gracious about our transition. So as time went on, exceptions to this norm became more glaring. Once I was on the phone with a health insurance representative to discuss some of Sarah's procedures and I gave her the gender dysphoria diagnosis code. But when she looked up what it meant, the elephant walked in and she promptly walked out, her voice turning flat and humorless. A particular party comes to mind, a first time for many to finally meet Sarah. If I didn't know any better it almost seemed like people were staking out positions. Some stuck beside us throughout the day, while others never made contact. I began to see these exceptional people in a different light around this time. After all we'd been through, I was getting pretty tough, and now they seemed weak and deficient.

· · · · · · ·

Unforeseen obstacles and puzzling questions popped up all year long. One day people may come into our house who won't know about the former existence of Steve, and so I've started removing family pictures from the walls. Will it be strange that only Jeff's image is present? Will someone someday want to see a baby picture of Sarah? What name do we call Sarah when referring to past events? Is it possible to say, "Sarah made this when she was a Cub Scout?" In the beginning of the journey, she told us, "I am still the same person I have always been: always your son, also your daughter." She assured us that we could call her any name we wanted. Today, when asked about how to refer to her in her past, she says she prefers Sarah. I perceive a subtle change in her attitude about our family's shared past—our paradoxical, parallel pasts.

I've stood with her as she stripped away her facial hair, tossed out her boy clothes, and sealed off Steve's birth certificate. All that represented her former identity as Steven has been erased. Very soon now, Steven's history will be all that I'll have left of my former child. It is starting to feel like she wants me to replace that aspect of Steven too. But when I look back to earlier days with Sarah, I can't find her. Looking backward in time, I only find Steve, who is missing today, and will never be found going forward.

As much as I may wonder about the childhood she could have had if she'd been able to personify Sarah, I mourn the only identity I ever knew her to be. I asked her if she would ever dress like Steven again for me because I am her mom, to help me to see that my child Steven is still in there. This should be a familiar concept to transsexual people. Closeted trans people will sometimes dress to feel the rightness of the alignment they see reflected from a mirror. Back when she was the dissonant one, she could dress as a woman, look in the mirror and see the person she knew herself to be. Is it such a stretch to see the similarity of these therapeutic exercises?

She replied, "You have no idea how painful that would be for me—to be perceived as a boy." But she misses the point; or misses the point of view of her mother. I would not want this exercise to perceive her as a boy, but only as the child I once knew and loved, the one she claims is still in there, and the one I sometimes still deeply mourn. I raised and loved a sweet gentle soul, a disheveled, quirky, nerdy young man, a kind hearted genius admired by many but inexplicably included by few. No matter how enigmatic aspects of his childhood were, perhaps even because of these subtle mysteries, this was the person who I remember raising, who I protected and cherished, and who I miss.

I waited twenty years to see this magnificent flower of happiness bloom from within Steve. It's most bizarre that the dream of happiness I'd always wanted for Steve finally did come true, but at the cost of Steven himself. I don't want a sad person to be the top layer of my child. But I do want to feel that the layer I once knew—the essence of Steven—is what made Sarah who she is today. I continue to try to get her to understand that from my perspective I grapple with a strange kind of death, and that she is the one who holds the power to attest to be—and help me to see—the only person I ever knew my child to be. If she has grown around the fundamental aspects of my former child, then she has not erased them but merely layered over them. I need help to substantiate this obscure state of mind I live in, somewhere in between the death and rebirth of my child. She finally said she could do this dressing-up exercise for me (to help me merge the "two people"), but doubted it would work anymore. She believed the hormones had already changed her face too much. I stared at her round and delicate face, graced with enormous blue eyes and impeccably clear, smooth skin. I searched in vain for the angular lines, the diamond shaped face that used to be Steve. And I didn't press her again.

· · · · · · ·

In early 2010, a judge granted Sarah's request for a legal name change. We ordered new birth certificates and we selected the option to permanently seal the original data. Sarah obtained a new driver's license. She registered her name change with the Social Security Administration. The University of Michigan renamed her records and transcripts and issued her a new picture ID. She got new bank accounts, new check books, new credit cards. By midsummer, mail (and junk mail) started to arrive for Sarah Baker by the tons. With her new birth certificate and a letter from her endocrinologist declaring her gender to be female, Sarah applied for a passport with a gender marker "F". Thanks to the Obama administration, the State Department under Hillary Clinton implemented a policy to allow US passports to reflect gender identity correctly, just in time for us. Sarah's first official picture ID with an accurate gender indicator arrived, fittingly, on Christmas Eve 2010.

The year 2010 had come and gone, and by medical standards, "The Real Life Test" was now technically complete for Sarah. She had met the requirements to be eligible for genital surgery. But 2010 was really a test for the rest of us, hanging on to the emotional ups and downs not so much to fight this change anymore, but to get used to it, to find our equilibrium, and to make peace with our new reality.

Chapter 16

In the Mind of the Beholder

One day, making tracks
In the prairie of Prax,
Came a North-Going Zax
And a South-going Zax.
And it happened that both of them came to a place
Where they bumped. There they stood.
Foot to foot. Face to face.

Dr. Seuss[1]

Sarah is on the inside looking out and I'm on the outside trying to look into her transgender existence, so it makes sense that our perspectives on transgender issues would at times be quite different. Open and honest communication with Sarah at these times has helped to build a bridge of understanding, though at the time of this writing (within the third year) it's still a wobbly bridge. Discussing our different views of how mainstream media sources depict trans people is fairly academic, impersonal, and interesting. We even reach agreement from time to time; or at least seem to grasp the other's point of view. But discussing our different perspectives of our own family transition is much more difficult for me, for obvious reasons, and also more personally important. It is unrealistic to hope we could ever see eye to eye at this level, but I do strive to reach a mutual acknowledgement that both points of view are valid.

Media Depictions of Transsexual People

Oprah Winfrey introduced the young, beautiful lesbian couple to the studio audience. Jane was brunette, Samantha a blonde, both of them were around 29 years old and recently proud new parents. The camera zoomed in to show flawless features, beautifully carved bodies. As Oprah began to talk about the new baby, the drum roll began: *this was their biological baby!* The camera panned the attentive audience as the climactic moment unfolded and Oprah drove it home: Samantha fathered the baby! The audience gasped, astonished and thoroughly impressed. Samantha, a transsexual woman who had the foresight to bank sperm before her transition, was the most beautiful, elegant creature in the room.[2]

In my mind, this depiction is a win for transsexual people. There is no better way to be presented to the world than by America's most beloved talk show host. But some trans people would disagree, claiming such depictions are an example of sensationalizing transsexualism. "This glamorous, token example does not represent the trans community at large. Every story is different," one might say. But I say that the stories *do* share the same concept. The condition of being transsexual is at the heart of each story and is not supposed to pertain to just one individual. The individual stories are showcased as examples to bring incremental conceptual changes to the minds of the cissexual audience. Anne Sullivan had to sign thousands of words to the blank Helen Keller before the epiphany at the water spigot. One day, watching or reading about some trans related story, the concept of transsexualism may suddenly be illuminated in another cissexual person's mind.

In her usual brilliant and sensitive way, Oprah Winfrey has helped to demystify transsexualism. By bringing numerous transsexual guests into millions of living rooms at a tangible level—a high school valedictorian, a star football player, a world famous, award winning novelist—she has helped people find compassion in their hearts for transsexual people.

I spent the first two years of my journey reading internet articles, books, and personal memoirs and watching movies, talk shows, and any television show that featured or addressed the subject of transsexualism. Each story brought me incrementally closer to understanding the condition. The diversity of the stories helped me understand that transsexualism is present in every corner of society, all around the world. For me, documentaries were therapeutic, and perhaps the most significant key to my coming to grips with my child's condition and the concept of transsexualism overall. Yet people in the trans community often criticize the media's stereotypical depiction of trans people. In my opinion, any decent exposure helps to demystify the condition. No matter how sappy or stereotypical the TV shows I watched were, I am an advocate of the trans community today because of each and every one of them.

Sarah has said, "The stories are real, but they only show what they think the public wants to see. They only show the pretty ones, the young ones, the ones who always knew since they were in preschool." But I say, showing what the public wants to see means the public will probably watch. A great way to reach the public is to start on common ground, presenting stuff the public is least likely to judge because they can almost relate, almost connect: "She is gorgeous! She is smart and successful! She could have been the guy next door!" One day they might wake up and realize that trans people live among us everywhere.

Showcasing Beautiful Women

Sometimes the person featured in a documentary is a 25 year old graceful, beautiful, shapely young trans woman. Although mainstream sources like to showcase very pretty transsexual women, not all trans people can afford surgery or even hormones.

I think society should be shown that if a person can transition early enough, he or she may have a better chance of a seamless transition. I say, tongue in cheek, that if the general cissexual public thinks the pretty ones are easier to accept, then adding coverage to insurance policies will end up helping everybody. Yet many insurance companies still have clauses which deliberately and specifically *exclude* coverage for trans related treatments.[3]

Sensationalizing Former Ultra-Masculine Guys

Mainstream media sources love to sensationalize the stories of trans women who had put effort into presenting as especially masculine men. Although Sarah has said these stories stereotype trans women, they also describe real people and real events. It is important for society to see how trans people sometimes struggle over half a lifetime to suppress their gender dissonance. They are not nutty people who just wake up one day and change sex on a whim. Society needs to see the story about a middle aged trans woman who used to be a body building man, a military man, or a football player. They need to know that people with transgender conditions walk among us and many still force it into the closet, sometimes by trying to smother the woman within themselves with an ultra masculine lifestyle. This condition could exist in the most unlikely of people we know—a fighter pilot, a crane operator, or even a husband or a son.

After learning the stories of middle aged people, a truly thoughtful audience might come to appreciate the huge advantage of transitioning young. One way to realize this advantage is to see and learn about how hard it is to make such a life change at age 40 or 50 when half a lifetime is gone. Some people have a wife and kids, established careers, and aging, masculine facial features. A compassionate viewer might say, "It's heartbreaking that a person like this is forced (by our culture) to live so long in misery." If showcasing older trans people convinces cissexual society that this medical condition could be treated when young, then young people will be able to live most of their lives as they are meant to be.

I had dinner one time in early 2011 with an old friend who seemed enchanted by our experience with Sarah. I showed her a picture of our young Sarah and she swooned at the very beautiful, lovely young woman in the picture. At some point during the meal, she brought up her neighbor, an "older man" whose wife had left him because he "cross dresses." She expressed her opinion that this was not at all the same thing as Sarah's condition. Her face grimaced a bit as she talked of seeing him at the mailbox lately in a skirt and heels. My stomach sank at her interpretation. It seemed like an unintentional double standard. I pointed out that the odds were pretty good that her neighbor was transsexual just like Sarah, and as simple as this statement was, I think it may have reached her. She seemed startled but receptive to that possibility, and said, "I will try to be more understanding now that you point that out!" I think many cissexual people want to learn more about transsexualism. A little information can go a long way to dispel double standards and prejudice.

Objectifying Transitioning People

From Julia Serano, *Whipping Girl*, p. 63:

> I know that many in the trans community believe that these TV shows and documentaries following transsexuals through the transition process serve a purpose, offering us a bit of visibility and the rare chance to be depicted on TV as something other than a joke. But in actuality, they accomplish little more than reducing us to our physical transitions and our anatomically "altered" bodies. In other words, these programs objectify us.[4]

In my view, documentaries that give exposure to transsexualism are actually doing exactly the opposite of objectification: they strip away the one-dimensional notion that trans people are just about their bodies and physical alterations. They tell heart-rending stories of real people and put a human face on the condition. The programs remove the body-focus and exoticism from the image of transsexualism and replace it with the heart and soul of an intelligent human being.

Some also argue that the media discounts the pain of gender dissonance. But I never saw a single documentary that didn't delve into the extraordinary physical and emotional hardships of trans people's journeys. Indeed this has been exemplified by using phrases such as "hero's journey"[5] or "the most difficult path known to humanity."[6] Different complications of the journey have been brought to light with each story.

In one of our discussions about the prevalence of stereotypes and sensationalism in documentaries, Sarah wrote:

> In some ways, it might be true that the people producing mainstream TV documentaries are "on our side." After all, they don't want to murder us, and some people do. But it really isn't a matter of two sides and nothing in between. The people producing the documentaries are focused on making money and appealing to the public's desire to see "weird" things on TV. I agree that imperfect documentaries are better than no documentaries at all—but that doesn't mean we shouldn't talk about how they could be better. Criticism provokes change—no matter how positive or negative the thing being criticized is already.

> Publicity for trans people may be a force for positive change, but that fact does not exempt documentaries and TV specials from criticism. I don't think they "come at it from all angles"—at least not most of the time. They rarely show trans men, people of color, young adults. They're using real information about real people, but they choose which information to display and they choose which people to document.

In the beginning, when the stories were most critical to my healing, I would not have recognized a stereotypical image for the life of me. I didn't care if the stories were about black or white or young or old people, or if any of these people were good looking. I didn't care about their statistical representation. Perhaps it was the very stereotypical stories that many trans people scoff at that engaged my attention at a simple level and helped me the most at the start. The demands for accurate information to be presented are justifiable at an advanced level. But it is the concept of this condition that needs to be explained first and foremost to a new learner. I think a fundamental problem that gets in the way of progress is that many cis people still think trans people are simply deranged. Before they can begin to learn about the diversity of trans people's experiences (whatever their race or age) cis people must become convinced that transsexualism is a *real, legitimate medical condition that exists all around us.* Each story helps describe and publicize the concept of transsexualism by example. In the meantime, it seems the concerns of the trans community are starting to be addressed. Maybe it's because more trans people today are willing to share their stories, but lately I've seen plenty of documentaries featuring trans men and young adults.

There is no easy way to make a perfect show to optimize accuracy, dignity and viewership. Uninvolved critics may never be persuaded to think seriously about transsexualism no matter how perfect a TV show is. It is probably much more important to reach just one single parent than it is to try to reach a thousand uninvested naysayers or curiosity seekers, anyway. However it happens, be it documentaries or books or rich inner faith in our transgender loved one, once we parents are on board, we live out our lives with conviction. We take the beautiful, colorful thread of this conviction to the fabric of mainstream society, and we weave our bold thread right on through it.

Showing Before and After Pictures and Using Before and After Names

Some trans leaders believe that revealing "before and after" names or showing "before and after" pictures of trans people in television documentaries is a form of objectification. They argue that such pictures compel viewers to pigeonhole trans women as former men (or trans men as former women) and allow viewers to ignore the mind, subconscious gender, and psychological well being of the transitioning person being featured.[7]

Where I am today, I actually agree with not showing before and after pictures. But in the beginning, I did not understand how distracting or even offensive it might be, because it was not at all distracting to me. I still feel that it is important to reach the public by engaging their attention to draw them into a story. It seems critical to send the message that transsexualism could exist in the most unexpected of people, including people we know. Showing pictures and revealing birth names is a part of telling these stories.

Even in the early days, I'd witness a woman's transition on a documentary and transition right along with her. If they later showed her "before" picture as a man, to me, that was the startling picture. Some trans people may worry that the viewer will be hijacked by the masculine picture, and then, thereafter pigeonhole the trans woman as a man. But in my mind, I had already pigeonholed her as a woman.

The Value of Identifying Biological Causes of Transsexualism

In my few years of exposure, I've noticed that some trans people seem to discount the importance of identifying neurobiological and genetic links to their condition. "Why not just take us at our word?" they seem to ask (in some of the memoirs, and even in my own personal encounters). One time in a trans support group meeting, I suggested that identifying a biological connection would help mitigate stigma, but I was immediately and firmly shut down. This happened again on a panel discussion a year later. An audience member asked me about biological causal theories. When I began to explain what I knew about a few of them, the audience was riveted, but the LGBT member of the panel quickly dismissed the discussion as irrelevant. She reminded the audience that the world doesn't need biological proof that there are millions of LGBT people out there. I wrote a whole section in this memoir about theories of biological links to transsexualism. When Sarah read the first draft of that section, she suggested I trim it to a couple of lines.

Sarah's transition was a lot easier on me when I could attribute it to a biochemical origin. I didn't start out knowing what trans people inherently know about the organic nature of gender identity. They are living and breathing the organic connection, and indeed it's their impetus for transition. As a parent, I had to transition too, but without the biological impetus. Learning about many biological causal theories was my substitute for this natural impetus.

I believe the more physiological evidence there is to support the reasons behind transsexualism, the better for everyone involved. Besides just helping to give loved ones something tangible to grasp, it would also seem to help the greater cause. For example, biological evidence could challenge dangerous treatment methods which focus on blocking transition, such as reparative therapy. Physiological evidence could expedite the removal of Gender Dysphoria from the DSM and facilitate insurance coverage of trans related medical expenses. Because I feel so strongly about the importance of biological causal theories of transsexualism, I have outlined some in more detail in Appendix A.

· · · · · · ·

I have much to gain by trying to learn about transsexualism. I strive to learn more and to become a better ally. Maybe it's not quite fair to consider my opinion as anything close to representative of the part of the cissexual population that has no real personal interest in transsexualism. The gist of this chapter may really only be relevant to the inner circle of loved ones most closely involved in a journey of gender transition. This leads me to my next observation. From within my inner circle, I've observed another level of conflicting views.

Different Perspectives of Our Family Transition

I sense that many trans people feel a little exasperated by their parents' inability to rapidly and unquestionably grasp the concept of a transgender loved one. I have read some autobiographies where a trans person was surprised and disappointed by a mother's reaction, or by a spouse's reaction. This surprise seems to imply that they had expected unquestioning acceptance. But, then, why don't gender dissonant people just disclose their condition the minute they suspect it? Why hide it for all the growing up years, and often for decades beyond? While gender dissonant people have a right to hope for unquestioning acceptance and support, they also seem to know that many other reactions are possible. I think one reason why so many trans people wait until middle age before transitioning is because they already suspect it will be hard on loved ones.

From Julia Serano (*Whipping Girl*, p.85):

> Sometimes people discount the fact that trans people feel any actual pain related to their gender. Of course, it is easy for them to dismiss gender dissonance: It's invisible and (perhaps more relevantly) they themselves are unable to relate to it.[8]

I think a comparison can be made to us, the parents: "Some trans people discount the fact that their parents are devastated by the radical transformation, near-replacement of their child by a completely different one. It is easy for them to dismiss the parent's paradox: they themselves, as non-cissexuals, are unable to relate to a person who has never known gender dissonance." Many of them may not even be able to relate to the concept of being a parent. When a family goes through a gender transition, a dissonance exists at some level for us all, and I think it is crucial to recognize all of these forms of dissonance. The concept of a parent's dissonance could be used as common ground. But it seems some trans people merely tolerate parents who still have old pictures on their walls, rather than trying to understand what they may feel (and who they feel they raised).

In *Wrapped in Blue*, a memoir by trans activist and author Donna Rose, although Donna appreciated her mother's company at her genital surgery, she seemed worried her mom would say something inappropriate to the other trans people they met. She seemed bothered by her mom's progress in the transition and I sensed a communication gap.[9] In *Becoming Chaz*, the documentary, when Chaz Bono's girlfriend Jenny said she felt like she had survived a tornado, Chaz shook his head, rolled his eyes and said "Wow" as if to say, "Oh come on, it could not have been that bad."[10]

Loved ones have a unique set of difficulties that are usually not shared by trans people themselves. Many of us are struck from out of the blue, stunned by the prospect of going through a gender transition. Ted and I began with no driving inner force leading us to this path in life, no critical need, not even the faintest concept of changing one of our sons into a daughter. As the transition proceeded, we had no rewarding feedback coming from within, relieving our dissonance and making us whole. We started out already whole and had to move *into* the dissonance.

Speed of Light vs. Snail's Pace

As the months went by, Sarah became more comfortable with herself, and also justifiably more comfortable with the family team and our enthusiasm to be involved. But I think she sometimes assumed that we were progressing in lockstep. It was like she had lost sight of the fact that the transition was still relatively new to us, unaware of the magnitude of its emotional impact on us as parents. That train continued to move too fast, and even in year two, I still couldn't keep up with the rapid changes—especially the changes of her personality on estrogen, and her expectations of our pace and our progress.

It was nine months from the time we first learned of Sarah's gender dissonance to the onset of estrogen hormone therapy. To Ted and me, the events that took place in those nine months occurred faster than we could handle. She was moving like a speeding train.

We learned much later that Sarah was frustrated by the snail's pace and felt she had been extraordinarily patient with us. This was a glaring example of polar opposite views of the exact same shared experience. She even told me once that she considered herself to be generous to wait for us to catch up when we lost ground. Of all the startling interactions we've had to date, this one was the most disconcerting. We were working as a team, to optimize everyone's best interest, out of love, so we could *all* successfully make this transition. I would not personally use the word "generous" because it sounds too disconnected from the family relationship. For example, saying "I felt generous to pay for Sarah's therapy" simply would not sound right. I still believe it mattered to her that we all pop out the other side the same happy family we'd always been, with all of us completely transitioned. I talked to Sarah about bridging this gap in our radically different perspectives. Her chilly retort was, "OK sure; we're a team." And so, the bridge is still wobbly.

Sarah is so much further ahead on the journey, it sometimes seems like she's lost sight of those of us still scrambling to catch up, still back in the dust, trapped in confusion as we deal with our own transition. The teamwork thing can only work to a limited extent as those of us in transition all step at a different pace. With seven or eight years of suffering behind her now, Sarah is ready to move on.

While reviewing an earlier draft of this book, Sarah wrote:

> Trying to be understanding of your emotions is very different from holding myself back. I was not holding you to an *expectation* of progressing emotionally so much as giving you an *opportunity* to progress emotionally. It was necessary for me to guide you forward even if you did not want to come along right away.
>
> My pain could be alleviated by moving faster; yours could *not* be alleviated by moving slower. The only way to optimize everyone's best interest was to move at a pace closer to mine than to yours, because in the long

run it was the only way *any* of us would get out the other side. I think that's what I was trying to get at by saying it seemed "generous."

Anyway, I'm not offended by these paragraphs. I think they get the point across, and they describe a real experience we had. This is an important part of what your book is trying to convey.

Same Person or Different Person?

Sarah and I have intimate discussions as often as necessary to clear the air, to cleanse our souls and to further bridge communication gaps like the ones described in this chapter. On one occasion I talked again of how I viewed her as a fast moving train. She said that she didn't feel like a train at all, and did not see herself as moving anywhere. From her point of view, she never left. She's on the inside looking out and I'm on the outside trying to look in. I said to her, "In order for us to see who you really are, you impelled us to change our perception of you. How does this not change who you are from our perspective?" Therein lies the heart of the problem and the reason for the impasse at that place where we stood (and still stand), uncompromising, foot to foot, face to face.

A transsexual friend once commended me for being an ally. Although I am proud to be an ally, I also feel allegiance to the family members who are confused and devastated, as I was during the first year of this journey. I seem to be standing in the middle of a bridge connecting two worlds that sometimes don't want to work to understand one another. I am lucky because I can reach either side; I have a place on both sides, and I strive to improve my ability to liaison between them. But talking to each world about the other has so far remained somewhat challenging.

Trading Places

Chapter 17

A New Reality

Some journeys are sprints, others are marathons, but I think the special road we travel is going to ramble on forever.

By spring of 2011, we were well into the third year of the journey. Sarah finished up four years of undergraduate study at the University of Michigan with two majors and a minor and a 4.0, without missing a beat, in spite of the challenges of gender transition. The name "Sarah Ann Baker" has been officially recorded on the diploma and engraved on prestigious awards. After being pursued by some of the finest graduate schools in the world, she enrolled in an Ivy League PhD program from which she will emerge Professor Baker, and I now see the world as her oyster. I'll never worry again about her chance at success in her career and in life overall.

At the honors luncheon for the top of the U of M graduating class, Sarah was seated next to the dean of the College of Literature, Science and the Arts. This was an honor indeed, to be rubbing elbows with department deans and the university president (who was walking around shaking hands). I wondered if any of them knew the remarkable story of this young scholar. Every one of them there had access to records starting with high school transcripts of Steven A. Baker. She went from Steven to Sarah right there on that campus. Many friends might count themselves lucky to have witnessed this extraordinarily courageous accomplishment. But from this point forward, wherever life takes her, she will only be Sarah to whomever she meets.

One other student was seated at our table, and he and Sarah began to chat. They learned that a few years back, they had been in a favorite class together. The other graduate scratched his head, trying hard to remember Sarah. He finally said, "There were only three guys in the class, but there were, after all, about twenty women...." Perhaps that is why he could not remember Sarah, hunting through his recollection of all those twenty girl faces. Surely he would remember the guys since there had been only three of them. But the most remarkable part of this story was that I didn't even catch on. I too was thinking back to their freshman year, imagining a room full of girl student faces, Sarah's one of them.

The human mind is phenomenally resilient. I could grapple with the paradox of Steven growing up to be Sarah for only so long. As an alternative, I am starting to imagine the memory of Sarah growing up to be Sarah. People with suppressed memories may work with psychologists for years to unblock them, to confront hidden truths in order to heal and become whole. Yet here I am today, subconsciously and miraculously repainting the memories of the past twenty years; with Sarah's hidden truth finally out, what was true to me then is now hidden.

· · · · · · ·

In January of 2011, we got a call from a couple, our longtime dear friends, to tell us that their son had just tragically died at the age of 22. I imagine they will walk through the rest of their lives with one foot on earth and the other in heaven; a surreal existence, having to muster strength with every breath they take just to take another. There is no other essence that can step in and magically fill the space their son has left vacant. They will truly never be whole again. Yet it was this very friend, who had the capacity and perception to say to me one day, "In a way, you've lost a son too."

It was one of the kindest, most tender connections I've felt with another during this journey. It was not so much the recognition of the concept of the loss that touched me, but the person who delivered it, and her ability, even at her darkest hour, to see the thread that ties her story to mine.

Indeed, we have lost a son because Steven does not exist anymore. While it is true that the changes in our lives have been traumatic, I've gradually come to know that the loss does not feel the same today as it did two years ago—or maybe I just think about it less. My other foot is in the past, or in some surreal parallel world, but it is not in heaven. We still have the present, and we still have the future with our child who is no longer Steven, but is Sarah instead. We are getting used to living with the dichotomy of "we have her, but we had him." Everything else has resumed course, continuing—almost—as previously expected.

One by one, over the past couple years, all of my initial fears of what might come of this transition fell like dominoes. Sarah looked like a woman even before she started the real life test; At long last, in the right skin, those spectacular huge blue eyes are radiant. When she came out to her friends, virtually all of them showered her with support and admiration, and she has a lot more of them now. When Nathan's mother was brought into the loop she took the news with exceptional grace and compassion. I was relieved to learn this great secret was finally revealed to an important player in this story. Most of our family members are working hard to accept the transition, even some of the ones who are typically quite uncompromising. Sarah's odds of getting assaulted now seem no greater than anyone else's. Her future is as bright as it always had been but she is infinitely happier now that she can be the woman she is. She is living in an east coast cultural and intellectual paradise with her physicist boyfriend, who adores her and the ground she walks on. And with so many friends and research responsibilities filling her days, she still wants to spend time with me. How can it get any better than this?

At the start I didn't think I'd ever be the same again, and that sentiment remains true. Nothing in life stays the same anyway. But I can honestly say that I am finally just as positive about life as I had been before—maybe even more so. Now, within the third year of the journey, as I complete the first draft of my memoir, the worst days are finally behind me. I feel strong and happy again.

• • • • • • •

Ted and I started going to PFLAG meetings in February of 2011. This is a support organization for "parents and families of lesbians and gays", but trans people's families are represented too.

In a small breakout session at one of these meetings, Ted and I were given the floor to tell a bit of our story. At one point I mentioned that Sarah had visited a psychologist for a second opinion, and the transsexual people in our group were perplexed. "Who would order a second opinion?" they wondered as they glanced at one another. But I couldn't find words to admit to them that Sarah talked to a second therapist at *my* request. Two years ago I was the one who questioned all of this. I fought like the devil to find weak links, to find another reason for Steven's dissonance, because I didn't think my son was a daughter. I didn't know then what I know now, and their bafflement spotlighted how far I had progressed since then, as well as the radical difference in our points of view and the paths of our journeys. With an equal mix of embarrassment and odd suspicion, I silently wondered, "How can you not know that a parent might seek validation?" I wish I could have articulated how many more people accepted Sarah's condition once I explained to them what I had learned as a result of struggling so hard to resist.

A transgender group member went on to tell us that sometimes parents will mourn the loss of their former child, as in a death. Her own dad had gone away for a week to privately mourn. "A week?!" I exclaimed to myself, a little incredulous. "It took me almost two years!" I began to realize, "They think I have come for help with my process ... but I am only here today because I have survived the process," and for the second time in less than a minute I felt disconnected and inhibited. I wish I could articulate how tough it was for me to watch this happen to my child, and, how tough it was to have to transition too. I wish I could have told them that had I actually come to this meeting for help in the earlier days, I'd likely have left more depressed.

If I had spoken honestly, I might have hurt the feelings of these innocent victims of a tragic human condition. They've been hurt enough already and they come to PFLAG meetings to find sanctuary. But keeping my personal experiences to myself did little to bridge the cis-trans communication gap. I sacrificed honesty for politeness. So today I stand in between the two worlds, telling my story through writing with what I hope is a mixture of both.

A young activist couple came to the meeting one time. Their child displayed clear and consistent transsexual behavior right from the start of life as a toddler and so their story will always be a little different from ours. They have the chance to let this child grow up as he was meant to be. Of course I don't really know, but they also appeared to have had an easier time accepting transsexualism than those of us there with much older transitioning children. I can only speak for myself, but I spent the first twenty years of life raising a completely different child than the one I have today. In some ways it might have been easier to have raised Sarah right from the start, but such an experience might have had its own set of challenges. I'd probably be writing this memoir about life as a social activist instead. I can only imagine trying to get the school system to accommodate the needs of a growing trans child with kindness and discretion. In a conversation about gender congruent bathroom use, a child care director once shocked me by saying, "Wow. That's a lot to ask of society." Simple minded people may judge young parents and accuse them of forcing their child to be the other gender. But thinking people know it takes hard work to get a child potty trained, to finish homework. So why would it suddenly be easy to force a kid to change gender? Getting society to recognize transsexualism as a real medical condition may be a long and difficult process.

Narrow-minded criticism and a hostile society present nasty obstacles for parents of very young transsexual children. I hold those parents in the highest esteem; they have their work cut out for them, striving to improve the world their children will live in. I guess we all are coming at it from different angles, doing what we need to do to chip away at rigid attitudes about transsexualism and inform and reshape our culture.

• • • • • • •

When I began to write this memoir, I felt a great urgency to try to explain transsexualism to people on the outside, including the non-thinkers and naysayers—who I will call "the others." This mission had seemed to be entwined with my own well being in the early days, as though it mattered that other people understood the valid biochemical reasons for this condition. Did I think the others held a more stately position than open-minded people in life's hierarchy? Did I feel pressure to think their boxed in and rigidly defined rules determined who was normal and who was not? Did I somehow believe that lemmings were more respectable or smarter than free-thinkers? I suppose the others do hold considerable power in a country where the majority determines law and social policy and norms. There are politically good reasons to get the others to think, but none of those reasons are just about me anymore.

Another transition happened during this journey that was like a renaissance to me when I figured it out. I have grown immensely from this experience. I opened the door to a dimension of humanity filled with rich and beautiful stories from everywhere around the world through all the ages of time. I've learned of the stories of heart rending pain and tragic loneliness; I've been encouraged by stories of perseverance and sacrifice and hard-earned triumph. I've been moved by some of the greatest love stories imaginable. I am surrounded by some of the most incredibly brave and fascinating people on earth. One of them is my own daughter.

Now that I'm on the other side of my transition, I look at the others as though they are aliens from outer space. Instead of feeling an urgent need to bring them to a better understanding, I feel pity that their world is so limited, so restricted, so devoid of this richness. At this point I hardly need to finish this memoir for the others anymore. My attempts to explain transsexualism to people on the outside have started to seem futile. It might have to be enough just to seek a simple level of acceptance. Other than parents, therapists, and academics, there are likely few people willing to think deeply about transsexualism. It's just too hard. In this memoir, I have made analogies to being blind, yet not one time have I ever tied a wrap over my eyes and tried to experience it.

Still, I kept writing, if only just for me. It was an opportunity to process and express my emotions, to say things in subtle ways that I could never say to anyone's face. The writing has kept me busy, and has given me a sense of purpose. And even after I move to the next phase of my life, I can hand the bound words to anyone who asks, "So how did you feel about all this?" and not worry that the story will be lost to a fading memory or to evaporated passion. The journey was not easy and I would never want to pretend for one minute that it was—especially not to a parent who is just starting transition. Most parents at the start of this journey cannot just look at a happy ending and be convinced they will get there someday. But now that I've moved into brighter days, it's become harder to look back at the dark ones. I've had enough and I'm ready to move on.

• • • • • • •

Sometimes I wonder if another reason I needed to write this book was to keep Steven alive, to document his existence and our years as a family. Then Steven will somehow be immortalized; he'll never be gone. To this day I still carry pictures of Steven in my wallet, although they now seem a bit startling. The caller ID on my cell phone rings as Steven though it now seems a bit confusing. I find small ways to keep Steven alive while I continue through life with Sarah, loving her, so proud of her, and merging her with the memory of him. We move forward with Sarah, but look backwards to Steve. My new reality is a steady mental paradox, one with which I've learned to live.

Today, my sadness is dormant for the most part. If some trigger happens to roust it, I will momentarily be overcome with deep grief. Although Sarah is beautiful, wonderful, I say today and I will say forever, I miss you my Stevie, my sweet gentle soul, my love, my treasure, my Steve. I wonder if, when I am old and frail, I will still be looking for him, wondering where he has gone and when he will come back home to me. I flash forward to my deathbed, with Ted, Jeff and Sarah by my side. I imagine I will tell these three people in my delirium, "I used to have another child, a sweet and wonderful boy named Steve ..."

· · · · · · ·

At dinner one day in early 2011, Sarah announced her plans for genital surgery with the internationally acclaimed Dr. Marci Bowers, booked for the summer of 2012 in San Francisco. We kept on eating just like we had so long ago that Christmas of 2008 when Steve launched this journey by telling us he was bisexual. This time we were at least a little more ready. I no longer think it's possible for Steven to return, for Sarah to be a guy, for any of this to be a mistake. It is wonderful to see the happiest person on earth before me. Yet the words to describe the flurry of emotions set off by this latest announcement are still a mixed bag—excitement, agreement, melancholy, curiosity. I wonder if Sarah will remember what life had been like through testosterone lenses, misplaced though they were. However academic, her experiences being treated both as a man and as a woman will give her multidimensional insight about humanity.

We had been so average, so ho-hum for most of our lives, but now we are subjects of fascination and curiosity, agents of soul searching, examples of love and courage and pride and ability to live honestly. I get to tell about my beautiful daughter, and all the memories of her as a little boy, and with this memoir, I've now told about the time in between.

Sunrise, sunset, the days and weeks come and go. I weave the threads of my story into a tapestry of tragedy and comedy, of paradox and renaissance, of yesterday and today. I've been given a rare gift: it is a privilege to be a part of this phenomenal world. We live our new family life with Sarah now, and with the passage of time we are building new memories. Images of Steve are fading into the distance, or maybe more accurately, they exist in a separate chamber of my mind and my heart. I remind myself that we had a boy, who really was a girl, a courageous transsexual girl. We only thought we had a boy; she was Sarah all along. After this extraordinary journey of transition, our broken souls have mended, and Sarah now lives in a world that can finally see her.

Trading Places

Afterword
by Sarah Ann Baker

This book is not about me. The events in it happened to me, and I have my own memories of them and my own feelings about them, but presenting those memories and feelings would require a separate book with a separate purpose. Stories primarily about the experiences of transsexual people's family members have been overlooked and under-told; the motivation to share such a story is why I am writing this afterward, and why you are reading this book.

If you are a parent of a transsexual child and you have experienced emotional trauma during the process of reimagining your child's identity, I hope this book has given you the comfort of shared experience. If you experienced no such trauma, or experienced trauma for different reasons and in different ways, I hope this book has helped you understand someone dear to me with a perspective different from yours. If you are a transsexual person with parents, I hope this book has illustrated some of the pain they might experience, though their feelings are sure to differ from my mom's feelings in unpredictable but meaningful ways.

If you are a scholar or an interested member of the general public, I hope this book has helped to humanize the experiences of trans people and their family members, all of whom are profoundly affected by social stigma in ways you may not be able to comprehend without feeling them deeply yourself. If you are an uninterested member of the general public, kudos for getting this far.

To most cis people, gender seems like quite a simple concept. It is not. But gender *identity* can be described in relatively simple terms. Gender identity is a fundamental sense of self as male, female, or something else. Like our minds themselves, our gender identities are real, and we are the only ones who have direct access to them. Nobody else can know your gender directly. Nobody else can declare that it is or is not valid. Just as nobody can look at you and know intuitively whether or not you like carrots or believe in God, nobody can look at you and know that you are a man or a woman. When people look at me, they perceive me as a woman, but that is not why I am one. My identity comes from within. I simply *am* a woman. That is as objective a statement as can be made about a person—it is not a matter of perspective, it is just a statement of fact.

My incontrovertible femaleness did not make it impossible for others to perceive me as a man for many years. My sense of identity did not prevent me from experiencing uncertainty about whether their perspective or mine was more valid, and it did not prevent me from doubting whether I would ever stop pretending to be a man. When I finally did, my mom had to change the way she thought about my identity. Her mental and emotional transition has required time and effort. And while all of the details of this story are particular to us—our family, our personalities, our resources, our social context—it conveys at least one larger point: transitioning involves more than one person. It depends on communication, on making a concealed identity public, and so it shapes the experiences of many beyond the transitioner.

I cannot help that I am a woman. I also cannot help that I was initially perceived as a boy. Neither I nor my mom can help that she experienced consternation surrounding my transition. I can listen to her and acknowledge her pain, but I have no control over its source. I am a woman, and confronting that fact was enough to cause her to suffer—but it is an indisputable fact of the world, not a choice of framing or behavior. Sometimes my mom felt I was transitioning too quickly, but there was nothing I could do to change the fundamental reality that was troubling her. My identity itself, and not my volitional behavior or the pace of my transition, was her sticking point. She sometimes said that I was driving a train that was moving too fast for her. In reality, the tracks did not lead to where she thought she wanted the train to go; the speed of the engine had nothing to do with it. I did not give up on understanding her perspective, but I knew that I could do nothing more than continue to steadfastly express the truth about my self. The only real choice anyone made in this process was my mom's decision to share her experiences in print.

This book is not about me, but I can summarize what happened to me as my mom was going through the psychological events described in this book: my life began to make sense. And although my mom felt some foundational axioms of her social world unraveling around her at first, I believe her understanding of my life has begun to make sense as well.

If this book had existed when I came out to my parents, I would have given them each a copy.

• • • • • • •

If you have any comments or questions about this book, please send them to TradingPlacesBook@gmail.com. My mom and I would appreciate hearing your thoughts, and we will do our best to reply.

Trading Places

Appendix A
Theories About the Causes of Gender Dysphoria and Transsexualism

I am not a scientist, and the ideas reviewed here are complex. This is my best attempt to simplify and summarize my understanding of some of them. It is important to keep in mind that the possible biological origins of transsexualism are ambiguous and difficult to study, and work in this area is relatively new and rapidly changing. For this reason, it is likely that my summary of the evidence will seem outdated within a few years of this book's publication. Setting the details aside for a moment, the central point of this appendix is that transsexualism seems to have some complicated but very real biological causes, regardless of what those causes actually are.

Fetal Sex Hormone Wash

For decades, scientists believed the sole determining factor causing variance in gender identity development was the fetal testosterone hormone wash. All human embryos start out basically identical in the womb—with "female" bodies and brains exposed to high levels of estrogens—regardless of sex chromosomes (i.e., XX or XY). No genital differentiation occurs within the first twelve weeks of gestation. After the first trimester, male gonads start to develop in the fetus of a prenatal boy (usually associated with an XY karyotype, but not always). Between the first and second trimester, around week 14 in utero, prenatal gonadal androgen hormones are released to wash over and masculinize the brain. This critical testosterone hormone wash will—or will fail to—biochemically and neurologically masculinize the gender of the brain at this decisive time of fetal development in a baby that will be born with male genitalia.[1-5]

This early gestational testosterone surge is important for male sexual differentiation of the human brain.[5] Brain gender identity is likely determined at this point, regardless of how gonadal sex hormones affect genital development weeks later.

The gonads, genitals, and brain must all develop congruently to form a unified cissexual outcome. Hormones are the glue which links them together. If the brain fails to masculinize in a fetus that is developing male genitals, the result might be a transsexual girl: this person would have a neurologically female brain (or an innate female gender identity) and a male body.

Structural Differences in the Human Brain Related to Gender Identity

Evidence shows that prenatal sex hormones cause male and female mouse brains to develop differently in ways "such as sizes of particular regions of the brain, number of nerve cells, distribution of neurotransmitters, and even in development of behavior."[6] In humans, similar structural and functional sex differences may be the basis for gender identity.[7] These sexually dimorphic areas of the brain, developed very early in utero, may be the reason one ultimately "thinks" like a male or like a female. Indeed, studies show that certain brain structures in transsexual women are similar in volume and neuronal density to those of cissexual women.[3,8,9]

Preliminary physiological evidence was discovered in the Netherlands in 1995. A team of scientists performed autopsies on the brains of several male to female transsexual cadavers.[3] The team took slices of the cadaver brains and discovered that the region of their brains called "the central subdivision of the bed nucleus of the stria terminalis" or BSTc for short, was about the same size as that normally found in cissexual women.[3] The BSTc is a tiny region in the hypothalamus that some speculate might be linked to gender identity in all of us. The BSTc is about 50% smaller in average cissexual women than it is in cissexual men.

Research found that male-to-female trans women had female sized BSTc or smaller, and female-to-male trans men had male sized BSTc. Differences in BSTc size most likely occur during fetal brain development since the size of this structure doesn't seem to be changed by drugs or hormones after birth.[3,8] This further validates the theory that gender is determined in the brain prenatally.

Indicators Observed in Brain Scans of Living Transsexual People

Several other studies have scanned living transsexual people's brains. Such studies have identified a number of brain components on which transsexual brains look like cissexual brains of the identified gender rather than the gender assigned at birth.[8,10,11,12] Such results can be observed in indicators of how the brain processes audio and visual information[13,14] even before transsexual people begin hormone therapy.[15,16] However, brain scan studies have not always yielded consistent results.[17,18] This science is still in its infancy.

Sex Hormone Receptors in the Brain and a Genetic Link to Transsexualism

Evidence from a 2003 genetic study suggests that genes, activated prior to the fetal hormone wash, may directly induce "sexually dimorphic patterns of neurological development" in the brain.[6] These findings suggest that the prenatal sex hormone wash may not be solely responsible for the differences between male and female brain development.[6]

Dr. Eric Vilain, assistant professor of human genetics and urology at the David Geffen School of Medicine at UCLA said, "Sexual identity is rooted in every person's biology before birth and springs from a variation in our individual genome."[4]

"Our findings may explain why we feel male or female, regardless of our actual anatomy," said Vilain. "From previous studies, we know that transgender persons possess normal hormonal levels," he added. "Their gender identity likely will be explained by some of the genes we discovered."[4,6]

Other studies in humans have shown a link between genes related to androgen and estrogen hormone receptors and transsexualism.[9,19] Specifically, it seems that underactive androgen receptor genes (including complete androgen insensitivity syndrome) is related to female gender identity in (male to female) transsexual women.[9,19,20] In 2008, Australian researchers identified further evidence for these genetic links to transsexualism. The Australian team compared the DNA of 112 transsexual women to 258 control subjects to show that the transsexual women are much more likely to have a longer version of the androgen receptor gene.[9] Longer versions of the androgen receptor gene inhibit interaction and binding between the androgen protein and its receptor and co-activator. This will lead to reduced testosterone signaling during fetal development and may be responsible for under-masculinization of the brain during the fetal hormone wash.[9] Professor Vincent Harley from Prince Henry's Institute of Medical Research said, "Our findings support a biological basis of how gender identity develops."[21]

Multidimensional Factors

Congenital adrenal hyperplasia is a genetic condition characterized by high androgen levels during fetal development. Most people with XX chromosomes with this condition may not experience gender dissonance, but they are many times more likely to have a male gender identity than people with XX chromosomes without this condition.[5,9] These findings support the view that prenatal exposure to unusual levels of sex hormones may permanently affect brain gender identity.[5]

Reported concordant occurrences of gender dissonance in twin and non-twin siblings, in parent-child pairs, and in other familial cases suggest that transsexualism is likely hereditary; this further supports a genetic link.[5,9,19]

• • • • • • •

Joan Roughgarden's groundbreaking book *Evolution's Rainbow* provides a detailed study of the biology of gender. Reviewing decades of research, Roughgarden illustrates that gender variance, once viewed as rare and aberrant, is actually common and natural. The natural world is filled with beings that exist outside the typical male female binary categories. Gender variant humans "have something in common with approximately half of all species on the planet."[22,23]

The causes of gender identity, gender variance, and transsexualism, while rooted in biology, are almost certainly multidimensional.[24] Although research in this area is still under-funded, notable progress has been made in the last 20 years. Research findings continue to reveal biological factors and genetic triggers which may explain why transsexual people have the brain of one gender and the body of the other.

As mentioned in Chapter 16, I believe evidence for biological causes of transsexualism is valuable for everyone involved. Besides just helping to give loved ones something tangible to grasp, such evidence can also help refute transphobic voices and challenge doctors who try to block transition. Biological evidence could expedite the removal of Gender Dysphoria from the DSM psychiatric handbook altogether, and would facilitate justification for medical insurance coverage independent of psychological diagnoses. In short, biological research on transsexualism could help move transsexual health care awareness into the 21st century.

Trading Places

Appendix B

Transphobia in Science and Medicine

It was not in my original plan to include this kind of political commentary in my memoir. But I have read and learned just enough to know there are some arrogant people out there in influential positions who don't have our children's best interests in mind. Their transphobic messages need to be squelched and I want to do my part to help spread the word. A few decades ago it was believed by many cissexual "experts" that trans people were incapable of speaking for themselves. Even today, many "experts" think they know more about trans people than trans people know about themselves.

Kenneth Zucker is the head of a child and adolescent gender identity clinic in Toronto and has worked with transgender youth since the mid 1970s. Although therapists from the 1990s reported that up to 70% of trans patients had attempted suicide because of their gender dissonance[1], Dr. Zucker remained steadfast in his decades-long practice of blocking transition in young people. Dr. Zucker served on the workgroup which determined that transsexualism should be classified alongside paraphilias and criminal sexual behaviors in the 1994 release of the DSM-IV. In 2008, to the outcry of trans activists, he was appointed to the DSM-5 workgroup too. Unfortunately, Zucker was still a member of WPATH in 2013.[2,3,4,5]

Ray Blanchard is an American-Canadian sexologist. He served on the American Psychiatric Association DSM-IV subcommittee on Gender Identity Disorders (along with Zucker) which resulted in transsexualism being classified with paraphilias and criminal sexual behaviors. Despite widespread protests, he was assigned again to work on the DSM-5. He has declared that lesbian and bisexual trans women are really men with a mental illness called "autogynephilia." His double standard that frames being gay or bisexual as a mental illness for transsexual people but not for cissexual people has no scientific empirical basis.[3,6,7-15,18,19]

Anne Lawrence is a psychologist who sometimes works with Ray Blanchard. She also believes that all lesbian and bisexual trans women are really men with "autogynephilia" and are not actually transsexual. I don't think she really believes trans men exist at all, or at least she conveniently forgets about them most of the time. Her transphobia is particularly strange because she is transsexual herself. She has first hand experience living in a transsexual body, yet denies the existence of other trans people.[3,8-15,18,19]

John Michael Bailey is an American psychologist and author of the controversial 2003 book, *The Man Who Would Be Queen: The Science of Gender-Bending and Transsexualism.* Complaints have been filed against Bailey challenging his credentials and accusing him of overstepping professional bounds.[7,15-17] He appears to have the same mindset as Blanchard, describing transsexualism as a paraphilia while claiming to want to understand transsexual people better; this seems duplicitous to me.

People like these four who claim to be scientists seem extraordinarily arrogant, selfish and transphobic to me, more like ideologues—"gender supremacists"—rather than scientists. They seem fixated on defending traditional gender (and sexual) ideologies and on denigrating transgender and intersex people.[6,17] It seems easier for many of these ideologues to believe that trans people are simply lost souls than to admit their own mistakes at this stage of their careers. Some seem more concerned about protecting the rest of society than genuinely helping trans people. They all seem to think they know trans people better than trans people know themselves.

With the transgender movement twenty years underway, transphobic people and naysayers are rapidly losing their footing. Their unqualified voices are becoming the ones to ignore and trans people who speak for themselves are rapidly populating society's landscape instead. Trans people have moved into leadership positions in physical and social science, medicine, education, politics and law, and they are on the executive board of WPATH. Transsexual celebrities, artists, authors, and documentary and movie makers are creatively and effectively speaking for themselves as well.

Progressive parents are part of the movement to improve the lives of transgender children, young ones and old ones alike. Many of us can help improve our culture's understanding of transsexualism from the ground floor up, and we can make a powerful impact as examples. A new generation of children will grow up in a safer, more welcoming climate and they will speak for themselves. Transphobic voices will be left behind as the modern world moves forward.

Trading Places

Appendix C

What Percentage of the Population is Transsexual?

I thought I would find this condition to be extremely rare, but it is likely more common than cleft palate. Because transsexualism is frequently concealable, transsexual people make up a much larger portion of the population than most people think.[1,2,3,4] In 2001 the best available estimate of transsexual prevalence in the United States was 1 in 500.[5] In the last thirty years, prevalence rates have continued to rise with each successive report. By 2011, according to a growing number of statistically sound estimates, there could be as many as 1 in 333 individuals in the United States who consider themselves transgender.[4,6] In fact, in a random sample of individuals taken from the general population of Massachusetts in 2011, at least 1 out of every 200 respondents acknowledged being transsexual.[7] Evidence from multiple countries suggests the prevalence of transsexualism worldwide is at least 1 in 500.[4-6,8-11] There are probably just as many trans men as there are trans women.[12]

These numbers have been hard to obtain. Some unrelenting statisticians still base their count of transsexual people on the number of SRS surgeries performed in the United States—even though many (maybe most) trans people never even have surgery in the United States or anywhere at all. Last century, very few therapists helped patients access surgery. Many American insurance companies have built in exclusionary clauses *specifically to deny coverage* to transsexual people for procedures related to transgender health. Trans author and activist Donna Rose had a policy that flatly denied short term disability coverage to felons, criminals, and transsexual people—all in one clause.[13] It is financially impossible for some to obtain medical help for physical transitioning. Resourceful trans people are forced to seek surgery outside the country where the quality is just as good and the procedures are more affordable.

There is a broad spectrum of gender identity and expression. Some researchers have different ideas on who to count as transgender and this contributes to the variation in prevalence numbers reported. Some researchers like to estimate the prevalence of trans people by counting people who visit gender clinics for counseling or medical treatment. But for every gender variant person who has sought medical help, there might be 50 who have not.[4,14] Many trans people try to suppress their dissonance, and many choose to keep their transsexual status private for other reasons.

American society has created a hostile environment for trans people to come out and be counted. Many trans people live life in the closet out of fear of being disowned, murdered, or fired from their jobs (which is still legal in many states).[15-18] Hormones are usually more important to transition than SRS, and many people can't afford either anyway since most insurances won't pay. Even if there was a way to count all the trans people on prescribed hormones, many others have to get their hormones on the street or via the internet. Last century, many therapists would only allow "good-looking" trans people access to hormones. Even though this policy was cruel to suffering patients, the rest of society never had to know about the transsexual people who live among us since good looking ones blended in better. And to help protect the general public from becoming too squeamish or uncomfortable, transsexual people were instructed by their doctors never to reveal their status. In years past, transsexual people were nearly impossible to count.

Many past researchers grossly underestimated the prevalence of transsexualism: they decided who qualified as transsexual, they used unsound survey methodology and ancient data, they decided to look in places trans people were least likely to be found, they counted only the few that they could find, and they excluded all trans people who choose to conceal their transsexual status.[4,5,11,19] A logical thinker will realize that numbers from years past such as 1 in 80,000 are bogus and farcical. I am not even trying to count, and even within my own community I witness numbers of trans people closer to 1 in 400, not including people I see at trans-related events. Our local high school has had about one transsexual student in every graduating class (of about 400 students) over the last several years.

It is also estimated that as many as 1 in 100 births are intersex (with physiological characteristics that differ from standard male or female) and about 1 in 1500 people are born with ambiguous genitalia.[20] You and I don't know which people we meet are intersex or have ambiguous genitalia. We likely see them as either a man or a woman.

Most people, whether transgender, intersex, or cissexual, just want to blend into society and live their lives. With the current social climate trending to support civil and human rights for all LGBTQI people, floodgates are opening and prevalence numbers are rapidly increasing.

Trading Places

Appendix D

Why Doesn't Mainstream Society Know More About Gender Variance?

First they ignore you, then they laugh at you, then they fight you, then you win.

Mohandas Gandhi

We all probably interact with numerous transsexual people on a regular basis, simply assuming that they are cissexual. Why would there be any reason for trans people to broadcast their medical histories in casual interactions? In fact there are still several reasons why they would not. In the U.S. in 2011, a person could still be fired from jobs in 34 states if it was discovered they were transsexual.[1,3] 63% of Americans lived in areas that allowed discrimination based on gender identity or expression.[2,4] 78% of trans people in one large survey had been mistreated at work or denied work due to bias.[2] 19% of trans people sampled had been denied living in a house or apartment because of their gender expression, resulting in double the overall rate of homelessness in the US.[1,2] Of those who tried to access a homeless shelter, over half were harassed and one third were completely denied.[1,2] Only 11 states have passed hate crime laws enumerating protection for transsexual people, who continue to face unconscionable levels of abuse and violence due to hate.[4] They are among the most mistreated and misunderstood people in American society.[1-4]

Some therapists have speculated that many inexplicable teenage suicides in the last century had probably been due to being closeted transgender or gay individuals. Dr. Mildred Brown, gender therapist and co-author of *True Selves* in 1996, said that as many as 70% of her patients seeking therapy for gender dysphoria had attempted suicide.[5] In recent surveys, estimates of the prevalence of attempted suicide among transsexual people ranged from about a quarter to two fifths, still high compared to 1.6% for the general population.[2,6,7] We don't usually know about these people in society at large because they are pressured to stay in the closet, they are afraid to come out, or they choose suicide instead.

Gender variant people are everywhere among us, and have been documented in all of recorded history, all around the world. It is important to restate that transsexual people are not the same as people who are genderqueer or who are considered a third gender. I highlight gender variance (including third gender people) in other cultures not to pretend I know much about these cultures, but to exemplify the prevalence of gender variance around the world.

In some Native American cultures, "two-spirit" people are those who comfortably embody both genders. At one time they were considered especially gifted and were highly respected, even revered as uniquely spiritual as shamans or healers. Parents did not usually dissuade their children from living a two-spirit life. "Berdache" is another transgender term documented in the history of some Native American cultures. Berdaches were male-born Native Americans with a feminine spirit; they often filled the role of a wife and were usually considered a third gender. This, and most other aspects of those historic cultures were obliterated by the arrival of the puritan Europeans who, as we know, destroyed a lot of what they did not understand. But today, I understand (from various articles on the internet) that the two-spirit aspect of some Native American cultures is being revived.[8]

Transgender people have been recognized in India for thousands of years and some of them are known as Hijra. Hijra are usually considered a third gender, and in India's caste system, they are similar to untouchables. But they've made significant social advances in the last decade.[9] In 1999, the MacArthur Foundation helped set up Sangama, a rapidly growing support organization for sexual minorities in India. Today it is funded by the Bill and Melinda Gates Foundation and the Fund for Global Human Rights among others.[10] The status of Hijra is changing. Recently a resourceful Hijra got her own TV talk show, and many Hijra have moved into political office.

Certain Buddhists of Thailand believe that reincarnations include living once as a man, once as a woman, and once as transgender. Some say that the people of Thailand and Buddhists in general, are among the most compassionate and accepting of gender variant people in the world.

We are in the midst of a transgender movement in our modern American culture as well. Lobbyists are working hard to address the injustices mentioned in the first paragraph of this section, and a lot of progress has been made. There are transsexual people in high political offices, directing and acting in Hollywood, and teaching at universities all over the country. I've learned stories of doctors and lawyers and successful business people and acclaimed musicians. Oprah Winfrey regularly featured transsexual guests during her years as a talk show host. An increasing number of books, documentaries, movies and TV shows are about transsexual people. Trans people were even accepted at the 2012 Olympic tryouts. Exposure like this brings familiarity and I'm witnessing rapid and positive changes in cultural attitudes.[11,12] As more encouraging stories are told, I believe the time will come when transsexual people achieve an honored and respected status.

Trading Places

Endnotes

Chapter 1: Trading Places

1   Grant, Jaime M., Lisa A. Mottet, Justin Tanis, Jack Harrison, Jody L. Herman, & Mara Keisling. "Injustice at every turn: A report of the National Transgender Discrimination Survey," Washington, DC: National Center for Transgender Equality and National Gay and Lesbian Task Force, 2011. Retrieved March 2012, ⟨http://www.thetaskforce.org/reports_and_research/ntds⟩. In a 2008-09 survey of 6450 trans Americans, 41% reported that they had survived a suicide attempt, compared to 1.6% for the general population.

2   *Switching Sexes: The Aftermath.* Prod., writ. Bronwyn Emmet. Film Garden Entertainment. Discovery Production Services, L.L.C. for Discovery Health Channel, 2004. TV, Cable. Quote from Mikayla, a trans woman featured in this documentary.

3   *The Matthew Shepard and James Byrd, Jr. Hate Crimes Prevention Act* was passed by congress and signed into law by President Barack Obama on October 28, 2009. The Act expands federal hate crime law to include acts of hate motivated by a victim's race or disability, as well as gender identity or sexual orientation. It is the first federal law in U.S. history to enumerate and extend legal protection to transgender people.

4   Conway, Lynn. "How Frequently Does Transsexualism Occur?" 2001-2002. Retrieved 2009 from ⟨http://www.lynnconway.com⟩ and ⟨http://ai.eecs.umich.edu/people/conway/TS/TSprevalence.html⟩. Lynn Conway, a University of Michigan Professor of Electrical Engineering and Computer Science, estimates that 1 in 500 people suffer from gender incongruence.

5   Herman, Joanne. *Transgender Explained For Those Who Are Not.* Bloomington, IN: AuthorHouse, 2009. pp.5, 40. On employment discrimination against trans people in this country.

6   In 2010, President Obama appointed transgender woman Amanda Simpson to the post of Senior Technical Advisor to the Commerce Department. Associated Press on Amanda Simpson: "Tucson transgender woman now serving Obama administration." January 6, 2010. Information from Arizona Daily Star, ⟨http://www.azstarnet.com⟩ Retrieved 2010, ⟨http://bostonherald.com/news/us_politics/view/20100106tucson_transgender_woman_now_serving_obama_administration⟩.

7   Serano, Julia. *Whipping Girl: A Transsexual Woman on Sexism and the Scapegoating of Femininity.* Berkeley: Seal Press, a member of the Perseus Books Group, 2007. The term "cissexual" has become popular in trans culture largely because of the work of trans activist Julia Serano.

8   *Switching Sexes: The Aftermath.* Prod., writ. Bronwyn Emmet. Film Garden Entertainment. Discovery Production Services, L.L.C. for Discovery Health Channel, 2004. TV, Cable. Quote from Dr. Marci Bowers, "I think society needs to stop taking itself so seriously. People are people and this is just part of the human expression."

Chapter 2: Devastation

1   Sarah's bisexual announcement was meant to engage our attention and to analyze our reaction to unexpected news about her. Although being bisexual is not the same as being transgender, the experience of announcing being bisexual to parents can also be difficult.

Chapter 3: When She Was a He

There are no endnotes for Chapter 3.

Chapter 4: Dreams

1   Kübler-Ross, Elisabeth, and David Kessler. "The Five Stages of Grief." Retrieved February 2013, ⟨http://grief.com/the-five-stages-of-grief⟩. There are countless internet links about the stages of grief.

2   National Center for Transgender Equality (NCTE). Retrieved 2013,

⟨http://transequality.org/Issues/employment.html⟩. Regarding economic opportunity; as of 2011 only 16 states protected trans people from discrimination at work. The rate of unemployed trans people is higher than the national average. Extreme levels of poverty force many to turn to drug and sex trades.

3   Herman, Joanne. *Transgender Explained For Those Who Are Not.* Bloomington, IN: AuthorHouse, 2009. pp. 5,40. As of 2011, more than half the states can still legally fire a person for being transgender.

4   Beck, Aaron T. *Cognitive Therapy of Depression.* New York: The Guilford Press, 1979. p. 238. Concepts gleaned from this work: Sometimes you have to feel as bad as you possibly can before you can start to feel better again. A variation of the cliché: "it's always darkest before the dawn." Once you've depleted yourself of this dark thing, you may not be able to feel this bad again, even if you want to.

Chapter 5: The Devil's Advocate

1   Brown, Mildred L. and Chloe Ann Rounsley. *True Selves: Understanding Transsexualism for Families, Friends, Coworkers, and Helping Professionals.* San Francisco: Jossey-Bass Publishers, 2003. p. 220; quote on the value of learning. This material is reproduced with permission of John Wiley & Sons, Inc.

2   *Sex Change Hospital.* A series of six episodes. Dir., prod. Chris McKim. executive producers: Fenton Bailey, Randy Barbato, Jeremy Simmons. Ed. Afsheen Family. Consulting prod., perf. Dr. Marci Bowers. World of Wonder, for Channel 4 and Discovery Fit and Health, 2005. TV, Cable. Quote from Emeri Burks, a trans woman featured in one episode of this series: "It's frustrating as hell because what I've got to go on here is this intensely strong conviction ... that I am not a man."

3   Herman, Joanne. *Transgender Explained For Those Who Are Not.* Bloomington, IN: AuthorHouse, 2009. p. 28. On what it felt like to be gender dissonant.

4   Serano, Julia. *Whipping Girl: A Transsexual Woman on Sexism and the Scapegoating of Femininity.* Berkeley: Seal Press, 2007. p. 85. On explaining what it feels like to be gender dissonant. Reprinted by permission of Seal Press, a member of the Perseus Books Group.

5   Morris, Jan. *Conundrum*. New York: New American Library, 1975. pp. 33,41.

6   Morris, *Conundrum*, p.43

7   The World Professional Association for Transgender Health. "Standards of Care for the Health of Transsexual, Transgender, and Gender-Nonconforming People", Version 7. *International Journal of Transgenderism, 13*(4), pp.165-232, 2011. doi:10.1080/15532739.2011. 700873. Retrieved 2014, ⟨http://www.wpath.org/site_page.cfm?pk_ association_webpage_menu=1351&pk_association_webpage=3926⟩.

8   The Harry Benjamin International Gender Dysphoria Association's Standards of Care (HBIGDA SOC version 6) was the most common explicit protocol used by the medical community to treat patients with gender dysphoria when I wrote my questions for "The Devil's Advocate" in mid-2010. Since then, HBIGDA officially changed its name to the World Professional Association for Transgender Health, or WPATH. The Harry Benjamin "HBIGDA" nomenclature is still sometimes used when referring to the standards of Care (SOC), which are now administered by WPATH. In September 2011, WPATH released SOC version 7.

9   The Harry Benjamin International Gender Dysphoria Association's Standards of Care For Gender Identity Disorders, Fifth Version. June 15, 1998. (HBIGDA SOC Version 5) Retrieved 2009, ⟨http://www. hbigda.org/soc⟩. Some of the standard medical protocol I talk about in this chapter came from HBIGDA SOC Version 5.

10 In 2009, I downloaded and printed HBIGDA Standards of Care Version 5 (1998), unaware that HBIGDA Standards of Care (SOC) Version 6 (2001) was available. In September 2011, after I wrote the draft of "The Devil's Advocate," SOC Version 7 was released and is called the WPATH Standards of Care.

11 Aruna, N., Rao M. Purushottam, Rajangam Sayee "46,XX/46,XY Chimerism—A Case Report. *Journal of the Anatomical Society of India, 55*(1), pp.24-26, 2006. Retrieved ⟨http://medind.nic.in/jae/ t06/i1/jaet06i1p24.pdf⟩.

12 "Family Secrets." (story of Chloe Prince.) *Primetime, ABC News.* Dir. George Paul. Prod. Naria Halliwell. Writ. Kim Powers, Juju Chang,, Naria Halliwell, Jessica Velmans. Ed. Bud Proctor, Tim Kelly. Narr. JuJu Chang. ABC Primetime Limited Series, ABC Television Network, 2009. TV. About one out of every 500 boys is

born with Klinefelter syndrome, or XXY Karyotype. While many people with Klinefelter syndrome are not gender dissonant, others are. This TV documentary is about a transsexual woman with Klinefelter syndrome.

13   Hare, Lauren, Pascal Bernard, Francisco J. Sánchez, Paul N. Baird, Eric Vilain, Trudy Kennedy, & Vincent R. Harley. "Androgen receptor repeat length polymorphism associated with male-to-female transsexualism." *Biological Psychiatry, 65*(1), pp. 93-96, 2009. doi:10.1016/j.biopsych.2008.08.033

14   Serano, *Whipping Girl*, p. 85. On cognitive dissonance, a term coined by Leon Festinger in his "Cognitive Dissonance Theory," 1957.

15   Serano, *Whipping Girl*, pp.123-124, 135, 137. Description of trans women needing to conform to their doctor's expectations to be taken seriously. One woman had to put on a dress and heels to convince her therapist that she was transsexual.

16   Boylan, Jennifer Finney. *She's Not There: A Life in Two Genders.* New York: Broadway Books, 2003. p. 21. "...it had everything to do with being female."

17   *Sex Change: Him to Her.* Writ. Ben Ulm. Prod. Vanessa Cole, John Grassie, John Luscombe, Eileen O'Neill, Sophie Seaborn, Donald Thoms, Ben Ulm. Narr. Greg Stebner. Ed. Philippa Rowlands. Produced by Beyond Productions PTY Limited For DHC Ventures, L.L.C. Discovery Health Channel. ©MMIV Beyond Properties Pty Ltd., 2004. TV, Cable.

18   *The Oprah Winfrey Show*: "Paul to Kimberly" episode. Prod. Sheri Salata. Harpo Productions for ABC Television Network, 2010. TV. Paul was the star quarterback in high school.

19   Green, Jamison. "Remembering Alexander Goodrum." *The Channel* (Newsmagazine of Trans Gender San Francisco). 21(11) p.14, November 2002. Retrieved 2010, ⟨http://www.tgsf.org/d/gwen_channel.pdf⟩.

20   The Harry Benjamin International Gender Dysphoria Association's Standards of Care For Gender Identity Disorders, Fifth Version. June 15, 1998. (HBIGDA SOC Version 5) Retrieved 2009, ⟨http://www.hbigda.org/soc⟩. *Section I. Epidemiological Considerations*, "Natural History of Gender Identity Disorders," p. 11. *Section VI. Psychotherapy With Adults*, "A Basic Observation," p. 19. My personal interpretation of these sections led me to believe some people can live with therapy alone.

21 Conway, Lynn. "Basic TG/TS/IS Information." Part 1: Gender Basics & Transgenderism. Subheading: *Counseling and medical treatment of transgender and transsexual women*. 2000-2006. Retrieved 2009, ⟨http://ai.eecs.umich.edu/people/conway/TS/TS. html#anchor282430⟩.

22 *American Psychiatric Association: Diagnostic and Statistical Manual of Mental Disorders, Fifth Edition (DSM-5)*. Arlington, VA: American Psychiatric Publishing, May 27, 2013.

23 *Gender Dysphoria*. American Psychiatric Publishing: A Division of American Psychiatric Association. Retrieved July 18, 2013, ⟨http://www.dsm5.org/Documents/Gender%20Dysphoria%20Fact% 20Sheet.pdf⟩. This publication talks about how Gender Dysphoria has a chapter of its own in the DSM-5. WPATH and trans activists worked to improve the depiction of transsexualism in the DSM before the fifth edition was released.

24 Rose, Donna. *Wrapped in Blue: A Journey of Discovery: A Memoir*. Scottsdale, AZ: Living Legacy Press, 2006. p.75. On estrogen and the sense of well being.

25 Serano, *Whipping Girl*, p.67. When testosterone was dominant, "...it was as though a thick curtain were draped over my emotions." Reprinted by permission of Seal Press, a member of the Perseus Books Group.

26 Roughgarden, Joan. *Evolution's Rainbow: Diversity, Gender, and Sexuality in Nature and People*. Berkeley: University of California Press, 2009.

27 O'Hanlan, Katherine A., M.D. "Origins of Diversity of Sexual Orientation & Gender Identity and How Discriminations Impact Health," from her presentation to the American Medical Association, 2010.

28 Zhou, Jiang-Ning, Michel A. Hofman, Louis J.G. Gooren, Dick F. Swaab. "A sex difference in the human brain and its relation to transsexuality." *Nature, 378*, pp. 68-70, November 2, 1995. Retrieved March 2012, ⟨http://www.nature.com/nature/journal/v378/n6552/ pdf/378068a0.pdf⟩.

29 Dewing, Phoebe, Tao Shi, Steve Horvath, & Eric Vilain. "Sexually dimorphic gene expression in mouse brain precedes gonadal differentiation." *Molecular Brain Research*,118, pp. 82-90, October 21, 2003. A study done in 2003 at UCLA found a possible genetic cause of transsexualism. Researchers identified 57 genes that seem to be

linked to the brain's gender identity development and differences in male and female brains. This UCLA discovery supports the theory that gender identity is hard-wired into the brain long before birth.

30 Kruijver, Frank P. M., Jiang-Ning Zhou, Chris W. Pool, Michel A. Hofman, Louis J. G. Gooren, & Dick F. Swaab. "Male-to-female transsexuals have female neuron numbers in a limbic nucleus." *The Journal of Clinical Endocrinology & Metabolism, 85*(5), pp. 2034-2041, 2000.

31 Hare, Lauren, Pascal Bernard, Francisco J. Sánchez, Paul N. Baird, Eric Vilain, Trudy Kennedy, & Vincent R. Harley. "Androgen receptor repeat length polymorphism associated with male-to-female transsexualism." *Biological Psychiatry, 65*(1), pp. 93-96, 2009. doi:10.1016/j.biopsych.2008.08.033

32 Henningsson, Susanne, Lars Westberg, Staffan Nilsson, Bengt Lundström, Lisa Ekselius, Owe Bodlund, Eva Lindström, Monika Hellstrand, Roland Rosmond, Elias Eriksson, & Mikael Landén. "Sex steroid-related genes and male-to-female transsexualism." *Psychoneuroendocrinology, 30*(7), pp. 657-664, 2005. doi:10.1016/j.psyneuen.2005.02.006

Chapter 6: From Winter to Spring

1 *The Jungle Book.* A play adapted by Monica Flory, based on the stories of Rudyard Kipling. Produced by special arrangement with Playscripts, Inc.

2 PFLAG stands for "Parents, Families and Friends of Lesbians and Gays." It is a national support group, with local chapters everywhere in the United States, for families of lesbian, gay, bisexual, transgender, and intersex people. Headquartered in Washington D.C., this non-profit organization has over 200,000 members in the U.S.

3 Beam, Cris. *Transparent: Love, Family, and Living the T with Transgender Teenagers.* Orlando: Harcourt Books, 2007.

Chapter 7: From Summer to Fall

1 Following my disclosure to Judy in 2009, I learned that Judy had a third friend (besides Alice and myself) with a young adult transsexual child—a son in his twenties. I became friends with both of these

parents in the years after that. When I am in their company I become normalized; now everybody has a transgender loved one. Our shared discordance kind of synchronizes and morphs into a mellow harmony. Because of the respite it brings, the bond that ties us together seems to transcend every other aspect of our relationship.

2 Conway, Lynn. "How Frequently Does Transsexualism Occur?" 2001-2002. Retrieved 2009, ⟨http://www.lynnconway.com⟩, ⟨http://ai.eecs.umich.edu/people/conway/TS/TSprevalence.html⟩.

3 *I Love Lucy*: Season 2, Episode 1. "Job Switching." Dir. William Asher. Writ. Bob Carroll Jr., Madelyn Davis, Jess Oppenheimer. Perf. Lucille Ball. Desilu Productions. Columbia Broadcasting System (CBS), 1952. TV.

Chapter 8: Liberation

1 Brown, Mildred L. and Chloe Ann Rounsley. *True Selves: Understanding Transsexualism for Families, Friends, Coworkers, and Helping Professionals*. San Francisco: Jossey-Bass Publishers, 2003. p. 24; Nature vs. nurture. This material is reproduced with permission of John Wiley & Sons, Inc.

2 Walker, Jesse. "The Death of David Reimer: A Tale of Sex, Science, and Abuse." *Reason.com*. May 24, 2004. Retrieved March 2012, ⟨http://reason.com/archives/2004/05/24/the-death-of-david-reimer⟩.

3 "Who was David Reimer (also, sadly, known as 'John/Joan')?" *Intersex Society of North America*. Retrieved March 27, 2012, ⟨http://www.isna.org/faq/reimer⟩.

4 Brown and Rounsley, *True Selves*, p.195. On acceptance by grandmothers. This material is reproduced with permission of John Wiley & Sons, Inc.

Chapter 9: Making Peace with Religion

1 Jefferson, Thomas. *Notes on the State of Virginia*. London, 1787. Query 17 "Religion," p. 285. Retrieved 2013 from the Electronic Text Center, University of Virginia Library, ⟨http://web.archive.org/web/20080914030942/http://etext.lib.virginia.edu/toc/modeng/public/JefVirg.html⟩.

2   *Michigan Senate Bill 045* (2011) "Matt's Safe School Law." Sponsored by Senator Glenn Anderson (D) District 6. Retrieved March 2011–March 2012, ⟨http://www.legislature.mi.gov/(S(ohkaes55wsulu355c1c h0q45))/mileg.aspx?page=getobject&objectname=2011-SB-0045⟩.

3   *Michigan Senate Bill 0137* (2011). Sponsored by Senator Rick Jones (R) Senate District 24. Retrieved March 2012, ⟨http://www.legislature.mi.gov/(S(ebhkpe45i4ogkc45jdjhapbz))/mileg.aspx?page=getobject&objectname=2011-SB-0137⟩.

4   "Michigan's 'Matt's Safe School Law' Allows Bullying With Religious, Moral Reason." *Huffington Post.* November 2011. Retrieved November 2011, March 2012, ⟨http://www.huffingtonpost.com/2011/11/04/michigans-matts-safe-schools-law-allows-bullying_n_1076494.html⟩.

5   "Michigan Senate passes a weak anti-bullying bill that makes exceptions to allow bullying." *The Ionia Sentinel-Standard.* By Equality Michigan. November 3, 2011. Retrieved March 2012, ⟨http://www.sentinel-standard.com/newsnow/x1054790072/Michigan-Senate-passes-a-weak-anti-bullying-bill-that-makes-exceptions-to-allow-bullying⟩.

6   *King James Bible.* 1611, 1769. Retrieved 2012, ⟨http://www.kingjamesbibleonline.org/1611-Bible⟩ and retrieved 2011-2012, ⟨http://www.online-literature.com/bible/bible.php⟩. Bible passages and references made in this chapter are from the *Oxford King James Bible* unless otherwise noted. The King James Bible is public domain. More recent Bibles, translated by modern writers, are copyright protected.

7   Leviticus 20:13. "If a man also lie with mankind, as he lieth with a woman, both of them have committed an abomination: they shall surely be put to death; their blood shall be upon them." or, Leviticus 18:22. "Thou shalt not lie with mankind, as with womankind: it is abomination." Some speculate that this text was simply meant to be about preservation of a pure Jewish blood line through procreation, and not about morals at all. Others think the text was meant to condemn male cult prostitution, acts of lust, rape, and pedophilia. The internet holds thousands more interpretations and opinions about this text and others.

8   Leviticus 20:9. "For every one that curseth his father or his mother shall be surely put to death: he hath cursed his father or his mother; his blood [shall be] upon him."

9   Leviticus and Deuteronomy are rife with scientific errors and violent

messages, rules and abominations barely mentioned today. Deuteron-omy 22:20-21 say to stone impure brides to death. Deuteronomy 7:1-2 and Deuteronomy 20:10-17 say to destroy other nations and to take women and livestock as plunder. Leviticus 13 is an entire chapter about leprosy. Leviticus 12:1-12:8 give instructions for women to sacrifice lambs, pigeons, and/or turtledoves after giving birth as a penance. Leviticus 11:19 says it is a sin to eat certain fowl like "bats."

10   Romans 1:24-27. "Wherefore God also gave them up to uncleanness through the lusts of their own hearts, to dishonour their own bodies between themselves: Who changed the truth of God into a lie, and worshipped and served the creature more than the Creator, who is blessed for ever. Amen. For this cause God gave them up unto vile affections: for even their women did change the natural use into that which is against nature: And likewise also the men, leaving the natural use of the woman, burned in their lust one toward another; men with men working that which is unseemly, and receiving in themselves that recompence of their error which was meet." Retrieved 2011-2012, ⟨http://www.online-literature.com/bible/Romans⟩. To me, it seems like Paul is scolding people for having sex, period, especially if it was not for procreation. This may be true, since being celibate was considered more pious at one time.

11   Paul's views on homosexuality have been obscured by the mistrans-lation of Latin 'para physin' to 'unnatural' instead of 'atypical or unusual.' Even with the mistranslation, there is no ethical condemna-tion associated with the message.

12   The way I interpret Romans 1:24-27, Paul cautions against lustfulness and prostitution in both opposite and same sex relationships. After all, within the first several hundred years after Christ, celibacy was considered a holier form of existence than marriage. Women even had to repent for giving birth. Fundamentalists today who proselytize that marriage must be between one man and one woman might have been heretics back then. Paul notes that same sex relationships were "atypical" pretty much the same way it was "atypical" for a man's hair to be long or for a woman's hair to be short. Nobody was to be killed for being atypical.

13   1 Corinthians 11:14-15. Chapter 11 talks about Paul's recommenda-tions for hair length and covering.

14   1 Corinthians 6:9-10. "Know ye not that the unrighteous shall not inherit the kingdom of God? Be not deceived: neither fornicators, nor

idolaters, nor adulterers, nor effeminate, nor abusers of themselves with mankind, Nor thieves, nor covetous, nor drunkards, nor revilers, nor extortioners, shall inherit the kingdom of God."

15 I interpret 1 Corinthians 6:9-10 to say that effeminate people shall not inherit the kingdom of God along with people who masturbate, adulterers, alcoholics, people who swear and scold, and a variety of others. This batch alone would indicate virtually everyone in modern society would be disinherited from God's kingdom. Some authors who have modified the Bible decided to change the word "effeminate" to "homosexual." These self serving editions are copyright protected.

16 Matthew 4:8. The earth would have to be flat in order to see the whole world from a mountain top.

17 Bells, Mary. "Galileo Galilei: The Vatican's Reaction to Galileo Galilei." *About.com, Inventors.* n.d. Retrieved 2011, ⟨http:// inventors.about.com/od/gstartinventors/a/Galileo_Galilei_3.htm⟩. In early 1600, Galileo Galilei, a religious man, wrote that the earth moved about the sun. He was tried for heresy for saying the interpreters of the Bible could make mistakes and that its text shouldn't be taken so literally. Giordano Bruno, a fellow astrologer of the same era, was burnt to death for thinking outside church doctrines and saying the earth moved about the sun.

18 Exodus 21:20-21. This passage refers to beating slaves with a rod for a day or two. Although slavery unfortunately still exists, it has formally been outlawed in every country on earth as of 2012.

19 Exodus 35:2 declares that no work should be done on Sunday under penalty of death.

20 Acts 8:26-39 and Matthew 19:11-12. Examples provide evidence that gender variation has always been a part of everyday life, even in biblical times. Gender variant people were baptized into the church.

21 Roughgarden, Joan. *Evolution's Rainbow: Diversity, Gender, and Sexuality in Nature and People.* Berkeley: University of California Press, 2009. pp. 8-9, 358-362, 373-376, and part 3 overall (pp 323-399) Joan Roughgarden examines the Bible in detail. Hebrew and Christian Testaments welcome gender variant people.

22 Roughgarden, Joan. *Evolution's Rainbow,* 2009. Joan Roughgarden is a professor of Evolutionary Biology at Stanford University.

23 Leviticus 13. An entire chapter of 59 verses outlines extraordinarily detailed rules about handling people with Leprosy. In the 21st century,

Leprosy is called Hansen's disease and it is medically treated. Some estimate that gender variance exists in at least 1 in 500 people. In 2013, only about 189,000 cases of Hansen's disease were reported worldwide, which is about 1 in 40,000 people. Retrieved 2013, ⟨http://www.who.int/lep/en/⟩.

24   From 1400 BCE to 200 CE, to the King James versions of 1611 and 1769, and through copyright protected editions published today, there are over three thousand years of biblical translations, editing and censoring, based on the knowledge and philosophy and cultural opinions of the times. Most modern religious scholars generally believe the old books were written by priestly groups of men and various independent and anonymous authors who claimed to be divinely inspired to write in God's behalf. The Bible is believed to be a collection of letters written by men who thought they knew what God wanted.

25   *A Girl Like Me: The Gwen Araujo Story*. Dir. Agnieszka Holland. Writ. Shelley Evans. Prod. Gloria Allred, Fran Rosati, Zev Braun, Philip Krupp. Perf. Mercedes Ruehl, JD Pardo, Lupe Ontiveros. Braun Entertainment Production. Sony Pictures Television Inc. for Lifetime Movie Network, 2006. TV, Cable.

26   Brandon Teena was a young transsexual man who was raped and murdered on December 31, 1993 in Humboldt Nebraska. His story has been documented in *The Brandon Teena Story* and the Academy Award-winning 1999 film, *Boys Don't Cry*.

27   Matthew was gay, not transgender, but his brutal murder was due to a hateful mindset that often targets both groups of people. Retrieved 2013, ⟨http://www.matthewshepard.org⟩. A Baptist minister, on the self proclaimed basis of his religious beliefs, sought to erect a statue to *celebrate the brutal murder* of this innocent young person, just because he was gay.

28   Stout, David. "House Votes to Expand Hate-Crime Protection." The New York Times. May 4, 2007. Retrieved January 29, 2013, ⟨http://www.nytimes.com/2007/05/04/washington/04hate.html?_r=0⟩. Regarding right wing opposition to the *Matthew Shepard and James Byrd, Jr. Hate Crimes Prevention Act*. James Dobson, founder of the socially conservative "Focus on the Family" opposed the Act, and claimed the bill's real purpose was to "muzzle people of faith who dare to express their moral and biblical concerns about homosexuality."

29 *Her Name was Steven.* The story about transsexual City Manager Susan Stanton. Dir. Dave Timko, Jody Gottlieb. Prod. Bud Bultman, Rose Arce, Amanda Sealy, Steve Keller, James Evans, Jack Austin, Mark Nelson TimeWarner, Cable News Network Television, 2010. TV, Cable. "If Jesus was here tonight ... " quoted from a speech delivered by Pastor Ron Sanders of the Lighthouse Baptist Church.

30 Leviticus 21:18-23. These verses state that any man with a blemish or a handicap or bad eyesight or a flat nose is profane and shall not approach the alter to offer the bread of his God.

31 Ring, Trudy. "Transgender Name Changes Not OK With Bible-Quoting Oklahoma Judge." *The Advocate.com.* September 16, 2012. Retrieved 2012-2013, ⟨http://www.advocate.com/politics/trans gender/2012/09/16/oklahoma-judge-cites-bible-denying-transgender-name-changes⟩. This 2012 article is about an Oklahoma judge who refused to allow a transsexual person the right to change her name. This district judge, a former state legislator, actually quoted some biblical passages, interpreted them for the court as the basis for his decision, and declared that our DNA shows what God wants us to be.

32 Heywood, Todd A. "Paul Scott targets transgendered people in race for Secretary of State." *The Michigan Messenger.* January 1, 2010. Retrieved 2010 & March 26, 2012 ⟨http://michiganmessenger.com/ 33506/paul-scott-targets-transgendered-people-in-race-for-secretary-of-state⟩. Current Michigan law allows trans people to update the gender marker on their driver's license after certain qualifying surgeries. Paul Scott sought to revoke this hard-earned right and the dignity it represents.

33 In 2011-2012, Rep. Michele Bachmann (R-Minnesota) ran for the Republican candidacy for president of the United States on a Christian platform. She and her husband owned a Christian clinic in Minnesota, offering various mental health treatment, including dangerous reparative therapy for homosexual people (i.e., to pray the gay away). Bachman seemed to interpret the bible in ways that best suited herself: when asked if she obeyed her husband, as the bible widely dictates, she explained that she and her husband have chosen to interpret *that* part of scripture to mean "mutual respect" in a marriage. The same election year, Rick Santorum ran for the Republican candidacy for president of the United States, also on a Christian platform. He stated he wanted to "throw up" at the idea of separating church and state. He firmly believed his religion should be foisted on the people

of the United States. If elected, he planned to immediately eradicate equal rights for people in the LGBT community. Mitt Romney was a ringleader in a gang of bullies in high school. The bullies targeted a handicapped teacher and a gay student. Today, the other participants in this ring recall the incidents with deep regret and shame, but Mitt Romney doesn't remember any of it. See the additional footnotes below for more information about these three Republican candidates.

34 Ross, Brian and Rhonda Schwartz, Matthew Mosk, Megan Chuchmach. "Michele Bachmann Clinic: Where You Can Pray Away the Gay?" ABC The Blotter, July 11, 2011. Retrieved 2012-2013, ⟨http://abcnews.go.com/Blotter/michele-bachmann-exclusive-pray-gay-candidates-clinic/story?id=14048691⟩.

35 Marrapodi, Eric. "Bachmann faces theological question about submissive wives at debate." *CNN Belief Blog*, August 12, 2011. Retrieved August 2011, ⟨http://religion.blogs.cnn.com/2011/08/12/bachmann-faces-theological-question-about-submissive-wives-at-debate⟩.

36 Ephesians 5:22-24. In Paul's Letter to the Ephesians, a wife must submit to her husband in everything.

37 Goodman, Lee-Anne. "Santorum says he doesn't believe in separation of church and state." The Canadian Press. Associated Press. February 26, 2012. Retrieved March 2012, ⟨http://news.yahoo.com/santorum-says-doesnt-believe-separation-church-state-164307440.html⟩. This article documents how Rick Santorum wanted to throw up at JFK's speech about keeping religion out of public state.

38 Horowitz, Jason. "Classmates recall Romney's pranks-and darker incidents." The Washington Post, May 10, 2012. Retrieved 2012-2013, ⟨http://seattletimes.com/html/politics/2018185202_romneyprep11.html?prmid=obinsite⟩. Mitt Romney was a mastermind in a prank to tackle and cut the hair of a gay classmate. He also masterminded a prank to set obstacles in the path of a visually impaired teacher causing the teacher to trip and fall.

39 Kaleem, Jaweed. "Luis Leon, Episcopal Priest, Will Deliver Obama's Inauguration Benediction, Replacing Louie Giglio." *The Huffington Post*, January 15, 2013. Retrieved January 16, 2013 ⟨http://www.huffingtonpost.com/2013/01/15/luis-leon-benediction-obama-inauguration-louie-giglio_n_2468824.html⟩. St. John's Church (an Episcopal parish in Washington D.C.) welcomes openly gay members, has had a gay bishop, and has announced that it will bless same sex partnerships and ordain transgender priests beginning 2013.

40 Roughgarden, Joan. *Evolution and Christian Faith: Reflections of an Evolutionary Biologist.* Washington D.C., Island Press. 2006. The Bible actually teaches us to live with and embrace the diversity among us. Dr. Joan Roughgarden is a professor of Evolutionary Biology at Stanford University, the author of several books, a Christian, and a transsexual woman.

41 Roughgarden, Joan. *Evolution's Rainbow.* pp.8-9, 358-362, 373-376, and part 3 overall (pp. 323-399). Hebrew and Christian testaments welcome gender variant people.

42 Acts 10:47-48. Peter would not deny baptism to anyone. It was not his place, nor any human's place, to allow or deny Gods blessings to another.

43 Romans 14:5. Think for yourself. "Let every man be fully persuaded in his own mind."

44 Jefferson, Thomas. *Notes on the State of Virginia.* London, 1787. Query 17 "Religion," p. 286. Retrieved 2013 from the Electronic Text Center, University of Virginia Library, ⟨http://web.archive. org/web/20080914030942/http://etext.lib.virginia.edu/toc/modeng/ public/JefVirg.html⟩.

Chapter 10: Queer Clarification

1 Grant, Jaime M., Lisa A. Mottet, Justin Tanis, Jack Harrison, Jody L. Herman, & Mara Keisling. "Injustice at every turn: A report of the National Transgender Discrimination Survey." Washington, DC: National Center for Transgender Equality and National Gay and Lesbian Task Force, 2011. Retrieved March 2012, ⟨http://www.thetaskforce. org/reports_and_research/ntds⟩. Gender identity definition.

2 Serano, Julia. *Whipping Girl: A Transsexual Woman on Sexism and the Scapegoating of Femininity.* Berkeley, CA: Seal Press, a member of the Perseus Books Group, 2007.

3 Bornstein, Kate. *Gender outlaw: On men, women, and the rest of us.* New York, NY: Vintage Books, 1994.

4 Harrison, Jack, Jaime Grant, & Jody L. Herman. "A gender not listed here: Genderqueers, gender rebels, and otherwise in the National Transgender Discrimination Survey." *LGBTQ Policy Journal at the Harvard Kennedy School, 2,* pp.13-24, 2012.

5   Raj, Rupert. "Towards a transpositive therapeutic model: Developing clinical sensitivity and cultural competence in the effective support of transsexual and transgendered clients." *International Journal of Transgenderism,* *6*(2), pp.1-38, 2002.

6   Serano, *Whipping Girl.* Julia Serano popularized the term "cissexual" and the reasons why it is important in her book *Whipping Girl.*

7   Samons, Sandra L. *When The Opposite Sex Isn't: Sexual Orientation in Male-to-Female Transgender People.* New York, NY: Routledge. Taylor & Francis Group. L.L.C. October 15, 2008.

8   American Psychiatric Association: *The Diagnostic and Statistical Manual of Mental Disorders, Third Edition (DSM-III).* The American Psychiatric Association, 1986. The first edition DSM was revised in 1973 and Homosexuality was reclassified from "Mental Disorder" to "Sexual Orientation Disturbance" for the DSM-II. By 1986, with the release of the DSM-III, the condition of "homosexuality" was removed from the manual entirely.

9   In a major victory for the gay rights movement, The Defense of Marriage Act (DOMA) was overturned on June 26, 2013. By mid 2013, 13 states and Washington DC had legalized gay marriage. Eight other states recognized some form of same-gender union. I wrote this book during a period of rapid change.

10   *American Psychiatric Association: Diagnostic and Statistical Manual of Mental Disorders, Fourth Edition (DSM-IV).* The American Psychiatric Association. Washington D.C., 1994.

11   *American Psychiatric Association: Diagnostic and Statistical Manual of Mental Disorders,* Fourth Edition, Text Revision (DSM-IV-TR). The American Psychiatric Association: Washingon D.C., August 2000. Sexual and Gender Identity Disorders, p.535. Retrieved 2009 and March 2012, ⟨http://www.psych.org/mainmenu/research/dsmiv/dsmivtr.aspx⟩.

12   *American Psychiatric Association: Diagnostic and Statistical Manual of Mental Disorders, Fifth Edition* (DSM-5). Arlington, VA.: American Psychiatric Publishing, May 27, 2013.

13   *Highlights of changes from DSM-IV-TR to DSM-5.* American Psychiatric Publishing. A Division of American Psychiatric Association. Retrieved July 3, 2013, ⟨http://www.dsm5.org/Documents/changes%20from%20dsm-iv-tr%20to%20dsm-5.pdf⟩.

14 *Gender Dysphoria*. American Psychiatric Publishing: A Division of American Psychiatric Association. Retrieved July 18, 2013, ⟨http://www.dsm5.org/Documents/Gender%20Dysphoria%20Fact%20Sheet.pdf⟩. This publication talks about how Gender Dysphoria has a chapter of its own in the DSM-5.

15 Serano, *Whipping Girl*, pp.87-88. On the $10 million incentive to permanently change gender, and on other hypothetical examples.

16 *The Barefoot Contessa*. Food Network Television. Ina Garten is the host of this popular cooking show which routinely features gay guests and their partners. Set in the prestigious Hamptons, this show recognizes successful gay residents living in ocean side estates. Ina does a great job inviting many different kinds of American families to appear as guests on her show.

17 A few recent examples of primetime television shows featuring gay people include *Modern Family* (voted most popular TV comedy 2011-2012), *Brothers and Sisters*, *Ugly Betty*, *The Good Wife*, and *Glee*. A gay character was even introduced one time on the conservative and popular *NCIS* in 2012.

18 Ken Mehlman is a former chairman of the Republican National Committee. Among many other political posts, he was also President Bush's campaign manager in 2004.

19 Cohen, Jon. "Gay marriage support hits new high in Post-ABC Poll." *The Washington Post. ABC News Poll*. March 18, 2013. Retrieved March 30, 2013, ⟨http://www.washingtonpost.com/blogs/the-fix/wp/2013/03/18/gay-marriage-support-hits-new-high-in-post-abc-poll⟩.

20 Dea, Robin A., MD. "Gender identity and the transsexual individual." *Sexuality, Reproduction & Menopause*, 7(1). pp.23-25. February 2009.

21 PFLAG stands for "Parents, Families and Friends of Lesbians and Gays." See Chapter 6, Endnote 2.

22 Herman, Joanne. *Transgender Explained For Those Who Are Not*. Bloomington, IN: AuthorHouse, 2009. pp.5,40. Describes discriminatory laws against trans people in this country, such as how it is still legal in many states to fire people if they are transgender.

23 National Center for Transgender Equality (NCTE). Retrieved January 2012-January 2013, ⟨http://transequality.org/Issues/discrimination.html⟩. Regarding discrimination in employment.

Chapter 11: Merry Christmas 2009

1 Shirley Ardell Mason (1923-1998) a.k.a. "Sybil Dorsett" was a famous psychiatric patient who was alleged to have 16 dissociated personalities. A book and two movies have been made about her.

Chapter 12: The Yin-Yang Milestones

1 World English Dictionary. Definition of "identity." Retrieved 2011-2013, ⟨http://dictionary.reference.com/browse/identity⟩.

2 Merriam-Webster. Definition of "identity." Retrieved 2013, ⟨http://www.merriam-webster.com/dictionary/identity⟩.

3 Oxford English Dictionary, Third Edition. Definition of "identity." Oxford University Press, November 2010. This entry relates "identity" to ideas like "oneness," "individuality," "what a person or thing is."

Chapter 13: Conceptualizing Gender Dissonance

1 Serano, *Whipping Girl*, pp.87-88. Julia asks her audience who would take ten million dollars to live as the other sex for life.

2 *The Miracle Worker*, based on the book, "The Story of my Life," by Helen Keller. Dir. Arthur Penn. Writ. William Gibson. Prod. Fred Coe. Perf. Patty Duke, Anne Bancroft. Playfilm Productions for United Artists, 1962. Motion Picture.

3 Festinger, Leon. *Cognitive Dissonance Theory*. 1957.

4 As my child became whole, I became the fragmented one instead. I would do almost anything to rectify my disharmony except wish it back on my child.

Chapter 14: Affirmation

1 *Sex Change Hospital*. A series of six episodes. Dir., Prod. Chris McKim. executive producers: Fenton Bailey, Randy Barbato, Jeremy Simmons. Ed. Afsheen Family. Consulting prod., perf. Dr. Marci Bowers. World of Wonder, for Channel 4 and Discovery Fit and Health, 2005. TV, Cable.

2 *Switching Sexes: The Aftermath*. Prod., writ. Bronwyn Emmet. Prod. Robin Sestero, Eileen O'Neill, Pamela Deutsch, Susie Miles, Joy

Hart Gregory. Ed. Shaun Gildea. Narr. David Healy. Film Garden entertainment. Discovery Production Services, L.L.C. for Discovery Health Channel, 2004. TV, Cable.

Chapter 15: The Year Long Test

1 Harris, Thomas Anthony, M.D. *I'm OK, You're OK*. New York: Harper & Row, 1967. This book was a popular self-help book during the late 1960s and early 1970s and became a philosophical reference for many young baby boomers. Popular culture of that era was so influenced by it that many aging boomers today still use the name of the book as a cliché. This book remains a best seller today.

Chapter 16: In the Mind of the Beholder

1 Geisel, Theodor Seuss, a.k.a. Dr. Seuss. *The Sneetches and Other Stories*. Includes "The Zax." Random House, 1961.

2 *The Oprah Winfrey Show*: The Farewell Season. "A Modern Family" episode. One segment featured a lesbian who "fathered her own child." Prod. Sheri Salata. Harpo Productions for ABC Television Network, 2010. TV.

3 Rose, Donna. *Wrapped in Blue: A Journey of Discovery: A Memoir*. Scottsdale, AZ: Living Legacy Press, 2006. p. 293. In her book *Wrapped in Blue*, trans woman Donna Rose talked about her Herculean battle with insurance. Her policy excluded certain benefits for trans people. These exclusions were listed along with the clause that excluded treatment for felons—but only if the felon was injured *while* committing the crime. Trans people were unconditionally excluded.

4 Serano, Julia. *Whipping Girl: A Transsexual Woman on Sexism and the Scapegoating of Femininity*. Berkeley: Seal Press, 2007. p. 63. Regarding her take on TV documentaries and how the media objectifies transitioning women. Reprinted by permission of Seal Press, a member of the Perseus Books Group.

5 *Sex Change: Her to Him*. Writ. Ben Ulm. Prod. Vanessa Cole, John Grassie, John Luscombe, Eileen O'Neill, Sophie Seaborn, Donald Thoms, Ben Ulm. Narr. Greg Stebner. Ed. Philippa Rowlands. Produced by Beyond Productions PTY Limited For DHC Ventures, L.L.C. Discovery Health Channel. ©MMIV Beyond Properties Pty Ltd., 2004. TV, Cable. About a hero's journey.

6 *Switching Sexes: The Aftermath.* Prod., writ. Bronwyn Emmet. Prod. Robin Sestero, Eileen O'Neill, Pamela Deutsch, Susie Miles, Joy Hart Gregory. Ed. Shaun Gildea. Narr. David Healy. Film Garden entertainment. Discovery Production Services, L.L.C. for Discovery Health Channel, 2004. TV, Cable.

7 Serano, *Whipping Girl*, p.63. On showing before and after pictures.

8 Serano, *Whipping Girl*, p.85. On feeling actual pain related to gender. Reprinted by permission of Seal Press, a member of the Perseus Books Group.

9 Rose, *Wrapped in Blue*, p.333. On Donna's concerns about her mother at her surgery.

10 *Becoming Chaz. The Documentary Club with Rosie O'Donnel.* Dir., prod. Fenton Bailey, Randy Barbato. Prod. Chaz Bono. Prod. Mona Card, Howard Bragman, Dina Lapolt. Ed. Cameron Teisher. World of Wonder Productions, Inc. OWN: The Oprah Winfrey Network, May 10, 2011.

Chapter 17: A New Reality

There are no endnotes for Chapter 17.

Appendix A: Theories About the Causes of Gender Dysphoria and Transsexualism

1 O'Hanlan, Katherine A., M.D. "Origins of Diversity of Sexual Orientation & Gender Identity and How Discriminations Impact Health," from her presentation to the American Medical Association, 2010.

2 Roughgarden, Joan. *Evolution's Rainbow: Diversity, Gender, and Sexuality in Nature and People.* Berkeley: University of California Press, 2009. Joan Roughgarden is an evolutionary biologist and Professor of Biology at Stanford University.

3 Zhou, Jiang-Ning, Michel A. Hofman, Louis J.G. Gooren, Dick F. Swaab. "A sex difference in the human brain and its relation to transsexuality." *Nature, 378*, pp. 68-70, November 2, 1995. Retrieved March 2012, ⟨http://www.nature.com/nature/journal/v378/n6552/pdf/378068a0.pdf⟩.

4 University of California, Los Angeles. "Brain May 'Hard-Wire' Sexuality Before Birth." Printed on website of *Science Daily.* October

22, 2003. Retrieved March 26, 2012, ⟨http://www.sciencedaily.com/releases/2003/10/031022062408.htm⟩.

5   Swaab, Dick F. "Sexual differentiation of the human brain: relevance for gender identity, transsexualism and sexual orientation." *Gynecological Endocrinology: 19,*(6), pp.301-312, 2004. doi:10.1080/09513590400018231.

6   Dewing, Phoebe, Tao Shi, Steve Horvath, & Eric Vilain. "Sexually dimorphic gene expression in mouse brain precedes gonadal differentiation." *Molecular Brain Research, 118,* pp.82-90, October 21, 2003. A study done in 2003 at UCLA found a possible genetic cause of transsexualism. Researchers identified 57 genes that seem to be linked to the brain's gender identity development and differences in male and female brains. This UCLA discovery supports the theory that gender identity is hard-wired into the brain long before birth.

7   Swaab, Dick F., Wilson C. J. Chung, Frank P.M. Kruijver, Michel A. Hofman, Tatjana A. Ishunina. "Structural and functional sex differences in the human hypothalamus." *Hormones and Behavior, 40*(2), pp.93-98, 2001. doi:10.1006/hbeh.2001.1682.

8   Kruijver, Frank P. M., Jiang-Ning Zhou, Chris W. Pool, Michel A. Hofman, Louis J. G. Gooren, & Dick F. Swaab. "Male-to-female transsexuals have female neuron numbers in a limbic nucleus." *The Journal of Clinical Endocrinology & Metabolism, 85*(5), pp.2034-2041, 2000.

9   Hare, Lauren, Pascal Bernard, Francisco J. Sánchez, Paul N. Baird, Eric Vilain, Trudy Kennedy, & Vincent R. Harley. "Androgen receptor repeat length polymorphism associated with male-to-female transsexualism." *Biological Psychiatry, 65*(1), pp.93-96, 2009. doi:10.1016/j.biopsych.2008.08.033

10 Kranz, Georg S., Andreas Hahn, Pia Baldinger, Daniela Haeusler, Cecile Philippe, Ulrike Kaufmann, Wolfgang Wadsak, Markus Savli, Anna Hoeflich, Christoph Kraus, Thomas Vanicek, Markus Mitterhauser, Siegfried Kasper & Rupert Lanzenberger. "Cerebral serotonin transporter asymmetry in females, males and male-to-female transsexuals measured by pet in vivo." *Brain Structure & Function,* 2012. advance online publication. doi:10.1007/s00429-012-0492-4

11 Berglund, Hans, H., Lindström, P. P., Dhejne-Helmy, C. C., & Savic, I. I. "Male-to-female transsexuals show sex-atypical hypothalamus

activation when smelling odorous steroids." *Cerebral Cortex, 18*(8), pp.1900-1908, 2008. doi:10.1093/cercor/bhm216

12 Luders, Eileen, Francisco J. Sánchez, Christian Gaser, Arthur W. Toga, Katherine L. Narr, Liberty S. Hamilton, & Eric Vilain. "Regional gray matter variation in male-to-female transsexualism." *Neuroimage, 46*(4), pp.904-907, July 15, 2009. doi:10.1016/j.neuroimage. 2009.03.048

13 Govier, Ernest, Milton Diamond, Teresa Wolowiec, & Catherine Slade. "Dichotic listening, handedness, brain organization, and transsexuality." *International Journal of Transgenderism, 12*(3), pp.144-154, 2010. doi:10.1080/15532739.2010.514219

14 Schöning, Sonja, Almut Engelien, Christine Bauer, Harald Kugel, Anette Kersting, Cornelia Roestel, Pienie Zwitserlood, Martin Pyka, Udo Dannlowski, Wolfgang Lehmann, Walter Heindel, Volker Arolt, & Carsten Konrad. "Neuroimaging differences in spatial cognition between men and male-to-female transsexuals before and during hormone therapy." *Journal of Sexual Medicine, 7*(5), pp.1858-1867, 2010. doi:10.1111/j.1743-6109.2009.01484.x

15 Gizewski, Elke R., Eva Krause, Marc Schlamann, Friederike Happich, Mark E. Ladd, Michael Forsting, & Wolfgang Senf. "Specific cerebral activation due to visual erotic stimuli in male-to-female transsexuals compared with male and female controls: An fMRI study." *Journal of Sexual Medicine, 6*(2), pp.440-448, 2009. doi:10.1111/j.1743-6109. 2008.00981.x

16 Rametti, Giuseppina, Beatriz Carrillo, Esther Gómez-Gil, Carme Junque, Leire Zubiarre-Elorza, Santiago Segovia, Ángel Gomez, & Antonio Guillamon. "The microstructure of white matter in male to female transsexuals before cross-sex hormonal treatment. A DTI study." *Journal of Psychiatric Research, 45*(7), pp.949-954, 2011. doi:10.1016/j.jpsychires.2010.11.007

17 Savic, Ivanka, & Stefan Arver. "Sex dimorphism of the brain in male-to-female transsexuals." *Cerebral Cortex, 21*(11), pp.2525-2533, 2011. doi:10.1093/cercor/bhr032

18 Wisniewski, Amy B., Mary T. Prendeville, & Adrian S. Dobs. "Handedness, functional cerebral hemispheric lateralization, and cognition in male-to-female transsexuals receiving cross-sex hormone treatment." *Archives of Sexual Behavior, 34*(2), pp.167-172, 2005. doi:10.1007/ s10508-005-1794-x

19   Henningsson, Susanne, Lars Westberg, Staffan Nilsson, Bengt Lundström, Lisa Ekselius, Owe Bodlund, Eva Lindström, Monika Hellstrand, Roland Rosmond, Elias Eriksson, & Mikael Landén. "Sex steroid-related genes and male-to-female transsexualism." *Psychoneuroendocrinology, 30*(7), pp.657-664, 2005. doi:10.1016/j.psyneuen.2005.02.006

20   Wilson, Jean D. "The role of androgens in male gender role behavior." *Endocrine Reviews, 20*(5), pp.726-737, October 1, 1999.

21   "Transsexual gene link identified." *BBC News Online: Health.* October 26, 2008. Retrieved 2009 & March 26, 2012, ⟨http://news.bbc.co.uk/2/hi/health/7689007.stm⟩.

22   Roughgarden, *Evolution's Rainbow.*

23   *Sex, Lies, and Gender.* Dir., prod., writ. David Elisco. Edit. Mickey Green. Narr. Peter Coyote. Features Tiger Howard Devore, PhD., Dr. Joan Roughgarden. National Geographic Explorer, National Geographic Television, 2009. TV Documentary. In this program, doctors explain that gender variance is not aberrant but natural and the magnitude of diversity in gender and sexuality is large—about half the species on earth. Dr. Roughgarden led the first exhaustive sex, gender and sexuality survey of the natural world, from fungi to insects to plants to mammals, to research for her book, *Evolutions Rainbow.*

24   Erickson-Schroth, Laura. "Update on the biology of transgender identity." *Journal of Gay & Lesbian Mental Health, 17*(2), pp.150-174, 2013. doi:10.1080/19359705.2013.753393

Appendix B: Transphobia in Science and Medicine

1   Brown, Mildred L. and Chloe Ann Rounsley. *True Selves: Understanding Transsexualism for Families, Friends, Coworkers, and Helping Professionals.* San Francisco: Jossey-Bass Publishers, 2003. p.76. On the percentage of transgender patients who have considered suicide.

2   Kenneth Zucker is a professor of Psychiatry and Psychology at the University of Toronto and the head of the child and adolescent gender identity clinic at Toronto's Centre for Addiction and Mental Health. He served on the American Psychiatric Association subcommittee on "Sexual and Gender Identity Disorders" to update this classification for the release of the DSM-V in May 2013.

3 Wyndzen, Madeline H. *DSM-V WorkGroup for Sexual & Gender Identity Disorders: Appointment of Kenneth Zucker & Ray Blanchard.* May 7, 2008. Retrieved 2013, ⟨http://www.genderpsychology.org/ psychology/dsm_v_workgroup.html⟩.

4 Conway, Lynn., "Drop the Barbie: Ken Zucker's reparatist treatment of gender-variant children." April 5, 2007. Retrieved 2013, ⟨http://ai.eecs. umich.edu/people/conway/TS/News/Drop%20the%20Barbie.htm⟩.

5 Raj, Rupert. "Towards a transpositive therapeutic model: Developing clinical sensitivity and cultural competence in the effective support of transsexual and transgendered clients." *International Journal of Transgenderism, 6*(2), pp.1-38, 2002.

6 Ray Blanchard is an American-Canadian sexologist. He served on the on the American Psychiatric Association DSM-IV subcommittee on Gender Identity Disorders which then resulted in transsexualism being classified alongside paraphilias and criminal sexual behaviors.

7 Serano, Julia. *Whipping Girl: A Transsexual Woman on Sexism and the Scapegoating of Femininity.* Berkeley: Seal Press, a member of the Perseus Books Group, 2007. Chapter 7 (on Bailey and Blanchard).

8 Meier, Stacey Lawrence Colton, & Christine M. Labuski. "The demographics of the transgender population." In A. K. Baumle (Ed.), *International Handbook on the Demography of Sexuality.* pp. 289-327, 2013. Dordrecht, Netherlands: Springer Science + Business Media. doi:10.1007/978-94-007-5512-3_16

9 Meier, Stacey Lawrence Colton, S.T. Pardo, Christine Labuski, & J. Babcock. "Measures of clinical health among female-to-male transgender persons as a function of sexual orientation." *Archives of Sexual Behavior, 42*(3), pp.463-474, 2013. doi:10.1007/s10508-012-0052-2

10 Moser, Charles. "Blanchard's autogynephilia theory: A critique." *Journal of Homosexuality, 57*(6), pp.790-809, 2010. doi:10.1080/ 00918369.2010.486241

11 Nuttbrock, Larry, Walter Bockting, Mona Mason, Sel Hwahng, Andrew Rosenblum, Monica Macri, & Jeffrey Becker. "A further assessment of Blanchard's typology of homosexual versus non-homosexual or autogynephilic gender dysphoria." *Archives of Sexual Behavior, 40*(2), pp.247-257, 2011. doi:10.1007/s10508-009-9579-2

12 Serano, Julia M. "The case against autogynephilia." *International Journal of Transgenderism, 12*(3), pp.176-187, 2010. doi:10.1080/ 15532739.2010.514223

13 Veale, Jaimie F., Dave E. Clarke, & Terri C. Lomax. "Male-to-female transsexuals' impressions of Blanchard's autogynephilia theory." *International Journal of Transgenderism, 13*(3), pp.131-139, 2012. doi:10.1080/15532739.2011.669659

14 Wyndzen, Madeline H. *Autogynephilia and Ray Blanchard's misdirected sex-drive model of transsexuality.* 2003. Retrieved September 22, 2013, ⟨http://www.GenderPsychology.org/autogynpehilia/ray_blanchard⟩.

15 Wyndzen, Madeline H. "A social psychology of a history of a snippet in the psychology of transgenderism." *Archives of Sexual Behavior, 37*(3), pp. 498-502, 2008. doi:10.1007/s10508-008-9340-2

16 Serano, Julia. "A matter of perspective: A transsexual woman-centric critique of Dreger's 'scholarly history' of the Bailey controversy." *Archives of Sexual Behavior, 37*(3), pp.491-494, 2008. doi:10.1007/s10508-008-9332-2

17 John Michael Bailey is an American psychologist, a professor at Northwestern University, and author of the controversial book, *The Man Who Would Be Queen.* Complaints have been filed against Bailey challenging his credentials and accusing him of overstepping professional bounds.

18 Conway, Lynn. "With the theory of autogynephilia in disarray, Blanchard and Lawrence propose a theory that transsexualism is an 'amputation fetish', by 'lumping' GID, BIID and apotemnophilia." June 20, 2004 and January 17, 2007. Retrieved 2013, ⟨http://ai.eecs.umich.edu/people/conway/TS/Bailey/BIID/BIID.html⟩.

19 Wyndzen, Madeline H. "Everything You Never Wanted to Know About Autogynephilia* but Were Afraid You had to Ask." 2008. Retrieved 2013, ⟨http://www.genderpsychology.org/autogynephilia⟩.

Appendix C: What Percentage of the Population is Transsexual?

1 Meier, Stacey Lawrence Colton, & Christine M. Labuski. "The demographics of the transgender population." In A. K. Baumle (Ed.), *International Handbook on the Demography of Sexuality,* pp. 289-327, 2013. Dordrecht, Netherlands: Springer Science + Business Media. doi:10.1007/978-94-007-5512-3_16

2 Brill, Stephanie A. & Rachel Pepper. *The Transgender Child: A Handbook for Families and Professionals.* San Francisco, CA: Cleis Press. 2008.

3 Ettner, Randi. *Gender Loving Care: A Guide to Counseling Gender-Variant Clients.* New York, NY: Norton. 1999.

4 Winter, Sam, & Lynn Conway, "How many trans* people are there? A 2011 update incorporating new data." 2011. Retrieved October 5, 2013 ⟨http://www.transgenderasia.org/paper-how-many-trans-people-are-there.htm⟩.

5 Conway, Lynn. "How Frequently Does Transsexualism Occur?" 2001-2002. Retrieved 2009, ⟨http://www.lynnconway.com⟩, ⟨http://ai.eecs. umich.edu/people/conway/TS/TSprevalence.html⟩. Lynn Conway is an electrical engineering and computer science professor at the University of Michigan in Ann Arbor.

6 Gates, Gary J. "How many people are lesbian, gay, bisexual, and transgender?" Los Angeles, CA: The Williams Institute, UCLA School of Law. 2011. Retrieved 2012, ⟨http://williamsinstitute.law.ucla.edu/wp-content/uploads/Gates-How-Many-People-LGBT-Apr-2011.pdf⟩.

7 Conron, Kerith J., Gunner Scott, Grace Sterling Stowell, & Stewart J. Landers. "Transgender health in Massachusetts: Results from a household probability sample of adults." *American Journal of Public Health, 102*(1), pp.118-122, 2011.

8 Conway, Lynn. *Falsification of GID prevalence results by the APA Task Force on Gender Identity and Gender Variance.* 2008. Retrieved 2012, ⟨http://ai.eecs.umich.edu/people/conway/TS/Prevalence/APA/Falsification_of_GID_prevalence_results_by_the_APA_Task_Force.html⟩.

9 Olyslager, Femke & Lynn Conway. *On the calculation of the prevalence of transsexualism.* September 2007. Paper presented at the 20th International Symposium of the World Professional Association for Transgender Health, Chicago, IL. Retrieved 2012, ⟨http://ai.eecs.umich.edu/people/conway/TS/Prevalence/Reports/Prevalence%20of%20Transsexualism.pdf⟩.

10 Shields, John P., Rebekah Cohen, Jill R. Glassman, Kelly Whitaker, Heather Franks, & Ilsa Bertolini. "Estimating population size and demographic characteristics of lesbian, gay, bisexual, and transgender youth in middle school." *Journal of Adolescent Health, 52*(2), pp. 248-250, 2013. doi:10.1016/j.jadohealth.2012.06.016

11 Winter, Sam. "Cultural considerations for the World Professional Association for Transgender Health's Standards of Care: The Asian perspective." *International Journal of Transgenderism, 11*(1), pp.19-41, 2009. doi:10.1080/15532730902799938

12 Landén, Mikael, J. Wålinder, B. Lundstrom. (1996) "Incidence and sex ratio of transsexualism in Sweden." *Acta Psychiatrica Scandanavica, 93*, pp. 261-263, 1996. Retrieved 2013, ⟨http://ai.eecs.umich.edu/people/conway/TS/Prevalence/REFs/landen1996b.pdf⟩.

13 Rose, Donna. *Wrapped in Blue: A Journey of Discovery: A Memoir.* Scottsdale, AZ: Living Legacy Press, 2006. Short term disability insurance plan specifically excludes coverage for "sexual transformations." p.293

14 Reed, Bernard, Stephenne Rhodes, Pietà Schofield, & Kevan Wylie. "Gender variance in the UK: prevalence, incidence, growth and geographic distribution." Gender Identity Research and Education Society, June 2009. Retrieved 2011-2013, ⟨http://www.gires.org.uk/assets/Medpro-Assets/GenderVarianceUK-report.pdf⟩.

15 National Center for Transgender Equality (NCTE). Retrieved 2012-2013, ⟨http://transequality.org/Issues/discrimination.html⟩. Regarding discrimination in employment: trans people can still be fired just for being transgender.

16 Grant, Jaime M., Lisa A. Mottet, Justin Tanis, Jack Harrison, Jody L. Herman, & Mara Keisling. "Injustice at every turn: A report of the National Transgender Discrimination Survey." Washington, DC: National Center for Transgender Equality and National Gay and Lesbian Task Force, 2011. Retrieved March 2012, ⟨http://www.thetaskforce.org/reports_and_research/ntds⟩.

17 Herman, Joanne. *Transgender Explained For Those Who Are Not.* Bloomington, IN: AuthorHouse, 2009. pp.5,40

18 National Center for Transgender Equality (NCTE). Retrieved 2013, ⟨http://transequality.org/Issues/issues_hate_crimes.html⟩.

19 Conway, Lynn. (2008b). *Open letter to Alan E. Kazdin, Ph.D., President, American Psychological Association.* Retrieved March 25, 2012, ⟨http://ai.eecs.umich.edu/people/conway/TS/Prevalence/APA/APA%20Letter%209-05-08.html⟩.

20 Intersex Society of North America (ISNA). Retrieved 2012-2013, ⟨http://www.isna.org/faq/frequency⟩.

Appendix D: Why Doesn't Mainstream Society Know More About Gender Variance?

1   National Center for Transgender Equality (NCTE). Retrieved 2013, ⟨http://transequality.org/Issues/discrimination.html⟩. Regarding discrimination in employment: trans people can still be fired just for being transgender.

2   Grant, Jaime M., Lisa A. Mottet, Justin Tanis, Jack Harrison, Jody L. Herman, & Mara Keisling. "Injustice at every turn: A report of the National Transgender Discrimination Survey." Washington, DC: National Center for Transgender Equality and National Gay and Lesbian Task Force. February 3, 2011. Retrieved March 2012, ⟨http://www.thetaskforce.org/reports_and_research/ntds⟩. In a 2008-09 survey of 6450 transsexual Americans, 41% reported that they had attempted suicide.

3   Herman, Joanne. *Transgender Explained For Those Who Are Not.* Bloomington, IN: AuthorHouse, 2009. pp.5,40

4   National Center for Transgender Equality (NCTE). Retrieved 2012-2013, ⟨http://transequality.org/Issues/issues_hate_crimes.html⟩.

5   Brown, Mildred L. and Chloe Ann Rounsley. *True Selves: Understanding Transsexualism for Families, Friends, Coworkers, and Helping Professionals.* San Francisco: Jossey-Bass Publishers, 2003. p.76. On the percentage of transgender patients who have considered suicide.

6   Clements-Nolle, Kristen, Rani Marx, & Mitchell Katz. "Attempted suicide among transgender persons: The influence of gender-based discrimination and victimization." *Journal of Homosexuality, 51*(3), pp. 53-69, 2006. doi:10.1300/J082v51n03_04

7   Grossman, Arnold H., & Anthony R. D'Augelli. "Transgender youth and life-threatening behaviors." *Suicide and Life-Threatening Behavior, 37*(5), pp.527-537, 2007. doi:10.1521/suli.2007.37.5.527

8   Galinski, Paul. "Two-Spirit People Embody Both Genders." November 5, 2008. A publication of *NorthEast Two-Spirit Society* (NE2SS). Retrieved 2010-2012, ⟨http://www.ne2ss.org/2008/11/06/two-spirit-people-embody-both-genders⟩.

9   Harvey, Nick. "India's Transgendered—the Hijras." May 13, 2008. *New Statesman.* Retrieved 2010-2012, ⟨http://www.newstatesman. com/world-affairs/2008/05/hijras-indian-changing-rights⟩.

10 *Sangama.* Retrieved 2012, ⟨http://sangama.org/about⟩. Sangama is an organization created to proved support and improve life conditions for gender and sexual minorities in India.

11 Conway, Lynn. "Transsexual Women's Successes: Links and Photos." ⟨http://www.lynnconway.com⟩. 2001-2012. Retrieved 2009-2013, ⟨http://ai.eecs.umich.edu/people/conway/TSsuccesses/TSsuccesses.html⟩.

12 Conway, Lynn. "Successful TransMen: Links and Photos." Retrieved 2013, ⟨http://ai.eecs.umich.edu/people/conway/TSsuccesses/Trans Men.html⟩.

Trading Places

Selected Bibliography

Print Sources

Beam, Cris. *Transparent: Love, Family, and Living the T with Transgender Teenagers*. Orlando: Harcourt Books, 2007.

Boylan, Jennifer Finney. *She's Not There: A Life in Two Genders*. New York: Broadway Books, 2003.

Boylan, Jennifer Finney. *I'm Looking Through You: Growing Up Haunted: A Memoir*. New York: Broadway Books, 2008.

Brown, Mildred L. and Chloe Ann Rounsley. *True Selves: Understanding Transsexualism for Families, Friends, Coworkers, and Helping Professionals*. San Francisco: Jossey-Bass Publishers, 2003.

Conway, Lynn. "How Frequently Does Transsexualism Occur?" 2001-2002. Retrieved 2009, ⟨http://www.lynnconway.com⟩ and ⟨http://ai.eecs.umich.edu/people/conway/TS/TSprevalence.html⟩.

Field, Genevieve. "Just Another Girl (who used to be a boy): Inside a sex-change story." *Glamour Magazine*. May 2010: 192-199.

Green, Jamison. *Becoming a Visible Man*. Nashville: Vanderbilt University Press, 2004.

The Harry Benjamin International Gender Dysphoria Association's Standards of Care For Gender Identity Disorders, Fifth Version. June 15, 1998. Retrieved 2009, ⟨http://www.hbigda.org/soc⟩. Retrieved March 22, 2012, ⟨http://www.tc.umn.edu/~colem001/hbigda/hstndrd.htm⟩.

The Harry Benjamin International Gender Dysphoria Association's Standards of Care For Gender Identity Disorders, Sixth Version. February, 2001. Retrieved March 12, 2012, ⟨http://www.wpath.org/documents2/socv6.pdf⟩.

Herman, Joanne. *Transgender Explained For Those Who Are Not.* Bloomington, IN: AuthorHouse, 2009.

Morris, Jan. *Conundrum.* New York: New American Library, 1975.

Rose, Donna. *Wrapped in Blue: A Journey of Discovery: A Memoir.* Scottsdale, AZ: Living Legacy Press, 2006.

Roughgarden, Joan. *Evolution's Rainbow: Diversity, Gender, and Sexuality in Nature and People.* Berkeley: University of California Press, 2009.

Serano, Julia. *Whipping Girl: A Transsexual Woman on Sexism and the Scapegoating of Femininity.* Berkeley: Seal Press, a member of the Perseus Books Group, 2007.

The World Professional Association for Transgender Health. "Standards of Care: for the Health of Transsexual, Transgender, and Gender-Nonconforming People," Version 7. Retrieved 2014, ⟨http://www.wpath.org/site_page.cfm?pk_association_webpage_menu=1351&pk_association_webpage=3926⟩. *International Journal of Transgenderism, 13*(4), pp.165-232, 2011, doi:10.1080/15532739.2011.700873

Film and Television Sources

A Girl Like Me: The Gwen Araujo Story. Dir. Agnieszka Holland. Writ. Shelley Evans. Prod. Gloria Allred, Fran Rosati, Zev Braun, Philip Krupp. Perf. Mercedes Ruehl, JD Pardo, Lupe Ontiveros. Braun Entertainment Production. Sony Pictures Television Inc. for Lifetime Movie Network, 2006. TV, Cable.

Becoming Chaz. Dir., prod. Fenton Bailey, Randy Barbato. Prod. Chaz Bono. Prod. Mona Card, Howard Bragman, Dina Lapolt. Ed. Cameron Teisher. Aired on *The Documentary Club with Rosie O'Donnel.* World of Wonder Productions, Inc. OWN: The Oprah Winfrey Network, May 10, 2011. TV, Cable.

Being Chaz. Dir., prod. Elise Duran. Prod. Chaz Bono, Fenton Bailey, Randy Barbato, Howard Bragman, Dina Lapolt World of Wonder Productions, Inc. OWN: The Oprah Winfrey Network, 2011. TV, Cable.

Boys Don't Cry. Based on the story of Brandon Teena. Dir. Kimberly Peirce. Prod. Christine Vachon. Writ. Andy Bienen, Kimberly Peirce. Perf. Hilary Swank, Chloe Sevigny. Fox Searchlight, 1999. Motion Picture, DVD.

Family Secrets. (The story of Chloe Prince.) Dir. George Paul. Prod. Naria Halliwell. Writ. Kim Powers, Juju Chang,, Naria Halliwell, Jessica Velmans. Ed. Bud Proctor, Tim Kelly. Narr. JuJu Chang. Aired on *Primetime, ABC News.* ABC Primetime Limited Series, ABC Television Network, 2009. TV.

Her Name was Steven. Dir. Dave Timko, Jody Gottlieb. Prod. Bud Bultman, Rose Arce, Amanda Sealy, Steve Keller, James Evans, Jack Austin, Mark Nelson TimeWarner, Cable News Network Television, 2010. TV, Cable.

I am Jazz: A Family in Transition. Dir., prod., writ. Jennifer Stocks. Figure 8 Films. OWN: The Oprah Winfrey Network. November 27, 2011. TV, Cable.

Normal. Dir., writ. Jane Anderson. Perf. Jessica Lange, Tom Wilkinson. Avenue Pictures Production. Home Box Office Films, 2003. Cable TV movie, DVD.

The Oprah Winfrey Show: "Inside Fascinating Lives." Prod. Sheri Salata. Harpo Productions for ABC Television Network, 2011. TV.

The Oprah Winfrey Show: The Farewell Season. "A Modern Family" episode. Prod. Sheri Salata. Harpo Productions for ABC Television Network, 2010. TV.

The Oprah Winfrey Show: "Oprah's Interview with Chaz Bono." Prod. Sheri Salata. Harpo Productions for ABC Television Network, 2011. TV.

The Oprah Winfrey Show: "Paul to Kimberly" episode. Prod. Sheri Salata. Harpo Productions for ABC Television Network, 2010. TV.

Sex Change: Her to Him. Writ. Ben Ulm. Prod. Vanessa Cole, John Grassie, John Luscombe, Eileen O'Neill, Sophie Seaborn, Donald Thoms,

Ben Ulm. Narr. Greg Stebner. Ed. Philippa Rowlands. Produced by Beyond Productions PTY Limited For DHC Ventures, L.L.C. Discovery Health Channel. ©MMIV Beyond Properties Pty Ltd., 2004. TV, Cable.

Sex Change: Him to Her. Writ. Ben Ulm. Prod. Vanessa Cole, John Grassie, John Luscombe, Eileen O'Neill, Sophie Seaborn, Donald Thoms, Ben Ulm. Narr. Greg Stebner. Ed. Philippa Rowlands. Produced by Beyond Productions PTY Limited For DHC Ventures, L.L.C. Discovery Health Channel. ©MMIV Beyond Properties Pty Ltd., 2004. TV, Cable.

Sex Change Hospital. A series of six episodes. Dir., prod. Chris McKim. executive producers: Fenton Bailey, Randy Barbato, Jeremy Simmons. Ed. Afsheen Family. Consulting prod., perf. Dr. Marci Bowers. World of Wonder, for Channel 4 and Discovery Fit and Health, 2005. TV, Cable.

Sex, Lies, and Gender. Dir., prod., writ. David Elisco. Edit. Mickey Green. Narr. Peter Coyote. Features Tiger Howard Devore, PhD., Dr. Joan Rough-garden. National Geographic Explorer, National Geographic Television, 2009. TV Documentary.

Super Surgery. Prod., writ. George Butts. Prod. Matt Chan, John Grassie, Lisa Hirotani-White, Christina Kindwall, Bob Reid, Donald Thoms. Screaming Flea Productions for DHC Ventures, L.L.C. Discovery Health Channel, n.d. (Viewed March 10, 2010) TV, Cable.

Switching Sexes: The Aftermath. Prod., writ. Bronwyn Emmet. Prod. Robin Sestero, Eileen O'Neill, Pamela Deutsch, Susie Miles, Joy Hart Gregory. Ed. Shaun Gildea. Narr. David Healy. Film Garden entertainment. Discovery Production Services, L.L.C. for Discovery Health Channel, 2004. TV, Cable.

Transamerica. Dir., writ. Duncan Tucker. Prod., writ. William H. Macy. Prod. René Bastian, Lucy Cooper, Sebastian Dungan, Linda Moran. Perf. Felicity Huffman. IFC Films and The Weinstein Company. February 14, 2005. Independent Film.

"Transgender Lives." *Our America with Lisa Ling*: Season 1, Episode 2. Dir. Heidi Burke, Michael Davie. Writ. Heidi Burke. Prod. Lisa Ling, David Shadrack Smith, Gregory Henry, Amy Bucher. Edit. Dena Mermelstein. Perf. Lisa Ling. OWN: The Oprah Winfrey Network. February 22, 2011. TV, Cable.

Transgendered and Pregnant. Dir./writ./prod. Suzanne Ali. Prod. Jud Cremata, Lee Toft, Kathi Kelly, Mike Mathis, Brian Puterman, Valerie Chow. Mike Mathis Productions, Inc. for Discovery Health. Discovery Communications, LLC, 2009. TV, Cable.

The Truth of My Sex. Dir./prod. Giles Harrison. Dir. Esther Ingram. Prod. Tina Fletcher-Hill, Erica Forstadt, Shirley Soloman, Julie Stern. Ed. Laura White. Narr. Karen Harrison. Perf. Dr. Tiger Devore. A BBC OWN: Oprah Winfrey Network Co-Production. BBC, 2011. TV, Cable.

Organizations

Affirmations. ⟨www.goaffirmations.org⟩.

The National Center for Transgender Equality. ⟨transequality.org⟩.

PFLAG Detroit: Parents, Families, & Friends of Lesbians and Gays. ⟨www.pflagdetroit.org⟩.

TransGender San Francisco. ⟨www.tgsf.org⟩.

WPATH: The World Professional Association for Transgender Health. ⟨www.wpath.org⟩.

Made in the USA
Monee, IL
13 April 2020